Bright Adults:

Uniqueness and Belonging across the Lifespan

Ellen D. Fiedler

Great Potential Press, Inc.

Bright Adults: Uniqueness and Belonging across the Lifespan

Edited by: Jessica Atha and Ann Grahl
Interior design: The Printed Page
Cover design: Hutchison-Frey

Published by Great Potential Press, Inc.
1650 N. Kolb, Suite 200
Tucson, AZ 85715
www.greatpotentialpress.com

18 17 16 15 14   5 4 3 2 1

At the time of this book's publication, all facts and figures cited are the most current available. All telephone numbers, addresses, and website URLs are accurate and active; all publications, organizations, websites, and other resources exist as described in this book; and all have been verified as of the time this book went to press. The author(s) and Great Potential Press make no warranty or guarantee concerning the information and materials given out by organizations or content found at websites, and we are not responsible for any changes that occur after this book's publication. If you find an error or believe that a resource listed here is not as described, please contact Great Potential Press.

Great Potential Press provides a wide range of authors for speaking events. To find out more, go to www.greatpotentialpress.com/do-you-need-a-speaker, email info@greatpotentialpress.com, or call (520) 777-6161.

Library of Congress Cataloging-in-Publication Data

Fiedler, Ellen D., author.
  Bright adults : uniqueness and belonging across the lifespan / Ellen D. Fiedler.
    pages cm
  Includes bibliographical references and index.
  ISBN 978-1-935067-41-2
  1. Gifted persons. I. Title.
  BF412.F54 2015
  305.9'089--dc23
                    2015014183

To my two highly gifted sons, Joel and Josh,
who launched me on this journey to understand
gifted children, adolescents, and adults.

Table of Contents

Acknowledgments

The journey to completion of this book has felt to me a lot like what sailors describe when they talk about sailing around the world. Like those who set off on such a voyage, I started out some years ago to write and speak on the topic of gifted adults—filled with hope and enthusiasm and only a few foggy concepts of what the route that led to this book might be like. Of course it's been all of that and more.

As time progressed and my book developed into what you now hold in your hands, numerous people shared in my journey to completion. Many contributed insights, incredibly meaningful perspectives, and guidance along the way.

Susan Daniels was the catalyst for my initial conceptualization of my model for considering giftedness across the lifespan. When she and Michael Piechowski began the book they co-edited that became *Living with Intensity,* Susan asked me to write a chapter on gifted adults. She suggested that I take a fresh look at the widely known theory of psychosocial development that Erik Erikson described in his 1951 publication, *Childhood and Society.* She thought it would be interesting if I wrote about how Erikson's stages of life might or might not apply to giftedness across the lifespan, and that launched me into the explorations that led to my writing this book.

Many who saw me through times that were like sailing peacefully along through fair weather and smooth seas are also those who were with me when I felt like I was slogging upwind into heavy waves and navigating through all kinds of adverse conditions. I wish to acknowledge a few of them here with gratitude and recognition for some of the ways they were on board with this project.

Ciro Mazzola, the gifted man who is the love of my life, has been along for each and every leg of my journey to completion of this book. He has been there for me and heard the frustrations I've experienced and witnessed the good times. I truly appreciate each and every way he has been able to support me in my efforts.

My good friend and colleague Michele Kane has contributed immeasurably to the development and completion of this book. She has always been willing to read whatever little chunk of it I was in a quandary about, finding myself uncertain about whether or not I was on target with what I was writing. For me, Michele epitomizes what Miraca Gross described as a "sure shelter" in a presentation that she gave in Melbourne, Australia, in 2001: a friend who provides unconditional acceptance, who faithfully keeps on being your friend no matter what, and who tells you honestly what they think.

I'm very grateful for my relationship with the other members of the Columbus Group as well and for the validation that they have given me for my efforts over the years. Besides Michele, I especially want to acknowledge Linda Silverman, Stephanie Tolan, Patty Gatto-Walden, and Anne Beneventi for their encouragement and their presence in my life, from when I was developing my early vision of what this book could be, during all of the time that this book was a "work in progress," and through its completion.

My dear friend Viviene DeOkoro has been an unfailing source of enthusiasm and encouragement throughout. Since Viviene lives in Jamaica and I'm in the United States, she and I only connect via email most of the time. However, she consistently appears on my screen just when I need her most. She has continued to be a steadfast supporter of my work, and I have regularly saved her messages on my desktop to reread whenever I was in the doldrums and having trouble making progress.

Jim Webb and the others from Great Potential Press were instrumental in steering me throughout this journey. Whenever I received their constructive comments, suggestions for improvements, and valuable feedback, I found that I could better move onward toward a finished product that would be worth celebrating. Jim's ideas and recommendations throughout the entire process, along with his kindly expressed concern for me when I unavoidably ran aground along the way, were very much appreciated. I'd specifically like to acknowledge the editorial expertise of Janet Gore, Jessica Atha, and Ann Grahl and the ways that their efforts served to improve this book.

Finally, I want to express my appreciation for all of the bright adults whose stories have served as beacons of light to illuminate the ideas I've included here. These include a host of long-term friends and family members, as well as newer friends and even casual acquaintances I've met over the years under wide-ranging circumstances and in all kinds of places during my travels. I am so grateful to them for being with me along the way and for sharing their life experiences with me.

CHAPTER 1

From the Crow's Nest

~ ~ ~

"There must be more to sailing than the mere setting out to sail from A to B to C. There must be exploration, not only of new areas of the ocean, but also of new parts of yourself."
—*Tristan Jones*

Introduction

Have you ever wished that you could look at your life from a distance? If you could, perhaps you would learn to find your way with greater perspective on the past and the future. Maybe then you would be more able to make decisions that would work well now and feel more comfortable with the life choices that you have already made or are considering.

Bright adults who feel that they are often out of sync with others or who live with someone like this are especially likely to want perspective. Some may feel different, peculiar even, when compared with other people, but they do not understand how their experiences are related to their brightness and creativity. They yearn to understand themselves and to find other people who think, feel, joke, and act in a similarly intense and maybe quirky fashion.

Perhaps you picked up this book to learn more about yourself and your own life, or maybe you were wondering about one or more of the bright and talented adults you know. Maybe you'll start with the idea of learning about someone else and discover things about yourself along the way. Lots of people never see themselves as bright, talented, or gifted until they start learning more about giftedness and how gifted people experience life. Whether you are reading for yourself or another, you are in good company.

Bright or gifted adults often search for answers about how to live their lives and directions they should go. People like this are usually intense, idealistic, complex, multifaceted, strong-willed, and impatient. In their lifelong journey, they seek to discover if they are "there" yet—that indefinable place where they can find meaning in their lives. Their search is often different from those of other people, and they wonder whether they will ever reach a destination that is right for them.

Many bright adults feel this way, especially when they don't want to follow a course that most people take. They feel like they are making it up as they go along, with numerous stops, starts, and midcourse corrections along the way. Some uncomfortably head in directions laid out for them by others, perhaps finding that they are living "lives of quiet desperation."[1] Others drift along with the prevailing winds and tides without the awareness that there might be alternate routes that would give them more meaning and satisfaction.

Charting a Course through Life

In some ways, life is a journey with fairly predictable stages, events, and destinations. As cultural anthropologist Mary Catherine Bateson said, "We remember our lives in terms of periods, with beginnings and endings, and we think in terms of watersheds and transitions, turning points and critical moments."[2] Childhood, middle school, high school, college, first job, marriage, travel, and career mark some of those time periods, turning points, and critical moments, and each has expectations, issues, and options, which are different for people who are brighter than average. Being aware of these stages and related aspects can help bright people navigate—and maybe even keep them from running aground along the way.

Regardless of our talents, intelligence, or ability, most of us focus on our own time frame—the 20s, 30s, 40s, or 50s—without thinking much about what lies ahead in the next decades or even what lies behind in the years gone by. Frankly, too, some of us would rather not spend much, if any, time looking back at the past, let alone focusing on the unknown future and what it might hold. However, it can be useful to have a broader view of an entire lifespan and to compare our lives to the journeys and paths mapped out by earlier travelers, particularly those whose passages differed from the average. This book offers a long-range look at the life stages and issues for bright adults—including exciting times, stormy seas, and periods of change.

Other authors who write about gifted adults generally overlook or ignore age-based stages of development.[3] However, my experiences have convinced me that life is different for bright, talented, and creative persons at each age and stage of life. Mine is not the first theory to focus on the importance of life stages that occur for all people. However, other authors who have written about these stages seldom incorporate information about gifted adults.

Bright adults have a lot in common with each other regardless of how old they are, and some issues they grapple with span all ages and stages of their lives. They typically experience complex emotions as they seek out acceptance, yearn for kindred spirits, and learn how to live with their intensity. Gifted adults are more likely to hunger for significant challenges, to need access to advanced resources, to seek universal principles, to question traditions, and to pursue meaning for their lives beyond the superficial.

Other issues—from understanding the implications of their abilities and uniqueness and the attitudes of other people to dealing with feelings of "differentness"—may not be the same in each stage of life. Of course, some experiences are shared by all people of similar age, regardless of how bright they are. However, life stages for gifted adults are not necessarily the same as life stages for the average adult. In the same way that gifted children often hit their life stages earlier and more intensely than other children, so do gifted adults.[4]

Stages of Development—My Model

If we look at what life is generally like for bright adults, we can gain better perspectives about their journeys and typical waypoints along their routes. From my years of work with gifted and talented children and adults, and building on the work of others, I have created a model that describes typical issues and experiences bright adults may experience at various ages and stages of life. (If you'd like more information about how I developed this model, see Appendix 1.)

We will start our journey across the lifespan by looking at differing points of view regarding giftedness and common issues and concerns, regardless of age, before narrowing our focus and considering the experiences of bright individuals just as they enter adulthood—the "Seekers," ages 18 to 25. We will follow them into their journey as "Voyagers," from ages 25 to 35. Then we will head through two segments of the middle years—"Explorers," from ages 35 to 50, and "Navigators," from ages 50 to 65. Next we will look at two separate groups of bright adults during the later years—the "Actualizers," from ages 65 to 80, and the "Cruisers," from age 80 and beyond. We will finish with thoughts about those I have labeled the "Invisible Ones"—those whose gifts are lost or hidden or those who have run aground.

Young Adulthood

○ **Seekers**—Usually ages 18–25: On a quest to find their place in the world.

○ **Voyagers**—Usually ages 25–35: Purposely journeying through life to establish themselves.

Middle Adulthood

○ **Explorers**—Usually ages 35–50: Matching their lives to their identity and priorities.

○ **Navigators**—Usually ages 50–65: Using prior knowledge, including self-knowledge, to fulfill their goals.

Late Adulthood

○ **Actualizers**—Usually ages 65–80: On a path of self-actualization as well as helping others actualize their goals and dreams.

○ **Cruisers**—Usually age 80 and beyond: Using minds that remain intensely active regardless of physical changes; knowing who they are and what they want in their remaining years.

○ **The Invisible Ones**—Found within any of the other fundamental six ages and stages of life: Adults whose giftedness is no longer recognized or recognizable.

Please know that the time frames I have suggested for each life stage are generalizations. The designated time periods and issues aren't carved in stone. They simply describe what most gifted adults have in common at these approximate ages and stages of life. Some people encounter these issues earlier, some later, and some cycle back to revisit one or more of the earlier stages depending on the circumstances of their lives, their unique experiences, and their individual perspectives.

What Does "Gifted" Mean?—A Brief Explanation

When I talk about people who are bright, talented, and gifted, the first question I am asked is, "What do you mean 'gifted'?" You may be wondering that, too. Sometimes people mistakenly assume that "gifted" is equivalent to "genius." "Bright" and "talented" blend into gifted, and the next chapter goes into that in more detail. For now, I will highlight some aspects that relate to all of this.

Newer definitions of giftedness are significantly different from those that focus primarily on achievement and performance, a viewpoint still held by many people in the world, including quite a few educators and legislators. But the abilities and talents of many adults are not necessarily apparent to others around them or even to themselves, especially if they do not have opportunities to highlight their characteristics and capabilities. As Willem Kuipers, a counselor for gifted adults, said, "If those adults do not produce as expected or become unable to do so, they may get rated as not gifted, after all."[5]

Our perception of giftedness needs to focus on the individuals rather than on their performance. Viewing giftedness through this lens helps us gain a better perspective on our own experiences and how they relate to our lives and the lives of the people we know. It takes more time and consideration to comprehend the inner awareness and understanding of bright adults, especially those who deliberately hide their deepest thoughts and feelings, such as the "Invisible Ones" whose giftedness is no longer recognizable.[6]

Perspectives on Others and Ourselves

Don't be surprised to find yourself wondering if much of the book isn't true for everyone in the world. The fact is that our personal frame of reference for the way we view ourselves primarily originates from other people like us—friends, family, and people we know or have read or heard about in the media who share our background, experience, interests, goals, and values. We grow up seeing the world through our own eyes, and we assume that our experiences, behaviors, and way of thinking are essentially the same as those of others. This excludes a vast number of people who are not much like us and are not in our lives or on our minds at all. This is as true for people in general as it is for highly gifted people, and it prompted psychologist Patricia Gatto-Walden to write, "…since their brightness is normal for them, they almost uniformly assume it must be normal in the world, which causes confusion."[7]

Each stage of life for bright adults has its own issues, satisfactions, and challenges. For some bright adults, life seems to be a voyage on calm waters. They fully enjoy the opportunities available to them, and regardless of ordinary ups and downs, their lives are marked by smooth sailing. Others strive against inner storms from time to time or outer turbulence that seems to assault them from all sides.[8] However, even the lives of those who battle stormy seas are not *always* problematic. Bright adults, in general, are quite likely to have good lives—but lives that are characterized by more intensity and complexity than those of others. Nonetheless, as psychologist Nancy Alvarado said, "An overemphasis on the positive aspects of being gifted does a disservice to the many gifted adults who are experiencing difficulties. It discounts their personal experience and places another expectation upon them: to be gifted, they must have better than average mental health, greater stability, and better coping skills."[9] This can create a burden that's pretty hard to bear.

Gifted children grow up to be gifted adults, whether they or anyone else recognizes that, and their experiences at each stage of their lives are worth considering. As author Stephanie Tolan asked, "How are we as adults to interpret the journey of our lives, our gifts, our complexities, our frustrations and failures? And what might we be?"[10]

Knowing what commonly happens for bright adults at various stages of their lives can help you feel more comfortable about your own journey. This book is designed to make navigating your life easier and to assist you as you contemplate life decisions and grapple with issues that commonly arise for bright adults. It is my intent to: 1) help shed new light on what life's journey is all about for bright and gifted adults, 2) provide greater clarity about life and its challenges for them, and 3) help them gain new insights so that they can better chart their course across the lifespan.

After reading the early chapters, which provide general information, you may wish to skip to the chapter about the age and stage of your life or the life of the person you had in mind when you picked up this book. Or you can read the chapters in chronological order and consider ages and stages sequentially before returning to relevant chapters.

Chapter 2

Bright, Talented, Gifted? Who Me?

~ ~ ~

"It takes several years for anyone to learn to handle a yacht reasonably well, and a lifetime to admit how much more there is to learn."

—*Maurice Griffiths*

"What do you mean *gifted*? I couldn't possibly be gifted. I'm not particularly talented or even all that bright." I once overheard two friends having this conversation in a coffee shop, and it seemed so implausible between these people who knew each other quite well. Each had always seen the other one as bright, talented, and creative and always just assumed that her friend was aware of her own giftedness. They were both surprised to discover that neither of them saw themselves as gifted. Amazingly often, traits of giftedness are readily apparent to others around us, but not to us.

Grappling with Giftedness

Giftedness seems like something that we *should* know about ourselves, especially when others around us do not have any doubt about our abundant abilities, gifts, and talents. Even bright adults who were identified for gifted education programs during their school years are often oblivious to their own gifts and talents. As psychologist James Webb said, "Ironically, many, if not most, bright people—even those who are clearly gifted—are unaware of how different their mental abilities are from those of others and thus are also unaware of the implications that this difference has on their daily lives. Even highly gifted, creative adults often will insist that their abilities are common-place and not particularly unusual."[11]

Some bright adults acknowledge that they were gifted as young children, but they outgrew whatever abilities they once had. They say, "I used to be gifted," as if giftedness were something you can leave behind.[12] Or they might say that they merely worked harder than others and make statements like, "Anyone could do what I do if they just put a little more effort into it." Some think that they were incorrectly identified as gifted years ago, or they see themselves as imposters who fooled the system, their friends, and their family. One highly gifted young man rationalized his intelligence by saying that he only seemed to be smarter than others because he'd learned to read earlier. Even into adulthood, he did not see himself as gifted, even though his measured IQ put him in the one out of a million category. Still other gifted adults harbor a belief that no one is gifted unless they have superior abilities in *all* academic or professional areas, rather than just one or two.

As the years go by, their denial often becomes more entrenched, as if acknowledging their capabilities is a blemish or some kind of error that they should conceal. After all, many of them have been told repeatedly that they shouldn't get a "big head" over their abilities. They have been criticized for being too intense, for thinking too much, for being too creative, for not fitting in, or even for being too sensitive. For some of them, giftedness is more of a burden than they can stand to bear, or perhaps they worry that other people in their lives might expect more of them than they can deliver. For many, "...their resistance can be attributed to fear of failure to live up to the label."[13] After all, they have often been taught that to whom much is given, much will be required.[14]

Why else do so many bright adults deny the very possibility that they might have unique abilities? At first glance, it seems like it could be modesty—a quality often appreciated and admired. However, this kind of modesty actually has a downside—hiding your true self and keeping others from knowing who you really are, as well as preventing full use of your talents and abilities. Modesty can interfere with your ability to know yourself if you think, "I'm not really that good at this; they're just being nice," or "I was just lucky." When it comes to the modesty of bright adults, a judicious "grain of salt" really is called for so that they do not lose sight of being authentic with themselves and others.

Bright adults often have an underlying reluctance to admit to their giftedness, because they are afraid of being seen as arrogant. They think that acknowledging their abilities might lead other people to scoff at them. The emotional intensity and sensitivity of bright individuals contributes to their reservations about even considering the possibility of being gifted. They are deeply concerned about the reactions of others. One highly talented and intelligent blues musician described it as "not having any skin"; he felt so easily wounded by what other people thought of him. It was terribly distressing for him; he continually felt stung by the real or imagined disapproval of others—people whose opinions mattered so much to him. Although they admired what he • could do, he was painfully aware of what he could not do.

Some bright individuals, unbeknownst to them, alienate others with their intensity; they seem to overwhelm other people with their energy, their idealistic sensitivity, and how deeply they care about so many things. As a result, these individuals can become isolated or depressed or antagonistic, or they may assert themselves in ways that often puzzle themselves as well as others.

Other gifted adults apologize for being who they are, and they keep other people at arm's length. Some become chameleons, masking their true selves from almost everyone other than those few rare people who accept them and do not criticize them for being who they are. One gifted adult described it this way, "I know too much. I remember too much. I learn too quickly. I make people uncomfortable. And it is hard to hide these things. I try. But it is also hard to spend your life hiding."[15]

The Chameleon[16]
Sometimes you see me; then you don't.
I know the tricks for blending in.
My color's bright,
A glowing hue,
Changing with your point of view.

My awareness, truly keen,
Makes me be sure
I'm seldom seen
Unless, unless it's safe for me—
Safe to be all I can be.

In surroundings where no threat
Causes me to fade and hide,
Filled with doubts
And deep despair,
Not quite belonging, anywhere.

If you will see me as I am
Then I can let you come inside,
Into a place
Where you can find
The treasures of my hidden mind.

I'll share my secret world with you,
Tell you my dreams,
My thoughts, my plans.
And then, at last,
Perhaps I can
Know who it is I really am.

—*Ellen D. Fiedler*

Intensity, Overexcitabilities, and Other Characteristics

The intensity of so many bright people underlies the accusations heaped on their heads of being "too much." So many of them seem to exhibit the overexcitabilities described by Kasimierz Dabrowski, a Polish psychologist and psychiatrist. The five overexcitabilities—intellectual, imaginational, emotional, sensual, and psychomotor—each have an upside and a downside. [17]

The various overexcitabilities can be thought of as different areas of intensity, and they show up in different ways throughout a bright person's life. For instance, someone with intellectual overexcitability typically has an insatiable thirst for truth and knowledge and is constantly in search of new information, but she may also be seen as argumentative, annoying, and hypercritical. A person who has imaginational overexcitability may delight in imagery and metaphor and be extremely creative with a rich fantasy life, but he also may have a lot of difficulty tolerating boredom and daydream often. Those with psychomotor overexcitability seem to be constantly in motion, highly energetic, and active, but their restless energy level can disrupt or overwhelm others. People with emotional overexcitability have great capacity for experiencing deep feelings. Their times of joy are greater, but so are their times of sadness, which can drag them down into a deep hole of sorrow.[18] The overexcitabilities create a paradox; if you live life to the hilt, each strength has an associated disadvantage that can be confusing for everyone concerned.

Emotional intensity, metacognition (thinking about thinking), and heightened sensitivity, along with enthusiasm, excitability, and expressiveness, are all typical of bright, talented, and gifted adults. Consider the following checklist of gifted characteristics. Do they apply to you or someone you know?

- ○ Makes keen observations

- ○ Extremely perceptive and insightful

- ○ Enjoys problem solving; prefers original, creative solutions

- ○ Easily connects seemingly unrelated ideas

- ○ Learns unusually quickly; has an excellent memory

- ○ Thoroughly enjoys discussing ideas

- ○ Is an independent thinker

- ○ Concerned about justice; lacks tolerance for unfairness

- ○ Self-critical; sets high standards for self and others

- ○ Has a somewhat quirky sense of humor

- ○ Exhibits a playful attitude or childlike excitement over simple things

- ○ Has a lifelong sense of wonder

- ○ Has a longing to find deeper meaning

○ Seeks excellence; sometimes seen as perfectionistic or judgmental

○ Has often felt misunderstood, different, or out of sync[19]

Even though not all of these descriptions fit every bright adult, they describe what life is generally like for gifted individuals.[20] Notice that very few of these words or phrases relate directly to achievement, academics, test scores, or eminence—the more frequently used yardsticks for measuring giftedness.

As the conversation in the coffee shop continued, it became clear that giftedness was being equated with noteworthy achievement when one of the participants said, "I couldn't possibly be gifted! I haven't accomplished anything that important." Unfortunately, many people think of giftedness in terms of a genius or a prodigy—someone who can produce major accomplishments like those of Einstein, Mozart, or Picasso. The underlying issue here actually is about the mental picture of what the term *gifted* means. Many folks seem to assume that it is a matter of either/or—either you're gifted or you aren't.

Broader Perspectives on Giftedness

It is important to know that within the framework of giftedness there is a continuum—or at least different levels.[21] A person can be mildly gifted, moderately gifted, highly gifted, exceptionally gifted, or profoundly gifted. The more highly gifted a person is, the more likely it is that she will seem "different" to other people and the more likely she is to have difficulty "fitting in," sometimes even within her own family. Moderately gifted people may unjustly compare themselves to those who are profoundly gifted. For instance, one young man with a measured IQ of 145 thought that he was just average because he was not as sharp as his father, an eminent physician with an estimated IQ of about 180. These bright adults do not recognize that their abilities still go far beyond those of most other people. Furthermore, IQ is only one way of defining giftedness and does not tell the complete story.

Identification of gifted and talented students in school often relies on data based on their performance in class and on standardized achievement tests. This carries over into adult life where recognition for someone's performance or achievement is what it takes to be considered gifted—in the media, in the corporate world, in sports, and in the entertainment industry—often validated with a sizable paycheck. As psychologist Rena Subotnik stated, "In adulthood, a gifted musician, scientist, or professional is one who is admired by members of his or her field for exceptional leadership or creativity."[22] If their performance does not match up to those criteria, bright people do not see themselves in the same league and say, "Me? I'm not gifted! I haven't done anything to speak of."

So many people are unlikely to value their own gifts and talents, because they compare themselves to others whose abilities and skills lie in specific, recognizable fields that are different from their own. Tolan wrote about how a famously successful and gifted novelist may feel inferior to a theoretical physicist or to the computer whiz who comes in to solve a technical glitch in her computer so that she can get on with her writing and meet a pressing deadline.[23]

The concept of success is often personalized. For some people, success means achieving in obvious ways. Others tend to focus on what they have not done rather than on the many meaningful contributions they have already made. Still others emphasize the goal of living a life with depth and meaning, regardless of external recognition. Some capable and accomplished people pay little or no attention to whether their efforts are recognized in the world and just go on doing whatever they feel is their calling in life.

A highly gifted pediatrician, who made groundbreaking contributions to her field throughout her life, wrote that she never knew she was gifted until her 80s when her daughter, a professor of gifted education, asked her to write a short article about how giftedness had affected her life. The daughter wanted to print her mom's story in a newsletter focusing on giftedness across the lifespan. Her mom was amazed to be asked to take part and astonished to discover that her daughter saw her as gifted. In her article, she reflected on years of feeling out of sync with others, even back to her days in school when she was labeled as the "teacher's pet." She described being puzzled by how other people reacted to her love of learning and her widely diverse interests ranging from ballet to literature to fishing. Once she had achieved success in her field, people seemed to accept her tireless dedication to medicine and eventually became comfortable with pigeonholing her as a woman doctor, even though it was pretty unusual for women to go into medicine in her time. However, people still seemed flummoxed by her intense pursuit of so many different passions.

This multitalented woman lived in a family filled with bright individuals.[24] This is often true of gifted adults. She and her family members were surrounded by others with no idea that they themselves were gifted. Being bright was simply "normal" for their family. In families where no one is especially informed about giftedness, the question of giftedness isn't even on their radar. The brightness of family members is not something they think about or talk about, even if one or more of them have significantly exceptional abilities.

Being Out of Sync

Eventually, gifted adults from families like these often begin to feel out of sync with others as they come into greater contact with the rest of the world. Then, as Tolan observed, "They may have spent their lives assuming that this difference was a deficit, a fault, even a defect of character or a sign of mental illness."[25]

Some bright people come from families where their everyday life and background do not reflect curiosity, an emphasis on education, or even encouragement for achievement. For instance, Vince was a gifted young man who grew up in a working class family. His father was a milkman and his mother worked stocking shelves for a hardware company. There were few books in their home, and their supper table conversations tended to be about mundane matters. When Vince was little, he begged and begged to go to school before the normal age; he was so hungry for learning. His parents intervened with the local parochial school and managed to get early entrance into kindergarten for him. However, he only went for one week before he dropped out, refused to go back, and complained that all they were doing there was "dumb, little kid stuff." His parents were baffled and had no idea what to do with him. Throughout his lifespan, Vince continued to have difficulty understanding himself and finding a place where he belonged.

Asynchrony and Giftedness

Equating giftedness with performance, especially achievement, is easily acknowledged and lauded by society. Although some in the field of gifted education still define giftedness as indicated by achievement, the Columbus Group put forth an alternative way of looking at gifted-ness, which has now become widely recognized and accepted.[26] This definition specifies that giftedness is more of an internal state of being, rather than a matter of external accomplishments that are validated by others. In other words, giftedness is about who you are rather than what you do. This definition describes giftedness as "asynchronous development in which advanced cognitive abilities and heightened intensity combine to create inner experiences and awareness that are qualitatively different from the norm."[27] In other words, it describes ways in which gifted individuals differ from others.

Another inside view of giftedness comes from the eminent edu-cator Annemarie Roeper, who co-founded one of the first schools for gifted children and established the *Roeper Review,* an important journal dealing with gifted education.[28] She believed that "Giftedness is a greater awareness, a greater sensitivity, and a greater ability to understand and transform perceptions into intellectual and emotional experiences."[29]

These definitions that focus on the inner life of a gifted person are quite different from a performance-based view of giftedness that relies on "evidence of high achievement capacity."[30] Prior to the Columbus Group discussion of asynchronous development and Annemarie's thoughts about giftedness, most people thought of giftedness as the ability to achieve at a high level in some field of endeavor. Some still do.

More specifically, asynchrony can be understood as being out of sync, especially internally.[31] This partially has to do with uneven development—meaning that someone who is gifted is developmen-tally advanced in one or more areas but may be just average or even behind in other areas.[32] For instance, Ingrid was a candidate for grad-uate school who scored in the 95th percentile on the verbal portion of the Graduate Record Exam, but only in the 30th percentile on the math portion. The program that she applied for was only concerned with her verbal score, so she had no problem being admitted, and she successfully completed her graduate degree several years later. You've probably known people who are highly capable in some aspects of their lives but struggle in others, including folks who are really smart in lots of ways but just don't seem to have any common sense. (Judgment in very bright people often lags behind their intellect.)[33]

Asynchronous development not only includes variations in ability, but also variations in how people experience life—the inner experiences and awareness that make it difficult for bright people to understand why others do not see the world the way they do. They think and feel deeply, far more so than is generally true for most people. The result is often feeling out of sync with those around them—another aspect of asynchrony.

As a result, bright individuals often feel like strangers in a strange land—sometimes even like an alien from a different planet—with little or no idea of what sets them apart from others. They don't understand why others "don't get it," and their attempts to use themselves as a yardstick to measure others generally fail miserably. They keep trying to make sense of the world and other people's reactions and behaviors based on how they themselves would react or behave, but it just does not work. The hours of bewilderment and rumination can go on and on, far beyond what anyone else might ever experience. Other people's underlying motivation is often unfathomable to bright individuals. This is especially true when these bright adults find themselves surrounded by people who do not share the same in-depth awareness and passionate idealism.

Since so many of the people around them do not understand them, bright people often are criticized for being "too much"—too sensitive, too intense, too curious, too worried about the state of the world.[34] According to clinical psychologist Mary-Elaine Jacobsen, "the chief complaint directed toward the gifted is that they think, do, say, imagine, or emote 'too much.' They are just 'too-too' in comparison to the norm."[35] And it can cause them to feel inadequate or to think, "Something must be wrong with me."

Because of their intensity, sensitivity, idealism, and concerns about fairness, bright people are much more likely to notice how tradition-bound, inconsistent, and absurd other people's behaviors often are. They tend to see the "big picture," how complex most issues are, and what the ramifications might be.[36] As psychologist, author, professor, and lecturer David Willings said, "The gifted person may see implications that other people do not see. He may see difficulties and complexities in a problem which to everyone else is perfectly cut and dried."[37] This creates a lot of confusion for someone who is gifted and can result in significant disillusionment with their friends or even with society.[38]

To top this off, bright people may be seen as having some sort of mental or psychological disorder, when in fact they may just be quirky—either a little or a lot. Many behaviors actually related to their giftedness are often misdiagnosed as some kind of disorder—attention deficit hyperactivity disorder (ADHD), bipolar, obsessive compulsive disorder (OCD), Asperger's Syndrome, depression, or others.[39] An incorrect diagnosis can lead to the prescription of inappropriate medication. The problem is further exacerbated by the fact that many professionals and clinicians—teachers, school nurses, pediatricians, psychologists, and psychiatrists—have no training in giftedness and, therefore, are not equipped to avoid these inaccurate diagnoses.[40]

Denying your own identity as being gifted is fraught with serious consequences. As Jacobsen eloquently reflected:

> ...not only because self-denial is a bad choice that causes persistent feelings of frustration and anxiety, but because inauthenticity threatens one's quality of life at the deepest level... When high potential is treated like a neglected tree, underfed and pushed out of the sun, it does not die off entirely. Nor does it thrive and bear wonderful fruit. It merely survives in an atrophied form, its vibrancy aborted.[41]

The process of understanding ourselves usually takes many years. It is a lifelong journey, typically with many joys and sorrows, highs and lows along the way. Most of us need time and experience to grow an awareness of our own abilities and what that means for living a satisfying, meaningful life.

Life Stages

Initially, I generated my model from developmental psychologist and psychoanalyst Erik Erikson's widely known theory of psychosocial development.[42] Then I added to Erikson's ideas from my own personal experiences and knowledge based on nearly 40 years of involvement in gifted education as well as ongoing dialog with colleagues. Other particularly influential foundations include Mary-Elaine Jacobsen's discussion of the lives of gifted adults; Marylou Streznewski's descriptions of gifted grown-ups; Willem Kuipers' descriptions of those he designates as extra intelligent, intense, and effective; and Gail Sheehy's writings about the cycles (and crises) of adult life.[43] All of these are valuable resources, and you will find ideas from each of these writers, as well as many other sources, interspersed throughout this book. I have also taken ideas from others who have written about stages of life that adults experience, selecting those that are especially relevant for bright, talented, and gifted adults.[44]

People may proceed through life's stages as a matter of their ongoing development and additional life experiences. It is a natural evolution, but thoughtfulness and reflection contribute to being prepared for the next stages of life and to smoother sailing through the sometimes stormy transitions from one time in your life to another.

Erikson's work, published in 1951, is often a key part of courses in psychology and child development. He described issues at each stage of life and divided the adult years into three stages of development: Young Adulthood—approximately ages 18 to 35, characterized by concerns with intimacy versus isolation; Middle Adulthood—approximately ages 35 to 55 or 65, characterized by dilemmas of generativity versus stagnation; and Late Adulthood—approximately ages 55 to 65 to death, characterized by challenges of integrity versus despair.[45]

Erikson's first stage of adult development—Young Adulthood—is still relevant in the 21st century, though his theory is less consistent with the lives of adults during their middle years and into late adulthood. Because Erikson's time frame was more appropriate in the mid-20th century when he formulated his theory than it is now, I have divided his Young Adulthood into two stages and expanded significantly on his ideas about the later years.[46] People live much longer and remain much more active now than they did in the 1950s when Erikson's theory was published. But, even then, bright adults often had significantly different issues and concerns to deal with than people in the general population. Erikson did not focus on those who were gifted. The inner experiences and awareness of bright and talented people, including their intensity, their insights, and their perceptions, have always set them apart from others.

Other authors have also taken an expanded view of adult development beyond the stages proposed by Erikson. For instance, the first of the phases of life that psychiatrist and professor Gene D. Cohen described are the years from the mid-30s to mid-60s.[47]

Although not specifically about gifted adults, Gail Sheehy's popular 1974 book, *Passages: Predictable Crises of Adult Life*, spoke well to the experiences of many bright people at various ages and stages of life. Her book, updated in 2004 with a new introduction, continues to offer timely information about each decade of life from the 20s through the 30s, into the 40s, and to some extent into the 50s and beyond.

Rather than looking specifically at life stages, Jacobsen especially focused on gifted adults as having potential for advanced development. She emphasized the importance of developing self-understanding in order to become liberated from the constraints that prevent them from being themselves. She called these gifted adults "everyday geniuses," a term that she coined to indicate that these people are those who can and will see beyond the obvious. Delving into their personality and psychology, she pointedly said that gifted adults are "the most under-identified group of potential achievers in our society."[48]

Streznewski zeroed in on three categories of bright adults whom she designated as "strivers, superstars, and independents." From interviewing 100 gifted adults and gathering stories of their experiences, she described what she called the "mixed blessings of extraordinary potential" at various ages and stages throughout the lifespan. She devoted one entire chapter to specific issues for gifted women and another one to what she called "The Dark Side," dealing with those situations where gifted individuals defy society's expectations of their achieving eminence in obvious ways, resisting the apparent lack of understanding or acceptance for characteristics and behaviors that differ from average people.[49]

Willem Kuipers created the acronym XIP to describe gifted adults, his abbreviation for "Extra Intelligent People." He stated that they "are a colourful [sic] lot; they can be brilliant, exasperating, full of ideas, dramatic, galvanizing or depressing, hilarious, persistently destructive, aloof or overwhelmingly helpful, and show many of these aspects even simultaneously." Further, he indicated, "The list can be much longer, but the shared aspects are 'intense,' 'uncommon' and 'diverse.'"[50] Kuipers described in detail the characteristics of these bright adults, the complexity of their lives, and the challenges associated with acknowledging and applying their abilities so that they can have happy and effective lives.

Stages for Bright Adults

My model starts out with Seekers—bright adults roughly between the ages of 18 and 25. They have finished high school, are now in college or graduate school, or they have started pursuing their first careers. They may be involved in romantic relationships, on their own, or in some cases even living at home with their parents. They are trying out different lifestyles, social settings, interests, and activities, and they are searching for their place in the world and for others who are on their wavelength—kindred spirits who can connect with them in meaningful ways, share their interests and their ideals, and perhaps even "get" them and their quirky sense of humor.

My second group of bright adults are the Voyagers—approximately from age 25 to 35. Some are in graduate school, and some are already moving ahead on the career path that they zeroed in on when they were Seekers, although they may be on their second or third job along that path. They value job security, but they will not stay at a job they do not like. Even though Voyagers have clearer ideas about what they want and do not want in their lives, including in their romantic relationships, they may still be continuing to search for a soul mate. Others may be in committed relationships or married—some with children and characteristically busy family lives—often struggling with the challenges of balancing a career with their family commitments and other personal interests.

The third group of bright adults in my model are the Explorers—roughly ages 35 to 50. By this point in life, they have a pretty good sense of who they are and have clearer ideas about what they do and do not want, based on things they learned earlier. During this time of their lives, they are greatly aware that what they want is not a question with one right answer. Some of them have started off in one direction and then decided that it was not quite right for them, even if it was appropriate for them at one time. Many Explorers are caught up in making significant midcourse changes that move them toward new goals. Some are exploring how to resolve a keen sense of dissatisfaction they feel, even though simultaneously finding themselves incredibly busy with their careers, family activities, and responsibilities. Although many Explorers seldom take time to reflect on their lives and how to make things better, others totally stop short and decide to alter the course of their lives drastically during this stage.

The next group are the Navigators, approximately ages 50 to 65. By this time, these bright adults have pretty much developed their goals and values. They have a clear course in mind for where they want their life's journey to take them during these years. They are more likely to be settled into their chosen careers—though sometimes it is their second, third, or even fourth career. Most of them know their capabilities and how to put them to use. And often they have moved beyond the point where their children take up significant amounts of their time, so they can set their sights on what they want for themselves. With clarity regarding their identity and the things they care deeply about, they can focus on what they would like to accomplish while there is still time. A sense of urgency often accompanies this stage of life—of wanting to make a difference while they can.

The fifth group of bright adults are the Actualizers—approximately aged 65 to 80. Their focus is likely on self-actualization, along the lines that Abraham Maslow described—finding meaningful ways to put their gifts and talents to use. [51] A common component of their lives is also helping others actualize their own lifelong goals and dreams—much like what Erikson meant when he coined the term "generativity" to suggest an emphasis on nurturing and guiding younger people at this time of life.[52]

Members of the last group in my model are the Cruisers. These gifted people, ages 80 and beyond, travel through life at a steady pace appropriate for them. Although they may occasionally feel some of the urgency that Actualizers do, Cruisers are generally not in a rush; they have developed greater perspective and patience. Although they are not particularly concerned with setting a course, exploring alternatives, choosing a designated route, or paying much specific attention to actualizing their potential, they often are still interested in guiding the next generation. For some, this time of their lives continues to be filled with vitality and involvement. For others, physical challenges may interfere with their being as active as they might like to be, and other constraints may limit what they can do and may weigh them down with despair as they contemplate how little time they have left. Cruisers primarily want to enjoy the rest of their life journey to the best of their abilities.

I include one more category in my model, and I call this last group the Invisible Ones. These are people who are bright, creative, and insightful, but who are overlooked by others who do not see them as gifted because they do not fulfill common expectations of outwardly recognizable achievement. They are not living up to their "full potential."

Often the Invisible Ones camouflage, deny, or downplay their abilities, perhaps sabotaging themselves or dropping out of traditional society. Some are so hurt and angry that their abilities emerge in anti-social and rebellious ways; others feel ground down by depression. Their giftedness may be barely visible even to someone who knows them fairly well. Some of them truly believe that they never were gifted. Others deliberately hide their abilities, conflicts, and loneliness, and they will only reveal themselves to one or two close friends. If their abilities and curiosity are unappreciated by their spouses or children, they may dumb themselves down just to get along at home or in the workplace.

We need to look at the lives of these Invisible Ones, at what may have happened to them, at why their true selves are hidden, and at how they may be coping. It is unlikely that they simply lost their abilities; it is more likely that a "Dark Side" of giftedness has taken over at least for a time.[53] Becoming invisible may be a temporary state of being for gifted adults related to their life situations. Some of them have become disheartened or disillusioned by life circumstances or because of roles they feel they must play—e.g., at work or among others who either are not like them or who do not accept them for who they are.

True for Everyone vs True for the Gifted

Whenever I give presentations about gifted adults describing what is going on for them at different times in their lives, someone usually asks me, "How is all this different from what goes on in every-one else's life?" They want to know how the experiences of bright adults are different.

Certainly we are all human, and everyone faces many of the same issues as we go through life. We all want acceptance and to find kindred spirits; we want challenge, stimulation, and opportunities. And we all seek meaning in life. However, how these issues play out in a person's life is different for a bright adult than it is for most people. Their heightened intensity, sensitivity, in-depth thinking, questioning attitudes, asynchronous development, and idealism affect every aspect of their lives. As a result, complications and challenges crop up at every stage of life for gifted adults.

Chapter 3

Compass Headings—Charting a Course across the Lifespan

~ ~ ~

"People are always blaming their circumstances for what they are. I don't believe in circumstances. The people who get on in this world are the people who get up and look for the circumstances they want, and if they can't find them, make them."

—*George Bernard Shaw*

"Are you happy?" It seemed like the umpteenth time his mother had asked Jason that question. She continued to ask him, no matter how old he was or how many years had gone by. He always had trouble responding, even though he knew that happiness was all his mother wanted for him. He knew that saying *yes* would set his mother's mind at ease. And yet all that question ever really seemed to do, regardless of how he answered it, was to make him catch his breath and stop and think. "What is happiness?" A string of other questions would then spring to mind. "What does happiness mean to me?" Happiness was not exactly the destination he was trying to reach. What he really wanted was to find his way to a satisfying, meaningful life. "Happy" just sounded too superficial.

He used to have a poster on his wall that said, "Life is a journey, not a destination," which came closer to the real answer to his mother's question.[54] He wanted to say something about how the twists and turns and unexpected course changes along the way had turned out to have a lot of meaning for him, regardless of whether he felt happy at the time. As he looked back at the challenges he had faced, he could see how each one had moved him forward—even when life was really difficult. However, he knew that this wasn't the answer that his mother wanted or needed to hear. So he would usually just smile and say, "Yeah, Mom, I'm happy" (thinking to himself, "Well, most of the time"), and he would leave it at that.[55]

Traveling Circuitous Routes

The routes traveled by bright, gifted, and intense adults through-out their lifespan are often circuitous. One of my favorite books, *First You Have to Row a Little Boat: Reflections on Life and Living* by Richard Bode, has a chapter titled, "The Shortest Distance between Two Points Is a Zigzag Line."[56] This aptly describes the indirect routes that many bright adults take as they journey through life, much like sailors tack-ing back and forth through the water to get to a destination upwind.

As mentioned before, some issues that bright adults encounter are distinctive for certain stages—categorized as Seekers, Voyagers, Navigators, Explorers, Actualizers, or Cruisers. The Invisible Ones, not surprisingly, face a variety of specific concerns throughout their lives unless something or someone breaks the cycle so that their gifts are no longer hidden.

Significant Needs and Issues throughout the Lifespan

This chapter focuses on challenges that transcend all ages and stages of life for gifted adults. These issues arise repeatedly as direct outgrowths of the differences between them and other people. The concepts here can help bright adults at any age chart their course and make changes to reach their goals.

○ *Acceptance*—meeting their needs for acceptance and belong-ing, a real challenge for gifted adults because of the ways they are different from others.[57]

○ *Meaningful connections*—finding kindred spirits, other people who are like them, who are on their wavelength, and who can connect with them in meaningful ways.

○ *Living with intensity*—accepting and coping with the higher levels of intensity that they experience throughout their lives.[58]

○ *Access to resources*—finding people, places, and things that let them pursue their passions, the things they care most deeply about.

○ *Relevant challenges*—having opportunities to use their minds to satisfy their thirst for knowledge, hunger for understanding, and quest for stimulating learning experiences.

○ *Finding meaning*—seeking and finding meaning in life; recognizing that their lives count for something and that their very existence has relevance in the world.

I think of these as compass headings because they help bright adults find direction in their lives if they are feeling lost or feel that their life is lacking. Let's look more closely at each of these, along with examples of how some bright adults have worked out their own solutions for handling these challenges.

Acceptance

Bright people often have difficulty finding acceptance from others. Sometimes bright adults assume that they cannot find acceptance because they never adequately developed their social skills. That may be true for some people, particularly the types of bright adults who are often referred to as nerds, dorks, or geeks; those who are introverted; or those who have Asperger's Disorder or fall somewhere on the autism spectrum. They may assume that something is wrong with them, especially if they grew up with no one else similar to them or anyone who really accepted them, quirkiness and all.

Most often, though, problems with acceptance arise from a mismatch between the person and the situation; these individuals have not yet found any kindred spirits or intellectual peers. Sometimes other people really are reluctant to accept gifted adults as they are. Perhaps others do not understand the advanced vocabulary that bright adults use, have trouble following their complex thinking processes, or do not appreciate their unique sense of humor. As was said before, people may dismiss gifted individuals as being "too much"—too intense, too emotional, too different, or too weird. Sometimes these people feel threatened by bright adults, as if being around someone with more knowledge or more sophisticated ideas diminishes their own worth as a person or undermines their chances of success and recognition.

If they have enough of these experiences, gifted adults may jump to the conclusion that others do not and will not accept them. The result then is that they protect themselves by withdrawing rather than finding ways to move along and gain acceptance. However, it does not have to be that way.

One bright man's strategy for finding acceptance evolved from his strong verbal abilities. He regularly uses some of what he'd learned "way back when" on the high school debate team where he discovered ways to disagree respectfully and diplomatically. For him, it helps to be articulate about his ideas, to "have his ducks in a row," and to be well versed in the facts about the topic of discussion, all while considering his audience and not using $500 words (highly advanced vocabulary that may come across as pretentious or arrogant). In this way, he can share his knowledge and perspectives without becoming either argumentative or defensive. He says to himself, "When all else fails, I just suggest that we 'agree to disagree,' and I walk away."

A bright woman who has often run into a lack of acceptance has come to the conclusion that there are three kinds of people in her world: 1) those who seem to be threatened by her or need to reject her or "bring her down a peg," 2) those who have puzzled looks on their faces when she tries to share complex thoughts and feelings with them, and 3) those whose eyes light up with recognition whenever they get into a conversation with her.

She does what she can to avoid or ignore the people in the first group when they snipe at her, choosing not to give them the satisfaction of getting a rise out of her. For the second group, the ones who are puzzled, she makes efforts to find common ground by listening to their thoughts and feelings and monitoring her own vocabulary to avoid talking over their heads in ways that create barriers and hinder her from connecting with them. She enjoys sharing activities with the people in this second group whenever they can find common ground—whether on the softball team, playing cards, or going to a *chick flick* together. Their conversations tend to center on activities they enjoy together, rather than deep philosophical or intellectual discussions. Although she says she would be starved for those other kinds of discussions if these were the only people in her life, she's happy to spend time with them. As with most gifted adults, she has different peer groups for different kinds of activities; the same people she goes to the symphony with are not necessarily the same people with whom she goes camping or attends sporting events.

She tries to spend as much time as possible with the third group of people, the ones more similar to her. She says, "They 'get me' so I can totally be myself with them." Whenever she needs to get an "acceptance fix," she reaches out to the people in her third group. She uses the phone, texts, email, social networking sites, video chats, and instant messaging, or she makes plans to get together in person—for lunch or coffee or an event, such as the opera, a foreign film, or a lecture on a topic they both find interesting.

Many gifted adults are good at playing the chameleon. They try to find acceptance by blending in, which can be exhausting. People are multifaceted, and the key is to avoid pretending to be something you are not. Instead, by listening to others and finding the parts of yourself that can relate to them, you can make meaningful connections. However, if that really isn't working, it's okay to move along and try again somewhere else. It takes effort and a balance of accepting others as they are and looking out for yourself so that you can find the basic acceptance everyone needs.

Meaningful Connections

Gifted adults are often independent and self-sufficient. This is a strength, but one that can sometimes make it difficult for them to fulfill their social needs, especially if they have little in common with the people around them. Unless bright adults can make meaningful connections with others, they can slip into the depths of loneliness and despair, feeling like aliens who have landed on the wrong planet.[59] They do not need many; just having a few kindred spirits in their lives can make all the difference. Even having one good friend may be plenty. Many gifted adults, particularly those who are introverts, have difficulty finding others they feel close to—something that is easier for most people in the general population.

One bright, extroverted woman says, "I don't know what's so hard about finding other people who resonate with me and are great fun to be with. They're everywhere." A closer look at why she can say this reveals some fairly simple strategies. She routinely gets involved in groups doing things she really cares about. She has serious concerns about the environment, about endangered species, and about global climate change, so she became an active member of the Sierra Club; some of her friends laughingly call her a "tree hugger." When environmentally conscious candidates run for local, state, or national elections, she gets involved in campaigning for them. Between elections, she works with others to start petitions or to get an environmentally friendly referendum on the ballot. Through participating in these activities, she has met many fascinating people who share her interests, values, and goals and want to make a difference in the world, just like she does.

One bright, older man found people like him by moving to a community populated largely by retired college professors. Although he barely had a high school education, he figured that he would be more likely to find people there that he could communicate with, given the kinds of things he liked to discuss. Moving to this community allowed him to feel that he would be able to thrive throughout the rest of his life.[60] Although he was an introvert, being around others to whom he could relate paved the way for him to make meaningful connections.

Pursue your passions and you will often find a community that shares your interests. The Internet is a good starting place to find an online forum or information on real life activities, classes, groups, meetups, events, etc. But you can also reach out to people you know, making it easier to forge connections the old-fashioned way.

Living with Intensity

Bright adults regularly face criticism throughout their lives when it comes to their intensity, "never quite understanding why others don't understand who they are, how they think, and how they feel."[61] Intensity affects everything for them, sometimes giving them a chance to live fuller, richer lives than others could imagine, but at other times causing them to feel isolated, alone, and rejected, often because people do not seem to be able to handle being around them for long. This intensity relates back to Dabrowski's overexcitabilities—a concept that was introduced in Chapter 2.

For some, the intensity is intellectual—always wanting to know the *why* of things, pursuing ideas, and chasing interesting concepts. For others, it's psychomotor intensity—always needing to be on the move, talking fast, walking quickly, or even constantly jiggling their legs or feet while sitting still. For still others, it's sensual intensity—being highly aware of sights, sounds, smells, tastes, and touch; having to cut the tags out of their clothes; and avoiding places with annoying levels of sound or lighting. For others, it's imaginational intensity—always wondering about everything, envisioning endless solutions to problems, or being aware of potentially disastrous possibilities and worrying about them. And, for some, it's emotional intensity—feeling everything deeply and experiencing extreme highs and lows in response to life. It is important to realize that for some gifted folks, it's all of the above—they may experience all of these intensities or at least several of them at any given time.

High levels of intensity seem to prompt many to just go on living "under full sail," flying along even in heavy winds, and enjoying all that they experience because of their intensity. Others find they need to "shorten sail," taking precautions not to have their intense experiences affect them as much as they might if they merely barreled ahead. They head for safe harbors or quiet anchorages, seeking places of concealment and not letting anyone see the depth and breadth of their intensity.

A deeply intense, high-energy, gifted man who had dropped out of high school in ninth grade because he was so bored subsequently joined the Navy. He initially worked in administration until he got tired of what he describes as "clerical work." He then decided to train to be a Navy search and rescue diver. After doing that for many years and saving quite a few lives, he wanted new challenges and became an expert in explosives, defusing mines and other bombs. After 20 years in the Navy, he went back to school to get two master's degrees. He currently develops software programs for the online education of medical personnel in collaboration with his wife, who is a research nurse in a cancer hospital. This bright man lives "under full sail." He clearly enjoys his fulfilled life, but it's easy to imagine others being puzzled by why he has felt driven to do so many different things.

For years, a bright and creative woman quietly nurtured her intensity while living what seemed to be an ordinary suburban life with her husband and two dogs, enjoying frequent visits with her young grandchildren. Behind the scenes, she was a major force in the organization of a writer's workshop that met every week and where she also developed her own writing projects. She regularly provided design input for the beautiful hand-carved wooden signs that her husband creates in his business. In the summer, she worked with others to develop an arts and performance center in the resort community in northern Wisconsin where she and her husband have a second home. They now live there year-round and have opened a shop that features his work as well as that of other local artists and artisans. She writes a weekly column about the arts for a local newspaper and acts as the live events coordinator for the performing arts center that now offers performances from May through February. This gifted multitalented woman is loving her life now and lives it to the fullest using a wide range of her ample abilities, multiple interests, and organizational skills.

Access to Resources

Bright adults often find themselves frustrated when they lack resources, including time, money, teachers and mentors, training, and the tools or equipment needed for them to pursue their passions. They need access to resources to match the often complex vision of their goals. Sometimes they know what they need to move forward, but they may run into too many obstacles along their route, and being patient is not easy for them. Other times, even though they can envision their goal, they may not know what resources could be useful to them, let alone where to access them. They need information and open doors so that they can see their way to finding what they need.

A gifted artist had difficulty determining how and where to market his sculptures. He started going to gallery openings in a nearby city, talking to the artists who exhibited work there and asking questions about what they had done to get their pieces out in front of potential buyers. He learned there was a regional organization that kept an online catalog of artists' work where gallery owners and interior designers would check regularly to discover emerging artists.

This artist has now made some good connections and is well on his way to having a one-man show at a local gallery.

One bright woman reached a point where she wanted to pursue a career that had more meaning for her than the jobs she had worked while her children were younger. She needed resources to help her understand her options and how to combine the knowledge and skills she already had with whatever additional education or training she might need to move forward. Fortunately, her local community college offered career-counseling services, and a counselor helped her figure out how her interests and abilities might take her to where she wanted to go. In addition, she explored no-cost websites of state and federal governmental agencies that displayed labor-market information. After narrowing her options, she pursued volunteering and job shadowing to find a good fit suited to her current needs. She learned that she could access additional training she needed either locally or by taking online courses, and now she is well on her way to a satisfying career.

Relevant Challenges

Bright adults need day-to-day stimulation that provides challenge and newness. They need opportunities to communicate with others • about their ideas and to move on to find new things to learn once they have exhausted the current ones.[62] These important opportunities extend far beyond what others need, whether those challenges are at work, at home, in their communities, or during their leisure time.[63]

Work typically takes up much of daily life. Because it is usually highly structured, narrowly focused, regimented, and repetitive, the workplace is frequently problematic for gifted adults—as was true for one bright man who changed jobs quite often. He would get frustrated with the procedures of the organizations and his bosses who did not want to listen to "the new guy." Each new company provided novel challenges for a while, but he mostly felt that the jobs he worked were really only for basic income to support his family. His real interests were in writing after work and on weekends. He has written a novel and has already found an interested publisher. So far his two strategies to meet his need for challenge—changing jobs periodically and writing—are working for him. However, his approach causes consternation and concern for his wife who manages the family's finances.

A female lawyer in her 30s, who partnered in a law practice with her husband, took several years off to be with her two daughters when they were young. During that time, she created a ballet based on Shakespeare's *A Midsummer Night's Dream*, using music composed by Felix Mendelssohn. She built a stage in her basement, and produced and directed a benefit show using the neighborhood kids and her own daughters as the dancers. They performed it for friends and relatives and charged a nominal ticket price that they donated to charity. Her creativity in designing the sets and the costumes led her to become an amateur interior designer, decorating apartments for several of her colleagues from the law firm. In the meantime, she continued reading case law and conferring with her husband over the dinner table about interesting cases. This allowed her to keep up with her field and go back to the law firm once the children were in elementary school. She managed to make the transition back to full-time work as a lawyer, because she didn't totally lose out on what was happening in her profession during the years she stayed home to raise her girls.

You also can identify what you need to keep your mind alive and to remain enthusiastic. Then make the time in your life for the people and activities that fulfill your needs for stimulation and challenge. When left on your own to search for appropriate options, seek them out via the Internet, by reading thought-provoking books, or by listening to intriguing podcasts. Upcoming chapters will provide additional suggestions for meeting your requirements for engaging and challenging experiences.

Finding Meaning

Stephanie Tolan often ends her writings and her public talks with the following quote from Osho, a Zen master, "You are not accidental. Existence needs you. Without you, something will be missing in existence, and no one can replace it."[64] Tolan emphasizes the importance of creating our own stories about our lives and our world in order to find meaning in life.[65] James Webb, in his book *Searching for Meaning: Idealism, Bright Minds, Disillusionment, and Hope*, suggests the following questions for those confronting their search for a meaningful life:

○ What is the purpose of my life?

○ What is important?

○ What is worth living and working for?

○ Who am I?

○ What is the most worthwhile way for me to spend my life in the short time that I will be on this earth?[66]

With two gifted children, both of whom were struggling in a school with no programs to challenge them appropriately, one woman found her calling in life in the field of gifted education. The principal of her sons' school, who had called her into his office, asked her what she thought should be done for her kids. She replied, "I don't have any idea. Why are you asking me? You're supposed to be the experts! I'm just a mom." The principal said, "We don't know, either." She launched her search for answers by reading and asking questions about gifted children and their education. Even though her educational background and employment history were in journalism, she went back to school and earned a master's degree in elementary education as well as certification to teach. In every education course, she focused on meeting the needs of gifted students in that subject area. The projects and papers she submitted for her classes related to her purpose in life—determining how schools might best provide appropriately for gifted students, a passion that extended far beyond her concerns for her own two bright and talented children. She went on to become a teacher and subsequently became a coordinator for a gifted program.

This woman found meaning in her life by getting involved in gifted education. Many years later when her sons were grown, she told them, "Because of you, I got into doing the work I'm doing, and you and I have helped more gifted children together than any of us will ever know."

After having what he reported as "86 unrelated jobs," Mike Matoin found his niche as a Unity Church minister.[67] His down-to-earth approach built on all he had experienced in his life, including his time as a stand-up comedian—a talent that he routinely incorporated whenever he spoke. When he shared about his mistakes and life experiences, it was easy to see that he had found ways to answer the big questions about his own identity, what was truly important to him, what his purpose in life was, and how everything he had done contributed to where he found himself now. Mike created a community of people who could laugh with him about his very human foibles and who found a way to acknowledge and laugh at their own, so that they too could move past them to seek and find meaning in their lives.[68]

In one of my graduate courses, the instructor had us each write our own epitaph. This exercise can be a good way for bright adults to start reflecting on their life's journey. A similar but much more detailed activity to help you clarify your purpose in life and better understand its value is to write your own obituary. A brief search on the Internet quickly reveals many websites that can guide you in doing just that.[69] Rather than being depressing, this strategy can lead to insights about what is really important to you and what you want the meaning of your life to be.

Questions for Reflection

One source of valuable ideas for spinning out your thoughts about life can be found in Tolan's book *Change Your Story, Change Your Life* in the exercises pertaining to what she calls "Story Principle."[70] These are found throughout her book in the sections labeled "Putting It to Work." For example, she suggests that the first step is to discover the stories we are telling ourselves that are not helpful; her book includes specific advice on how to do that: listening to others, listening to ourselves, and experimenting with changing a fairly small story that you find you are telling yourself about something in your life. These and other exercises in Tolan's book and various questions such as the ones from Webb[71] and Raines[72] (later in the text) are good prompts for journal writing—a worthwhile strategy for bright adults to use regularly to reflect on their lives.[73]

Many bright, talented, and gifted adults find themselves confronted with so many options that are attractive to them that they become stymied. Because they have an abundance of abilities and interests, they do not necessarily know which course to take.

Dealing with Life's Dilemmas

A set of either/or issues is at the heart of the challenging choices that bright adults face. In Jacobsen's book *The Gifted Adult: A Revolutionary Guide for Liberating Everyday Genius*, these issues are summarized as nine quandaries for gifted adults.[74] In order to live satisfying, fulfilling lives, bright adults must grapple with and overcome these dilemmas:

1. *Either* define, accept, and develop your gifts, *or* deny your gifts by fulfilling the wishes of others.

2. *Either* honor your need for independence and find some true peers, *or* tolerate isolation, misunderstanding, or loneliness.

3. *Either* take reasonable risks and avoid those that endanger your mission, *or* play it safe on the sidelines, risking a life full of regrets.

4. *Either* manage the boundaries in interpersonal relationships to be wisely discriminating, *or* pass up intimacy altogether.

5. *Either* listen to inner guidance and activate your soul's intention, *or* refuse to hear and bury your creative spirit in a one-dimensional reality.

6. *Either* use your exceptional gifts to benefit humankind, *or* indulge yourself in spirit-devouring self-gratification.

7. *Either* value the different traits and abilities of others, *or* remain immaturely intolerant of others, chronically impatient, and perennially disappointed.

8. *Either* turn frustration and rejection into creative energy, *or* cling to resentment and surrender your dreams.

9. *Either* initiate a balanced plan of self-maintenance strategies, *or* wait for external sources to dictate and control your life.[75]

For bright adults, dealing with these dilemmas is likely to be a lifelong challenge because they recur in all aspects of life. But every challenge overcome is another instance of finding empowerment and satisfaction in everyday life.

Chapter 4

The Seekers—Heading Out

~ ~ ~

"Twenty years from now, you will be more disappointed by the things you didn't do than by the ones you did do. So throw off the bowlines. Sail away from the safe harbor. Catch the trade winds in your sails. Explore. Dream. Discover."

—Mark Twain[76]

"I don't get it," said the young woman to her best friend—someone she knew she could always count on. "I thought that once I finished high school everything would be great, but it's not. I still don't feel like I fit anywhere." Her friend listened as she went on and on, analyzing all the whys and wherefores that might be behind her dissatisfaction with life. It was a familiar story; sure, she and her friend had both had many great, exhilarating experiences, but both had also struggled through the trials and tribulations of being bright and out of sync with their classmates and educational system when they were young gifted students. Both impatiently hoped things would be better after high school graduation, or at least by the time they passed the magic milestone of officially becoming adults at age 18.

The Lady-in-Waiting

A major task for gifted children is learning to wait for others to catch up. Recently, a gifted adult described how for so much of her life she felt like a "lady-in-waiting." In grade school, she waited while others figured out solutions that were obvious to her—but she believed that in junior high it would be different.

In junior high, she spent as much time waiting as before, but things would be better in high school. In high school, she found herself even waiting for teachers to catch up. But surely in the adult world things would be different! So she dropped out of school and married an older, successful professional man. Now, within a fairly narrow circle of friends, she finally does not have to wait so much.

Gifted children soon recognize that much of their life is spent waiting, and that their time often is "wasted" by others. Somehow these children must learn to wait, and to "suffer fools gladly," a task that they will have to continue throughout their lives.[77]

A Quest for a Place to Belong

Having felt misplaced and misunderstood throughout their school years, bright young adults eagerly turn a new page in their lives once they put high school behind them. Eager to be grown-ups, they think, "Once I go to college or get a job, I'll find my place in the world—a place where I belong, with exciting and interesting things to do and think about. Then I'll make my own choices and I won't feel so alone. Things are bound to be different then!" These are the Seekers, filled with hope and searching for meaning in their lives—meaningful intellectual challenges and meaningful relationships with others who are like them.

Being on their own for the first time is often an intensely joyful time for gifted young adults, and some of them do walk right into wonderful new lives in college, graduate school, or their first real jobs. They finally feel in charge of their own lives, answerable only to themselves for their choices and their behavior. Although many challenges come along with their newfound freedom, Seekers tackle them with their characteristic intensity and a level of euphoria they have not experienced before.

Other bright young adults can see so many exciting possibilities for their lives that they feel overwhelmed and seriously question whether they are making the *right* choices. They change majors repeatedly in college or they drop out and then come back later (or never). They job-hop. Sometimes they spend hours agonizing over whether they should listen to their friends' advice about what to do rather than just deciding on their own.

The term Seekers certainly fits these bright adults ages 18 to 25, because they are on a quest to find somewhere in the world where life is • the way they think it really should be. At this time of their lives, they are typically idealists and "see themselves and the world in terms of how things might be or should be; so they cherish principles, emphasize values, and pursue goals and purposes that seem good and righteous."[78] They would like to think that they can join in with other idealists in making a difference in the world. They would like to think that there is somewhere they belong—where their abilities will be valued and their minds challenged, where they will be accepted and appreciated, and where they will find kindred spirits and friends. They are filled with optimism about moving into long-awaited adulthood, out on their own and finding their own niche where they can flourish.

For some, these hopes and dreams pan out. Entering college or making their first forays into a promising career does lead to academic challenge and fulfillment, good friends, and worthwhile romantic relationships. The Seekers connect with people who share their interests and get their jokes, people who are filled with expansive thinking and the intense pleasure of being free from the limitations and conflicts of their earlier years—a time of life when it seemed that there was hardly anyone like them anywhere. They find their college courses intriguing; they discover new interests and classmates and professors who challenge their thinking. They get together with people of different backgrounds and points of view unlike any they have experienced before. They talk (and sometimes argue) well into the wee hours of the morning over subjects that they care deeply about, and they often find their old beliefs and illusions being challenged. They go on dates with interesting people and discover new ways of relating to others. They get involved with a variety of causes and explore alternative lifestyles. Life is good—not without its ups and downs, but good. They have sailed into brisk, fair winds that take them to intriguing new destinations.

Searching Within

As they find kindred spirits in college and beyond, Seekers search within themselves to gain greater clarity about their own identity—to determine who they really are, to decide if they want to move away from home outside of the direct influence of their families, and to make decisions about where they want to be. Of course, most Seekers are aware of expectations—from family members, teachers, other authority figures, friends, and the culture that they grew up in. They often struggle to resolve the conflicting feelings they have between what they want to do and what they think they should do, based on subtle (and sometimes not-too-subtle) messages that their parents and others have been giving them throughout life.

For still other Seekers, a different reality tarnishes their dreams. The challenges to their previous ways of thinking are so new, different, and upsetting that they begin to question things that they have never before thought seriously about. The ideals, lifestyles, and values they previously took for granted may seem meaningless or wrong. Their newfound discoveries may cause them distress, and the result is a meltdown or disintegration, but one that can result in a positive and healthier reintegration later. The seas of existential angst are stormy indeed.

Some Seekers find that their childhood friends, parents, or other family members are uncomfortable with their new ideas, too. As Seekers explore new lifestyles, they are likely to question and challenge family and social traditions, often making others uncomfortable. In some cases, particularly for any who come from traditional homes, Seekers may experience a major break from their families, temporarily severing or restructuring relations in their search for independence. This can be an emotional and challenging time for Seekers and their families.

College Planning/College Life

Caught up in indecision, many Seekers spend hours brooding about which college to choose, what to major in, and what career to aim for, all the while struggling to resolve their concerns about whether they are making the *right* choices. Sandra Berger stressed the importance of learning decision-making skills and helping bright young people learn that *not* making a decision will also affect their future. She even offered a systematic 10-step process that skillful decision makers follow, including questions they can ask themselves to assess the advantages, disadvantages, and consequences of alternatives they are considering.[79]

Once they get to college, the sought-after stimulation of their classes does not always have the desired results. Some undergraduate students suffer through soul-sucking prerequisite courses that cover material they have already learned or otherwise find irrelevant, presented at a pace slower than the proverbial molasses in January. They have trouble finding others who take college as seriously as they do, and most of their classmates seem only to be interested in partying and in finding classes with instructors who are reported to give "easy A's." Other people they meet do not seem to share their concerns about the world and how it could be better. It is not unusual for these Seekers to come home for Thanksgiving or Christmas break and announce abruptly to their families that they are going to drop out of college—that they think it's dumb, boring, and meaningless and that they don't see any point in continuing to waste their time there. If their parents do talk them into staying in school, many of them do not find the satisfaction that they seek. Some of them slip into the party scene and hang out with the bar crowd until they flunk out.

Seekers who do stay in college may try out a succession of majors, torn between compelling and intriguing possibilities for widely differing careers. When I was working on my doctorate, one young college freshman wandered into my office one day, saying, "I saw the sign for this place. I think I used to be one of those 'talented students.'" I asked him what his major was, and he said that he hadn't decided. He said, "I'm really interested in music, but I find myself drawn toward history or maybe engineering, too." He was in a quandary, standing in front of a smorgasbord of possibilities, all of which he had ample capabilities of pursuing successfully—facing issues of multipotentiality,[80] having all kinds of different gifts and talents in all kinds of different areas.[81] As Berger reported, "Many multitalented students have heard the saying 'You can be anything you want' over and over. But that's precisely the problem: They seem to suffer from a wealth of abilities."[82] This may be why Felice Kaufmann, in her study of Presidential Scholars, found that 55% of these gifted students changed college majors, and 33% changed their majors two or more times; further, 10 years after college graduation, 29% of them doubted that they had made the correct career decision.[83] Seekers need help prioritizing.

Career Development/Life Paths

Some Seekers find smooth sailing as they move through the many transitions of life that mark their journey between the ages of 18 and 25, especially those from the middle and upper classes within the dominant culture with families who are supportive of them. These Seekers went to schools committed to providing challenges for them and other students who were identified for gifted programs and advanced classes. Their high schools and colleges provided career guidance, mentorship opportunities, and alumni connections for beginning careers. This is not necessarily the experience of all gifted students during their years in school, especially those who come from dysfunctional families, are homeless or live in poverty, or who go to inner-city or rural schools or any others where services for gifted students are nonexistent.

Some Seekers just drift for a while and go whichever way the winds of life take them. If opportunities are available, they may take advantage of them and sometimes things work out. Other times, they go along without taking time to reflect on how things might be different until many years go by, or else they excessively agonize about what they should do but do not take action to set a course that might work well for them.

Some college graduates find themselves moving back home with their parents after they finish school or when they take a "gap year" or two off from college to reconsider their options. They do it for financial reasons or because they are applying for jobs and have not landed a position yet. Some of those who take time out from college and move back in with their families are disenchanted with the majors they chose. Or they have become intrigued with possibilities outside of higher education. Some of them need to work for a while to get caught up financially or for their parents to deal with unanticipated financial setbacks or economic downturns. Having these young adults move back home has significant impacts and trade-offs both for them and their parents, some of whom may have been looking forward to becoming "empty nesters." Seekers living at home want to be autonomous and do not want their parents telling them what to do or trying to direct their lives. Parents figure that they have a right to speak up as long as the Seekers are living at home. Both parents and Seekers can easily slip back into old family patterns—regardless of whether those patterns are helpful or healthy for this time in their lives.

In considering the career development of gifted adults, Barbara Kerr and Charles Claiborn discussed the following issues: [84]

○ Resolving multipotentiality and the confusion of unraveling multiple options

○ Finding a mentor and the development of a reciprocal mentoring relationship

○ Getting advanced training

○ Maintaining productivity and overcoming blocks

○ Issues of underemployment.

Each of these is especially relevant for gifted Seekers as they wend their way through the years from ages 18 to 25. Finding their way to a meaningful career focus becomes especially important, and these tasks often influence each other.

Mentors

Finding a mentor is a significant factor that can prevent isolation and help Seekers develop their skills and resilience. Often, one mentor can also suggest other mentors for the next phase of a Seeker's life—e.g., when moving from undergraduate to graduate school or a career. A mentor can act as a kind of tour guide—someone who has taken the journey before and can draw on her knowledge and experience to point out sights and sounds and things to learn along the way.[85] But just as tours are influenced by the individual participants, interactions between the mentor and mentee become a unique learning experience the participants share.

The presence of an experienced and trusted mentor as an advisor is especially meaningful and relevant for helping Seekers resolve issues of isolation. This trusting relationship with an adult serves as a "polestar." Like the North Star in the northern hemisphere, a mentor becomes a fixed point of light to focus on even when everything else in the Seeker's life seems to be swirling out of control. A relationship with a mentor is even more helpful if it is long lasting. This person might be a parent, a favorite aunt or grandparent, a teacher, a coach, or anyone with whom the Seeker makes a solid connection. One group of bright teens, all part of a horseback riding club, were highly influenced by their riding teacher who would spend hours with them talking about all kinds of philosophical issues. After horse shows, they would have lengthy discussions with each other and their beloved teacher about whether life is fair—a topic near and dear to the hearts of so many bright adolescents and young adults. Those who are deeply concerned about morality and justice are especially in need of the guidance an understanding adult can give them. We'll take a closer look at mentorships in upcoming chapters.

Entering the Workforce

Whether Seekers enter the workplace right out of high school, take time out from college, or go to work immediately following undergraduate studies, some of them actually find what they have been looking for—intellectual stimulation and exciting new opportunities. They find their way to an interesting social scene, and a whole host of fun activities fill their days and nights after work. They are free to seek others with similar interests, passions, and thoughts.

But when it comes to work, many Seekers run into problems again. Entry-level jobs seldom provide the much-hoped-for opportunities and support for using their minds and exercising their creativity and problem solving abilities. Too often, bright individuals run into trouble communicating with supervisors who are startled by them and their insights as well as all they already know and can do—supervisors who are threatened by the talent, vision, competence, and confidence of these bright employees. Seekers may see ways the business could be operated more efficiently or in more socially responsible ways, and they have criticisms that others cannot accept. They have difficulties finding other people at work who are on their wavelength—people whose minds function as rapidly, diversely, and idealistically as theirs do and who care as deeply as they do about everything, including sharing similar visions of how the work should be accomplished.

Being overqualified for entry-level jobs can be another problem for Seekers, and fatigue and depression are common results.[86] Even those who are ready, willing, and able to make use of their unique gifts and talents in the workplace may find themselves stymied. They run into situations where their contributions are discounted because of their youth and inexperience, usually by those who consider years on the job a prerequisite for saying or doing anything worthwhile. Their knowledge and abilities exceed their credentials, but they find themselves in systems that assess abilities based on degrees and prior experience. The result is often that they feel isolated and lonely and their co-workers think that they are arrogant and antisocial.[87] "Who is this young upstart who dares to criticize the way we do things here?" The result can be frustration, resentment, and hostility. These Seekers fail to find exactly what they are most yearning for—significant work where others appreciate their talents and meaningful relationships where they can share their ideas and ideals safely. The outcome can be quite disillusioning.

Today's Seekers usually see work as a place to garner a skill set and then move on. They do not necessarily feel any particular loyalty to their employers. Most employers have had to accept that once Seekers obtain the skills they desire, they will likely be looking for new opportunities. However, some Seekers are those who place a high value on loyalty and feel uncomfortable about leaving an employer. They feel guilt and anxiety when they do decide to leave, even for a better position where their abilities are more likely to be appreciated and they can find new challenges and opportunities for growth and advancement in their chosen field.

Some fortunate Seekers do find jobs that seem to be a perfect match for them and their abilities. Their co-workers are on their wavelength, value their ideas and contributions, and help them "learn the ropes." One Seeker, with a bachelor's degree in home economics,[88] got a job in a major Midwestern city with a large public relations firm that had clients in the food industry. Her job as the firm's home economist was multifaceted—writing for all media, developing recipes, directing food photography, and making client contacts. The work was challenging, interesting, creative, rewarding, and full of variety, and the account executives she worked with welcomed her and supported her efforts.

However, even though the stars seemed to be aligned for her in her work life, problems arose with relationships in her personal life. Most of these were related to her intensity and being significantly out of sync with others, including in her love life. Her intellectual abilities and high energy level interfered with receiving acceptance from the men she dated; they had difficulty appreciating her for who she was. These difficulties plagued her for years, and she found herself trying to adjust to societal expectations of what she *should* be like while also attempting to figure out how she could establish her own authentic identity.

Searching for Kindred Spirits

Eric Erikson labeled young adulthood as a time of struggling with "intimacy versus isolation."[89] For Seekers, the potential for intimacy lies in finding one or more kindred spirits—someone with whom they can truly connect, someone who accepts, understands, and appreciates them. They search for other people who are compatible with them in college or at work, for friendships or a romantic relationship.

However, finding others who have much in common with them is especially challenging. Gifted individuals, already a minority group, are more likely to have difficulty finding a soul mate, partly because of the scarcity of others who are as bright as they are and partly because of the other significant differences between them and others. Their broad and sometimes esoteric interests, the intensity that permeates their lives, and the rapidity and depth of thinking and feeling of Seekers often sets them apart from others who just do not know how to respond to them. For instance, not many people will be fascinated about how solar flares might be the cause of lightning, or how Russian leaders have influenced the country's economy through the years, or the details of the communication systems of bees. Finding people whose eyes don't glaze over when Seekers start waxing eloquently about their favorite subject can be a struggle for these bright, intense individuals, and they are often baffled by the ways that others react to them.

Romantic Relationships

In the midst of finding meaningful connections with friends and colleagues in college and the workplace, Seekers are searching for romantic relationships. Most find themselves getting into and out of relationships with their characteristic intensity—exuberant involvement and bliss, followed by disillusionment, sadness, angst, and despair. For them, falling in love is more like plunging headlong into a deep blue sea. Within the context of their relationships, nothing is taken for granted. Happy times are euphoric, and troubled times are dreadfully disastrous. When Seekers find someone who truly seems to be a soul mate, these relationships are extremely valuable for them.

Even the best of relationships, however, create additional complications in their lives. Although a good relationship is a tremendous source of support and satisfaction, it can also take a huge amount of time and energy, demanding attention otherwise required for day-to-day living and for making larger life decisions. This may be truer for women than for men. Men are still more likely to emphasize career and achievements than romantic relationships, sometimes to the distress of the women in their lives who wish they would pay more attention to the relationship. Whether the relationship ends up on the rocks or in a long-term commitment or marriage, continual interpersonal skills are needed in order to manage the needs, complications, disagreements, and other issues that are likely to arise—particularly if both people in the relationship are similarly sensitive, intense, and idealistic. Relationships take work, and gifted adults have their own unique challenges in romance. They are likely to overthink what is said to them and to infer hidden meanings, they may compare their relationship with that of couples in other cultures, or they may find themselves entangled intellectually or romantically with a co-worker— a situation that can often lead to complications in the workplace.

Seekers who understand and celebrate the factors that relate to their giftedness—intensity, sensitivity, idealism, rapid pace of learning—are better able to understand and make connections with others and to find common ground with them. Otherwise, Seekers have difficulty grasping why others are not much like they are, including a lack of wide-ranging interests. With their typical intensity and rapid pace of learning, they often find themselves going in so many directions at once that they run into other people who accuse them of having ADHD.[90]

Their heightened sensitivity combined with their tendency to feel deeply and agonize over decisions often pulls Seekers into "a whirlpool of conflicting choices, both personal and professional."[91] A significant portion of young adulthood has been characterized as the "Trying Twenties—a time when bright individuals are focusing on what they think they are supposed to do."[92] But the pervasive attitudes of the world may be diametrically opposed to what their hearts are calling them to pursue. On the one hand, they may aim for significant recognition and the outer trappings of success. Knowing that they have all kinds of options for careers, some bright Seekers focus on making money and achieving power. These particular Seekers gravitate toward careers that will have the biggest payoffs in worldly rewards—financially, in status or clout, or in recognition. On the other hand, what many other gifted Seekers really want is to pursue their passions, the things that they really care about, regardless of whether these most cherished dreams will bring them fame and glory and the "big bucks." These Seekers will have to deal with friends and family members who say things to them like, "How will you ever make a living?" "How will you ever support yourself?" "You'll never make decent money doing that!"

Developing Resilience

How Seekers face the challenges of the years between 18 and 25 may somewhat depend upon their background—on whether they have had successful family, academic, and social experiences during their school years and whether they have had support in making decisions.[93] Appropriate recognition and responses to their educational and social/emotional needs either in school or when being homeschooled generally help build a positive sense of self and a powerful capacity for coping with adult life, even given the challenges that Seekers typically face. Although coming from a supportive family helps, some Seekers grow up in families that cannot be supportive, for whatever reasons—limited resources (e.g., adequate time, energy, and money), long-standing authoritarian family patterns, lack of understanding about effective parenting for bright children, conflicts between parents, and basic belief systems about family roles and behaviors. One father, who was uncomfortable when his gifted stepchildren questioned his house rules, regularly told them, "As long as you put your feet under my table and eat my food, you'll do what I say and no questions asked!"

Those Seekers who come from diverse backgrounds and do not have support for their giftedness at school or at home are particularly likely to travel through stormy seas. The intensity of their behaviors and reactions makes the waters even more turbulent for them. As psychologist Daniel Keating pointed out, "The imbalance of race and ethnicity among individuals selected for gifted education programs remains striking."[94] Seekers from underserved minority populations include many who take to heart the ill-suited advice on what they should do, based on cultural norms that surround them. They yearn for a satisfying, meaningful life, one that has relevance for them, and wonder how they can go their own way regardless of traditional ideas that other people have about what their direction in life should be. Regardless of their background, Seekers need access to resources and adult support to know how to achieve their dreams. On the bright side, those Seekers who develop resilience earlier in life are better able to deal with adversity.

Resilience develops by overcoming challenges and difficulties, but sometimes young gifted adults need more than their own strength to move beyond their troubles rather than simply enduring them. A variety of factors can effectively assist Seekers in developing resilience. Among these are collaborative programs between home, school, and community; the presence of a mentor; informal sources of support; and opportunities for developing creativity.[95]

Although informal sources of support help young Seekers develop resiliency and prepare for careers, formal collaborative programs can provide a wealth of opportunities and support for educational experiences. One good example of such a collaborative program is service learning,[96] a recently adopted requirement for many high school students. Service learning can pave the way to the future by providing meaningful avenues for bright students who yearn for experiences with real world implications. For example, one young woman, who had done a prize-winning science fair project about eco-friendly architecture, completed her service learning requirement by working with a local architectural firm that specialized in designing buildings that focused on both functionality and sustainability. This kind of collaboration between a school program and the local business community shows how schools and businesses can work together to help Seekers develop skills while gaining insights into possible career paths—a key issue for this stage of life.[97] This is especially relevant during the transition from adolescence to early adulthood, with implications for Seekers that range from involvement in advanced education to exploring career options.

Productivity

Because of their intensity and multipotentiality, Seekers often find themselves pulled in many different directions trying to maintain productivity and overcome obstacles. This may result in a diversion from the course they have set to reach their long-term goals. Some Seekers did not have earlier opportunities to take on meaningful long-term projects—where they could totally immerse themselves, close their eyes to distractions, and sustain their efforts to complete all the tasks that were necessary. Seductive immediate interests and day-to-day responsibilities can easily deflect Seekers from even well-established plans for a productive work flow, and the more time that passes before they get back to their project, the more difficult it becomes to complete it. They are commonly accused of procrastination, but the threat to their productivity and the real source of their blocks may actually be self-criticism—the little voice in their heads that says, "You've never done something like this before. What makes you think you can do it? Who do you think you are?"

Relationship problems can also be a source of blocks to productivity for Seekers.[98] Gifted adults typically combine their characteristic intensity with a pretty big dose of perfectionism, desiring excellence in all aspects of their lives, including in their relationships. One of the peculiar quirks of human beings is that the closer we get to someone in a relationship, the more likely we are to expect the same things of them that we expect of ourselves. Then, when we run into trouble in our relationships, the resulting heartache makes it extremely difficult to concentrate on anything else.

Extroverted Seekers or those who grew up in families that emphasized socialization—being "popular," having lots of friends, and being in romantic relationships—are more likely to have problems if and when their relationships do not match up to the standards they have internalized, usually due to messages from their parents and the culture they live in. However, some Seekers—particularly those who are more introverted or on the autism spectrum—do not want to be bothered with relationships and are perfectly happy, even though they may feel twinges of discomfort because the culture they live in has always emphasized outgoing personalities and social success. In her best-selling book, *Quiet: The Power of Introverts in a World That Can't*

Stop Talking, Susan Cain champions introverts and offers support as they seek satisfaction in life; she writes pointedly about the valuable contributions of introverts and how they can find comfort in a world that idealizes extroverts.[99]

Waypoints and Strategies for Seekers

The following seven issues are waypoints that specifically mark the journeys that Seekers commonly take during this time in their lives:

1. Gaining greater clarity about their identity
2. Overcoming isolation
3. Finding relevant things to do and think about
4. Making college and career choices
5. Coping with entry-level courses and jobs
6. Finding like-minded mentors and colleagues
7. Dealing with newfound freedom.

The following sections offer recommendations to help Seekers navigate the challenges they face during this part of their journey. Each approach can be used by itself, or several can be combined in whatever ways seem most relevant for you.

Gaining greater clarity about their identity

During this time of life, bright adults are establishing their own identity and choosing directions that work for them. With their meta-cognition, heightened sensitivity, and deep feelings, they question why they seem different from others at the same age and stage of life.[100] Their asynchronous development contributes to the complexity of their lives, especially since they are increasingly aware that they are more mature than their chronological age in some ways but are far less mature and thus "younger" in other ways. The expectations that they grew up with may create confusion about their identity. They seek clarity about what feels right for them now. These strategies may help Seekers establish lucidity about their identity:

○ Keep a regular journal to help you sort out your thoughts and feelings about yourself and your life.[101]

○ Read self-help books, blogs, and websites, particularly those about similarly bright people.

○ Monitor and assess your own personal responses to different situations; recognize your intensity and impatience and give yourself time to adapt.

○ Label shades of feeling to reflect how intensely you feel about what's going on in your life—e.g., are you mildly, moderately, or extremely upset or angry (i.e., are you just somewhat irritated or really enraged…or?); embrace all feelings.

○ Recognize and accept the sensitivity that underlies your feelings.

○ Use an "Expectations Chart" to help you sort out conflicting messages from others in comparison with your own.[102]

By clarifying their own identity and how they feel about themselves in relation to other people and day-to-day events, Seekers can better chart their life course. For example, Bret felt bombarded by the opinions of others in his life—his parents and relatives, teachers, and friends. They all commented on how bright he was, and everyone seemed to have such specific ideas about him that he began to reach the point where he was beginning to wonder who he really was.

He began a journal to sort out his feelings about himself and the pressures to live up to what other people thought of him. He wrote nearly every night just before going to bed, and the more he wrote, the more he discovered. He found that he was flattered by compliments and devastated by criticism, and he began to see that he was giving other people too much power over him. He worked on sorting through what people said to him—paying attention to when their comments didn't really ring true for him and made him uncomfortable. He began to see the difference between how he saw himself and what other people said, saying to himself (or writing in his journal), "Well, that's their opinion, but I don't really see myself that way" or "I don't know if that's really true; only time will tell."

Overcoming isolation

Seekers often experience feelings of isolation and loneliness and concern about finding acceptance and meaningful relationships. They search for kindred spirits, others who share common ground with them—a crew to go along with them on their journey. For introverts who yearn for close connections with others, this can be quite a challenge, but it is worth the effort; extroverts put themselves out there with ease and feel more comfortable seeking common ground with people who are not noticeably similar to them. Here are some strategies to help Seekers overcome isolation:

- ○ Reflect on your passions (regardless of college major or career path); attend gatherings and join organizations for people who share your interests (the environment, politics, history, classical music, astronomy, etc.).

- ○ Join online groups and follow social media that focuses on people like you.

- ○ Listen to your intuition about others you meet in classes or at work; reach out to make contact with anyone who seems interesting to you.

- ○ Take noncredit courses and attend events centered on topics you would like to explore; talk to someone afterwards.

- ○ Accept invitations that sound somewhat interesting (but be sure to have your own transportation so that you can leave if you become uncomfortable).

- ○ Learn more about effective communication skills and practice regularly.[103]

Each of these tools can help Seekers find kindred spirits and ways to overcome isolation. For instance, Alisha was an introvert who had always loved the ocean and especially saltwater creatures—everything from sharks and whales to corals and the tiniest reef critters. When she had some spare time, she browsed the Internet to find intriguing sites with gorgeous pictures of marine life, and she visited aquariums whenever she had a chance.

She noticed an ad in the campus paper about scuba diving classes, and she decided to sign up, figuring that scuba diving was a good hobby for an introvert. After all, you could not do a lot of talking underwater. During her first dive trip, she entered into comfortable conversations with other divers during their surface interval between dives, starting with talking about what they had just seen on their last dive. Exchanges of email information followed with one or two of them, and she enjoyed keeping in touch with them after they all got back home.

Finding relevant things to do and think about

Bright Seekers hunger for worthwhile learning experiences and meaningful intellectual challenges. Too often they do not find these in everyday life, even in college classes or in the workforce. They need chances to exercise their creativity and problem solving abilities in ways that do not stifle them. Here are some suggestions:

○ Take online classes, including free courses offered by major universities.

○ Explore TED Talks and other stimulating programs and video presentations online.[104]

○ Read, listen to podcasts, participate in webinars, or attend conferences that relate to topics you are passionate about.

○ Peruse the bulletin board at your local library or at a nearby coffeehouse and seek out events that interest you.

○ Find outlets for your creativity (art, writing poetry, developing computer software, photography, composing music, etc.).

○ Get involved in organizations that welcome your participation and your input and ideas.

○ Avoid unnecessary time spent during leisure hours watching television or engaging in other mind-numbing activities.

By choosing the strategies that suit them best, Seekers can find things to think about and do that are meaningful for them. For example, Greg realized that he had become a football junkie and was spending far too much time vegging out in front of the TV. He decided to wean himself off of football by choosing only one game each week to watch, and he actually calculated how much time that freed up for him. So he decided to check out some of the online courses offered by different universities. He chose one about the history of sports that seemed particularly interesting—one that would even let him earn some credits. Although he did not know if he would ever use the credits he earned, he thought that taking an online course for credit would help him stick to his commitment to do something more meaningful with his mind than watching endless football games. He discovered that he had much more energy than in previous years, and he even got back into photography, which he used to dabble in before. He started taking pictures at local high school sports events and joined a camera club, competing with the other members every month for who brought in the best photograph—sometimes winning with an especially dramatic picture of a scoring play.

Making college and career choices

Seekers often face challenges finding where they belong. They need situations where their abilities will be valued in order to find a niche where they can flourish. Because of their multiple talents, they are often torn between compelling and intriguing options for widely differing careers ("overchoice"), and they need to figure out how to unravel numerous possible directions for using their wide-ranging skills. Others deal with basically the opposite side of the same problem: making a decision too soon—sometimes called "occupational foreclosure." Some pilots and sailors call this "goal-itis"—deciding on a destination and sticking to it, regardless of unfavorable weather indicating that they should head in another direction or postpone their journey until conditions are more favorable. Here are some guidelines for making college and career choices:

○ Identify your deeply held values and zero in on goals that focus on those values; search for meaning rather than a job.[105]

○ At the library or online, research college and career options that you are interested in.

○ Participate in individual or group college and career counseling sessions with someone knowledgeable about bright young adults.

○ Complete career interest profiles, such as the Holland Self-Directed Search, the Strong Interest Inventory, or other self-assessment tools; remember that these were not necessarily designed for gifted people. Reflect on the results in light of your own perspectives about who you are and what you want out of life.[106]

○ Job shadow or interview people who are currently working in fields that you are considering.

○ Learn about step-by-step approaches for making decisions and try one or more of them.[107]

○ Picture yourself choosing one of the options you are considering and determine how you feel about that one; then repeat this with others that appeal to you.

By considering what they most care about, exploring possibilities, and gathering information, Seekers can clarify the direction they want to take in life. For example, Alaina was torn between medicine and engineering. She completed short internships in each area and found a way to combine her interests by majoring in biomedical engineering. Mason wanted to be a veterinarian. However, after job shadowing the local vet for a month, and seeing what vets actually do, he changed his mind.

Coping with entry-level courses and jobs

Seekers frequently encounter situations in college or in the workplace that focus on material they already know or move at a pace too slow for them—a lot like being out in a sailboat when the wind dies and you are caught in the doldrums. These bright adults find themselves frustrated, wanting to get beyond the tedium of drifting aimlessly. They are stuck with basic undergraduate or graduate college courses that are often prerequisites for the classes they really want to take—i.e., courses specifically related to the majors that they want to pursue. At work, they face underemployment with supervisors who have little idea what they are capable of and simply want them to do the job for which they were hired without complaining or criticizing. They seldom have a chance to show what they really can do, because they are just starting out and have not yet "paid their dues." It is a big challenge for them to maintain enthusiasm and a reasonable level of productivity in basic college courses or in entry-level jobs in the workplace. Here are some suggestions:

○ Check which colleges or universities offer opportunities for testing out of entry-level courses and which accept a variety of ways for you to demonstrate what you already know and can do.

O Gather data to document your past experience and to demonstrate your abilities (including both paid and volunteer work); be prepared to present this information when it is appropriate.

O See what you can do to make the entry-level courses or jobs more meaningful—perhaps taking on related projects that pique your interest.

O Make an appointment with your college advisor or your supervisor at work and quietly, calmly, and respectfully discuss your concerns, asking for suggestions and offering any ideas that you can contribute; listen carefully to the responses and avoid becoming argumentative.

O Do what you can to find intellectual stimulation and outlets for your creativity so that you can keep your life interesting beyond the time that you put in at school or in the workplace, at least until you get beyond the introductory courses or the novice phase at work.

O Explore alternatives if you find yourself in an untenable situation after doing all you can to cope—e.g., choosing a different college, changing advisors or majors, or changing jobs.

Janna recently graduated from college with a degree in English. Her entry-level job with a big publishing company seemed to hold good potential for becoming challenging and absorbing even though it was not starting out that way. So she kept her eyes and ears open for whatever opportunities might present themselves.

One day Janna overheard a conversation about something that was in the works that she really wanted a chance to contribute to. Before she approached her supervisor about working on this intriguing new project, she decided to use ideas she had recently read about on the Internet for developing a "functional resume" to submit to her boss instead of the chronological one that she had used for her job application in the first place.[108] She used this format to highlight her skills and accomplishments from both paid work and volunteering—activities that showcased abilities that might not have been obvious to her employer. Because of this (and her enthusiasm), he was willing to let her work on the project on a trial basis.

Finding like-minded mentors and colleagues

Though often a challenge for Seekers, finding a mentor and like-minded colleagues can be challenging but is worth investing time and energy in. Good mentorships and a healthy relationship with colleagues need to be based on mutual respect and trust. Not all potential mentors and colleagues are a good match for gifted adults. Communicating with supervisors and colleagues who are threatened by bright adults and their knowledge and capabilities too often becomes a problem. Furthermore, mentorships or relationships with colleagues are seldom meant to last forever, and the dissolution of a relationship with a mentor or colleagues can be fraught with perils, worry, and painful feelings. Nonetheless, meaningful mentorships and satisfying relationships with colleagues are worthwhile and well within reach for Seekers. Here are some ideas to consider:

○ Know yourself, your personality, and your interests to help you make decisions about who might be an appropriate mentor or colleague for you.

○ Consider the reciprocity of the relationship—what you can bring to it, as well as what you are likely to gain from it.

○ Respond thoughtfully to people who come into your life as possible mentors or colleagues.

○ Take time to sort out the ways in which potential mentors might be on your wavelength.

○ Start slowly and see how it goes before you are too committed so that you can untangle yourself easily from the relationship.

○ Extricate yourself from situations in which your mentor or colleagues seem threatened by your knowledge and abilities.

○ Be prepared to wind the relationship down when it has run its course and served its purpose.

○ Celebrate the various ways that mentorships and relationships with colleagues contribute to enriching your life.

Takeisha, who was considering several different graduate school programs, scheduled a long lunch with a trusted and knowledgeable friend who had been her mentor for quite a while, was a specialist in her field, and knew the key people in it. He pointed out that in one program she was considering, she would need to defer continually to the major professor and would never find her own voice. He said that another university program she was thinking about seemed to produce a series of clones. He advised her to choose the last one that was on her "short list," because that one involved working with someone who would encourage her to be the best that she alone could be. As a result of her friend's candid comments, she chose the one that helped her develop her own identity as fully as possible.

Dealing with newfound freedom

Being a bright adult at this stage of life brings greater opportunities for making independent decisions. Many younger Seekers are living away from home for the first time, while others have returned to their parents' homes, but all in this age group face adult decisions about living arrangements, managing their time for leisure and various commitments, and handling their finances. These challenges continue as time goes by with greater responsibility landing on their shoulders. Here are some approaches that may be useful:

○ Practice systematic strategies for making decisions.[109]

○ Prioritize how you want to spend your leisure time.

○ Write descriptions of what you want your living arrangements to be like, considering various options—what's available, how much you are willing or able to spend, whether you want to have a roommate, proximity to places you want to go, options for dealing with transportation issues, etc.

○ Use whatever system works best for you for managing time—blocking out specific times on your calendar for specific activities, big projects, meetings, exercise, etc. Never skip using that time in the designated way without replacing it with an identical block of time during the same week.

○ Try various approaches for organizing your life; implement the ones that seem to work best for you.[110]

○ Check out practical books about dealing with finances; select one or two that seem to be relevant for you and implement ideas that seem to be a good fit.[111]

Jeff felt like "he'd gone to Heaven" because he had just finished his undergraduate degree in journalism and found a really exciting and challenging job with an advertising agency in a major metropolitan area. There were so many things to do and see there that he was almost overwhelmed by opportunities. It was much different from his life in the small town where he grew up or even in the city where he went to college. At first, he tried to do absolutely everything, but before long, he was pulled in too many directions and was not getting to do many of the things he really cared about.

So Jeff began listing his options and prioritizing them. Work came first, because he really wanted to be successful at his job. He also realized that he needed to be sure to get enough exercise—something that often got short shrift. Because he preferred to live alone, he decided to move to a studio apartment, which also was close to public transportation so that he could get to work easily. He found a place that was close to reasonably priced restaurants, a grocery store, a park where he could run, and an inexpensive gym where he could work out in bad weather. He realized that he could sell his car and rent one whenever he needed to go someplace farther away, like going back home to see his family. By thinking more systematically about himself and his needs, he discovered he could manage his life well and still find time for spontaneous fun with new friends he had made in the city.

A Paradoxical Time of Life

Seekers are continually confronted with paradoxes. On the one hand, their lives are filled with the joy of launching themselves into the novelty of college, new jobs, or fresh relationships. On the other hand, Seekers run into many challenges while finding their way, establishing their own authentic identity, and making myriad decisions that can have huge implications for the rest of their lives. Sometimes it is really uncomfortable for them, and they wish they could just go back to childhood or adolescence when the choices were so much simpler and clear-cut. Seekers sometimes get nostalgic for the days when they lived at home where so many of their basic needs were met. But then they start thinking about how much better it is to be in charge of their own lives and to make their own decisions about what to do, how and where to live, and who they want to be. It's like the difference between being part of the crew on a racing sailboat where the captain is always giving orders versus having your own boat and being the one to decide on the best strategies for winning the race. You may need to make course corrections along the way and you may make mistakes, but you can always chalk them up to "learning experiences."

CHAPTER 5

The Voyagers—
On with the Journey

~ ~ ~

"Cruising has two main pleasures. One is to go out into wider waters from a sheltered place. The other is to go into a sheltered place from wide waters."

—*Howard Bloomfield*

"Our voyage had commenced, and at last we were away, gliding through the clean water, past the reeds. Care was lifted from our shoulders, for we were free from advice, pessimism, officialism, heat, and hot air."

—*K. Adlard Coles*

Kari and her husband were hanging out at home, having a glass of wine and talking about their life together since their wedding a year ago. After finishing her bachelor's degree in political science, Kari had plunged into the nonprofit sector, enthusiastically working with an organization that focused on ameliorating poverty in the inner city. That is where she and her husband met, and they started living together soon after.

It had been five years since Kari graduated from college, but now she was thinking about going on to pursue a law degree. Because of her strong concerns about tenants' rights, she wanted to go into court and fight for people who were having legal struggles with their landlords, including those threatened with eviction due to gentrification and

67

urban development. But she and her husband were in a quandary. Although he supported her ambition to become a lawyer, they had married because they both wanted to start a family. However, she was not yet pregnant, and they were not sure they should begin having children if she attended law school.

Kari and her husband are part of my second group of bright adults—the Voyagers, approximately 25 to 35 years old. They, like many Voyagers, are already immersed in careers that they started when they were Seekers. Some Voyagers who go to college take a direct route through school and into the workplace; others pursue a more circuitous course, but once they start on a career path, they typically immerse themselves, enjoying the many challenges that come their way. Still others enter college because it is expected of them, only to stop for a while or drop out permanently. And some take a different route altogether—one that does not involve enrollment in higher education but still builds on their passions or concerns about the world they see around them.

I call them Voyagers because these bright adults start this part of their journey with more purpose than they had as Seekers, even though they are not necessarily tied to specific destinations. Like sailors who take long-distance voyages, they have general ideas of where they want to go, but they are willing to modify their plans based on new information, including unfavorable conditions or appealing destinations that they discover along the way.

Most people in the general population usually do whatever is expected of them or step into their circumstances in life simply because an opportunity came their way. Voyagers are far less likely to go whichever way the wind blows; instead, they make conscious choices, considering the implications of their alternatives. Bright adults tend to examine every facet of the possibilities before them—sometimes even to excess—and then do what they can to make a good match with who they are and what they want out of life, even when they seem to land someplace on their journey by serendipity.

Voyagers differ from other people in their intensity, complexity, and drive—all characteristics of gifted adults. This intensity is manifested in their energy and sensitivity, and complexity includes complex thinking and perceptivity.[112] Each of these characteristics, which set Voyagers apart from others, has implications for them and their identity as they journey through the stages of their life.

Identity and Authenticity

Building on experiences they had as Seekers, the identity of Voyagers becomes more clearly formed. They are more aware of what they want in their lives and make decisions based on that. At this stage of life, bright, intense, complex adults usually have a better understanding of their hunger for intellectual stimulation and their yearning for meaningful ways to use their abilities. All of this influences the directions that they choose in life and how they respond to the opportunities available to them. Because they have a clearer understanding of their multipotentiality, Voyagers consciously decide which of their wide-ranging abilities they will focus on, at least for now. They tend to move forward with a fair degree of confidence and increased clarity about the career path they want to follow at present, and compared to when they were Seekers, they are less likely to be ambivalent about the next steps they need to take.

Their focus on achievement and developing their potential, while satisfying to them, may also create issues for their sense of identity. Kaufmann studied a group of Voyagers—gifted adults who had been named Presidential Scholars in high school, selected from the upper one-half of one percent of National Merit Finalists. When she surveyed them at ages 26 to 32, she found that, despite their career aspirations, focus, and success, many had experienced sadness and disappointment. This was interwoven throughout their responses about personal matters and "apparently stemmed from some of the subjects' history of over-reliance on academic skills to provide them with an identity."[113] Though most had won many academic awards and received accolades, they found few similar external rewards in the workplace. It was as if they had become "trophy-addicted" and struggled with the relationship between their achievements and their sense of identity.

Kaufmann's results poignantly echo those of Annemarie Roeper about the importance of educating children for life.[114] More recently, Lisa Rivero similarly wrote about the issues and pitfalls inherent in overemphasizing academic success and raised the question of "College

Prep or Life Prep?" She advocated that preparation for life should be given more emphasis for gifted students than it has in the past.[115]

For bright women, the sense of identity can be particularly complex. Psychologist Barbara Kerr, describing challenges that gifted women in this age group face in the 21st century, said, "For smart young women in their late 20s and early 30s, the pressure to both marry *and* have a successful career is immense. Most talented young women expect that they will be able to have children, a career, and partners who will share equally in the household responsibilities."[116]

Bright men and women in this age group want to have it all—a successful career, a happy family, and healthy work and personal relationships. It's a lot for Voyagers to accomplish in these years that seem jam-packed with challenges on every front.

Decisions, Decisions

This stage of life is another paradoxical time for bright and gifted adults, though the paradoxes they face are different from those for Seekers. On the one hand, their values and interests are much clearer now than they were earlier, and they consider their life possibilities on their journey against these. On the other hand, this may also lead them to be more critical of the "practical" opportunities available to them and more frustrated with the decisions they face when these opportunities do not seem to match their personal values.

Their pursuit of life satisfaction, along with their visionary ideas, intensity, and multiple abilities, often leads them to change jobs, although they usually continue on the same career path, just in different positions and often with different employers. This group of bright adults will not continue working in a job that they do not like, including one that has become stultifying or boring, and they job-hop from one position to another even though it may cause dismay for their family members, friends, and acquaintances. If they are prevented from moving away from such jobs, they will likely feel unhappy and even depressed.

Boredom is a serious problem that is common for bright adults, and the abilities and competence of Voyagers make them more likely to experience dissatisfaction. They often battled boredom in elementary, middle, and high school and in college classes, hoping that things would improve when they graduated and started working. But even jobs that are interesting and challenging at first can become mundane after a while—especially when the jobs lack stimulation, challenges, and new things for gifted adults to think about and do.[117] Their impatient idealism and sense of urgency may not only prompt them to want to change jobs, but also may interfere with their interactions and efforts to collaborate with co-workers.

Some Voyagers drowning in boredom descend into the depths of "boreout"—the flip side of the well-known problem of burnout. Boreout is a condition recently recognized and is related to under-stimulation, especially in the workplace.[118] As physician and author Noks Nauta said, "Ironically, the symptoms of bore-out surprisingly resemble these of burnout—exhaustion and a depressive mood—and are often not recognized as coming from boredom."[119] Boredom and boreout can lead some Voyagers into self-medicating with addictive behavior—including substance abuse and more—as a way to deal with lack of stimulation either at work or in their personal lives.[120]

Voyagers yearn for new challenges as an end to boredom. Some find these by taking on new projects at work or by offsetting their job with exciting challenges outside of work. Many who have not yet found satisfactory jobs find ways to practice their passions—in the fine and performing arts, or in creating a business, or through one or more social causes—while dreaming about turning their heart's desire into a career.

Advanced Training—Yes or No? Now or Later?

A frequent decision that Voyagers face is whether to pursue advanced training, such as graduate school, medical school, or law school, or whether to wait a while and then decide. Some opt to work a few more years first and then see how they feel. Choosing between available alternatives is similar to the dilemma sailors face as they decide between staying in a safe harbor or setting out to sea. Both options are appealing, and each has its own pluses and minuses. Similarly, Voyagers may leave the security of a regular paycheck in an established work position to go back to school for a graduate degree or to become a doctor or a lawyer. Sometimes they decide on the challenging option to do both—work during the day and take graduate courses at night. With their advanced abilities, curiosity, and drive,

Voyagers can keep working wherever they are or head out into the uncharted waters of advanced training.

Most Voyagers who decide to go on for advanced training, especially those who trudged through unchallenging undergraduate programs, find that graduate school actually does become that long-sought-after haven. Perhaps they completed their bachelor's degrees in fits and starts with one interruption after another, and it may have taken years before they found their way into a graduate school program that appealed to them. But when they do find it, they are ready. Their focus on their vision and ideals helps them find what they have been seeking—meaningful learning experiences and like-minded mentors and companions.

However, even in graduate school, some Voyagers do not find the level of acceptance they anticipated and become disillusioned. Here is how one described her experience of feeling stigmatized early in her master's degree program.

A Room Full of Teachers

The look I received was incredulous; no, more than that, it was horrified.

It was the first day of class for one of my courses during the second year of my master's program. We went around the room introducing ourselves and saying a few words about our area of research. You know how it goes, "Hello my name is so-and-so and I do research in literacy/curriculum/social justice/policy." You can fill in the blank with almost anything.

This wasn't my first course; I'd been through this ritual several times. Without hesitation I smiled and said, "Hello, my name is Adrienne. My research is in gifted education, specifically gifted adults and the influence of giftedness on their pursuit of graduate education."

Horrified. That was the look I got throughout the room. It was so quiet that I could hear the big clock on the wall ticking off the seconds...so many seconds, too many seconds.

The stunned silence was broken by the most horrified of my classmates, who asked, "Are YOU gifted?" The words hung in the air, dripping with sarcasm and disdain, daring me to say it out loud.

"Yes, I was identified as gifted in elementary school." I could still hear the clock ticking.

Perfect little O's of shock formed on their faces. The faces of teachers.

I could hear their thoughts as if they had screamed them at me. How dare I?

How dare I presume to have been gifted?

How dare I presume to still be gifted?

How dare I say it?...

Even in grad school, where the intelligent, the capable, the educated congregate, I was an oddity.[121]

Despite her discouragement, this graduate student persisted. She was able to move beyond this disheartening time, finish her master's degree, and go on to a doctoral program. There she found a network of true peers and a sense of belonging that enabled her to be more resilient to these types of encounters, which still occurred occasionally. Issues related to uniqueness and to finding a sense of belonging are often particularly poignant for younger gifted adults.

Mentors

Meaningful relationships with mentors are particularly beneficial for Voyagers during this stage of their lives and can help them navigate turbulent waters. This was true when they were Seekers, too, but things are different for them now than when they were younger. As author Thomas Armstrong wrote, this time of life is marked by a greater sense of purpose and direction. His description of those moving out of their late 20s and into their 30s seems fitting for Voyagers and provides some insights into the worth of connecting with mentors:

You're no longer a novice or underling taking abuse from higher-ups, or at the very least, you're definitely fed up with this sort of treatment by now. You want to be taken seriously as a person in your own right and find your place as a full-fledged member of the adult community. Having a mentor—someone who knows the ropes—can be a great help in navigating your way through this labyrinth...They're able to open doors, offer encouragement in times of despair, and provide valuable advice not usually found in the "official" guidebooks to success.[122]

In *The Seasons of a Man's Life*, author Daniel J. Levinson described functions that mentors play: teacher, sponsor, host and guide, and even "exemplar"—an example to be admired and emulated. However, he stressed that the most crucial function of mentors is "to support and facilitate the realization of the Dream" for those they are mentoring—to believe in them and give their dreams their blessing.[123]

In his later book *The Seasons of a Woman's Life*, Levinson continued to emphasize the importance of mentoring as "a relationship in which the two participants conjointly initiate, form, sustain, exploit, benefit and suffer from, and, ultimately, terminate."[124] In other words, a mentorship is a joint venture that is launched, developed, kept alive, and used (or sometimes abused) by both parties. Most mentorships end eventually—either tacitly fizzling out or fading away by mutual consent, or sometimes ending explosively with fireworks and drama.

The relationships that Voyagers have with their mentors are not always smooth and pleasant, particularly as the Voyagers develop competence that begins to approach that of their mentors. The intensity, multipotentiality, idealism, and strong will so often characteristic of bright adults may make their relationships with mentors even more complex. Where things go drastically wrong is when mentors decide that they know what's best in ways that fail to acknowledge the capacity of their protégés to think for themselves. In the film *Good Will Hunting*, the math professor who wanted to direct Will's life was pointedly portrayed as a misguided sort of mentor who was sure that he knew exactly what Will should do. The math professor was portrayed in vivid contrast to the character of the counselor—as someone who was an excellent example of a mentor in a reciprocal mentoring relationship. The counselor's purpose was to help Will chart his own course in life. And, as is often true in good mentorships, the counselor simultaneously found his own life changed due to his interactions with Will.

Mentor relationships unfortunately can become tainted with jealousy as the protégé outpaces the mentor. Sometimes it is the mentor who feels threatened, but it also can be a problem for emotionally sensitive Voyagers who may perceive a need to dim their light so as not to outshine their mentor or any others around them. These Voyagers are in a dilemma—sensitive to the feelings of others, including their mentors, yet wanting and needing to make their own contributions.

As Barbara Kerr and Robyn McKay have noted, this can be an issue for gifted women in particular.[125]

Nell was completing her master's degree in a subject that she was passionate about, working with her mentor, a university professor and noted expert in that field. Everything went well as long as Nell was in graduate school. Because they seemed to have a good relationship, she and her mentor decided to write a book together after Nell finished her doctorate. That is when the difficulties began. The professor seemed unable to shift the interactions between them to resemble those of respected colleagues or peers, even though her former student had assumed that this was the way it would be. The professor acted as if her younger co-author was being outrageously arrogant and questioning her expertise, and the resulting pain and hurt feelings irreparably shredded their relationship.

Mentorships do not have to end that badly. Some shift and grow into a meaningful relationship as colleagues and respected friends. Years after finishing his degree, Brad kept in touch with his major professor—not as regularly, of course. But he always knew he could pick up the phone and call whenever he wanted to talk. From time to time, they would write a paper together to submit for publication or put together a proposal to co-present at a conference. Sometimes, they just exchanged emails to update each other on their lives.

Relationships—Sorting Them Out

Although Voyagers are well aware that they want other people in their lives to share their journey, they are less tolerant than they were as Seekers of others who are not as passionately idealistic, quick thinking, or focused as they are. Rather than acquiescing to those who are less in tune with their beliefs and priorities, as they did before, they are likely to be more discerning. Voyagers' friendships usually are anchored in relationships with people who share common interests and zeal—from work or graduate school or specific leisure activities, such as chess, photography, playing or composing music, singing in a choir, participating in team or individual sports, or pursuing wellness activities. Usually, their relationships are with other complex people with diverse interests, those who can quickly jump between various topics with sensitivity, intensity, and humor.

Informal sources of support are significant for Voyagers at this stage of their lives—just as they were for Seekers—particularly, as Kaufmann found, because they become so highly involved in their work and in pursuing achievements that they leave little time for social relationships. It might seem as if leisure-time involvements could help Voyagers connect with others like them, but this is not necessarily what happens. Kaufmann's follow-up research on Presidential Scholars at ages 26 to 32 revealed that 67% did not participate in any organized activities outside of work. Their most common explanations for this were "lack of time" and "no interest in being a joiner."[126]

Roger, a medical intern and talented pianist, said that his involvement in music helped him counteract what he described as "brain drain"—those times when he felt medicine was sucking every other thought from his mind so that he couldn't focus on anything else that he cared about. Though his piano activities were mostly solitary, he would get together, from time to time, with other musicians who encouraged his creative endeavors. He and the other interns in his program also provided a significant sense of connection and source of support for each other as they dealt with the weighty challenges they faced on their way to becoming doctors.

Some Voyagers do establish social relationships early on, and they use those connections to sustain them through tough times in the workplace or in graduate school, medical school, or law school. For them, friendships are vital. They realize how valuable it is to have one or two close friends whom they can rely on to share the ups and downs of their lives. This is not necessarily easy for them, especially for those who are "solo sailors"—introverts who find it difficult to reach out to others, who actually prefer their own company, and who find themselves drained if they spend too much time with too many people.[127]

Finding meaningful and enduring relationships is challenging. Gifted people are, by definition, a minority group, and the broad range of abilities and differences within the gifted population makes it even more challenging—everything from level of ability, to gender differences, to degrees of giftedness, to socioeconomic status, to differences in upbringing and family background, to racial/ethnic differences. Finding others who share your passions for esoteric subjects, such as medieval music, pre-Colombian art, or the search for extra-terrestrial life, adds another layer to the complexity of social relationships, and the intensity of all the persons involved can make for exultant highs but also for explosive fractures in relationships.

Running into snags with finding kindred spirits and meaningful relationships can wreak havoc in Voyagers' lives in subtle ways and can be another catalyst that leads them into unhealthy mental states and, sometimes, detrimental behaviors. An undercurrent of sadness can flow through the Voyager's day-to-day living, even if the source of it remains shrouded in fog for them.[128]

Romantic Relationships

When it comes to romantic relationships, some Voyagers are still playing the field and searching for a soul mate. Many have been disillusioned with the shallowness of romantic relationships up to now, and they want more. Their concepts of what they desire in a life partner tend to be more solidified during this stage of life. They are better able to see beyond superficial characteristics, such as looks or charm or even shared interests, and to consider more significant core factors like common values and beliefs—factors that might make someone a good partner for them.

As you reach the upper levels of giftedness, the issues become even more profound and challenging. For someone in the top one percent of the population intellectually, others at a similar ability level are rare. There is generally a "zone of tolerance" of approximately plus/minus 20 IQ points if a couple is to have a long-standing relationship, which usually involves sharing concepts, interests, passions, and jokes as well as valuing each other's abilities, intensity, and sensitivity. Otherwise, the relationship is likely to fizzle because you feel that your partner just doesn't understand you.[129] Think, too, about the decrease in likelihood of finding a romantic partner if you are GLBT[130] or if you live in a community where intellect, artistic abilities, or high levels of achievement are not particularly valued. The potential for finding someone who could be a good partner for you dwindles markedly, and this is without even considering factors such as personality, temperament, cultural background, etc.

Knowing that bright adults often feel they do not fit in and have trouble with relationships at work, it seems reasonable that Voyagers would benefit from a meaningful romantic relationship despite the difficulties with finding a suitable match. Whether or not they opt to live with their partner or if they choose to marry, having a soul mate can provide a safe harbor for bright, intense Voyagers.

Many Voyagers wait to marry until they are ready to have children. Others marry but defer starting a family until they have established themselves in their careers. Still others decide that they do not want to have children at all.

Those Voyagers who go into graduate school, medical school, or law school often defer serious involvement in romantic relationships because of the huge amount of time and energy their advanced study, internships, residencies, etc. require. Some Voyagers try to juggle both and hope that their relationships will be a source of support for them during this time. Sometimes this is true; other times not. What is predictable, though, is that Voyagers will experience intensity in their relationships as well as in their work, and if they understand this, they are more likely to be able to balance both aspects of their lives.

Sometimes both partners in the relationship are pursuing advanced study at the same time and have a lot of empathy for each other. It helps if they are willing to be flexible about their often conflicting schedules and about how particular they need to be about household chores, including decisions about meals and their standards of neatness and order.

Other Voyagers decide to take turns continuing their education, often with one going after an advanced degree and the other one working full-time to keep the couple afloat financially. Sometimes the one who works and provides the bulk of the income for both of them can begin to feel resentment and wonder when his or her turn will come— and sometimes it never does. Their relationship may falter when the one in school changes as a result and begins to feel that he or she has "outgrown" the other one. When one partner earns an advanced degree and the other does not, the educational and status balance between the two of them is upset, and there may be competition between them.

Despite their brightness, communication breakdowns are common and may require serious effort to mend; otherwise, the rift may become irreparable. Some bright couples who find themselves slipping into this unbalanced situation have used their strong problem solving abilities and understanding of their sensitivity and intensity to find solutions that prevent deterioration of their relationship. They create more opportunities to talk with each other about ideas, not just the usual mundane aspects of daily living, and in that way find that they can recapture the mutual respect for each other's fine minds that drew them together in the first place. John and Karen, who were one such couple, set aside Friday nights as their own special "date night." Sometimes they used the time to go to cultural events together and out for coffee afterwards to debate, discuss, and sometimes argue about their differing points of view regarding what they had just heard or seen.[131] Other times they just went out for coffee or long walks and talked, and all of this helped them recognize and appreciate each other's intelligence again.

Parenthood?

One question that ordinarily arises for adults at this age is whether to have children together, along with issues related to when and how it will affect their careers. Women particularly still struggle with these decisions.[132] Those Voyagers who are either in long-term committed relationships or married grapple with dilemmas about whether to have children at all. Some are idealistically concerned with population explosion. Others worry about bringing children into such a complexly troubled world. Still others recall the hurts of their own childhood as a gifted child, and they are concerned that their children might have similar experiences.

Simultaneously managing careers and parenthood is challenging for anyone, and particularly so for Voyagers who have high aspirations and goals. Voyagers in romantic relationships generally discuss these decisions at length, often even before they decide whether to marry or have children. Many of them defer having children until much later than others in the general population. Even then, if they do decide to have children at a later age, fertility issues may be a problem and pregnancy may not happen as easily as they thought it would. Their idealism and global concerns for children from other parts of the world prompt some Voyagers to adopt, including international adoption, rather than having their own biological children. Some adopt older children or children with disabilities who are less likely to be selected by other couples.

Singletons who are not in a committed relationship may conclude that they want to start a family, too, and this seems more common among brighter adults. Even though they do not have a partner, these Voyagers are determined to have both a career and one or more children. Faced with a ticking biological clock, some of them decide to adopt or opt for pregnancy through artificial insemination or surrogacy. These Voyagers find effective ways to use their intelligence and creative problem solving abilities to deal with the complexity of their lives, just as married couples do.

Once children are in the picture, Voyagers, like almost all parents, find that they must struggle to balance the demands of their careers and the things they want to do with and for their families, not to mention anything else they might like to participate in. They ask themselves, "Where should I focus my energies?" "How do I make it fair for everyone concerned?" "When do I get to think about myself and what I might really like to be doing outside my commitments?" Time for themselves at this stage of life is almost nonexistent.

Voyagers with children typically are quite involved with their families, and they are usually swamped with their kids' activities. Bright adults characteristically are concerned about issues of fairness, and they want to provide opportunities so that all of their children can develop their abilities to the fullest. These parents usually share child-rearing activities at home and try equally to attend their children's events, often finding that they are more intensely involved than other parents.

Despite their involvement, parents of gifted children can find their parenting to be a lonely experience, and this may be especially true at this stage of life. Even when their children are preschoolers, these parents often notice that their youngsters are ahead of many others in developmental behaviors, such as reading. They may observe that their children are especially strong-willed; concerned with fairness; active; and more sensitive than other children to sounds, odors, textures, and tastes. When they try to share their experiences with other parents, they are often met with blank looks or with comments that imply that their child's quirky behaviors warrant examination by a health professional. Voyagers may want to consider whether they, too, showed similar behaviors as children. They can benefit from gaining more information about young gifted children and perhaps from sharing parenting experiences with other Voyager parents.[133]

When their youngsters enter school, Voyagers frequently find that their children are substantially ahead of others developmentally, and it can be a challenge to persuade schools to provide an appropriate curriculum. Their children also are likely to gravitate toward older playmates or even adults in their search for peers who share their interests and abilities, and Voyagers need to be reassured that this is normal even though the judgment of their children will likely lag behind their intellect. In other words, Voyagers begin to discover that they have gifted children who are very bright, too, and whose intellectual, social, and emotional needs require attention. These challenges accelerate once their children are in school and parents have to confront issues of how the school is providing for them (or not).

Voyagers with school-age children tend to be intensely interested in their children's activities in and after school, and they get involved to the extent that their busy lives allow. However, time management often is an ongoing dilemma. On the one hand, they enjoy the benefits of active participation in their children's lives; on the other hand, significant time is required in the kinds of challenging careers that Voyagers yearn for.

Not surprisingly, these Voyagers may find themselves questioning whether their primary role is as a parent of a gifted child—something that can become such a compelling commitment that they may put their own goals and desires on hold. Can they acknowledge that they are gifted parents—i.e., gifted people who are also parents? And, if so, what does that mean for them?

Issues related to their own abilities, perhaps triggered by observing their own children, now surface vigorously, things that they either hadn't considered before or thought had been laid to rest. This is similar to the story that Elizabeth Meckstroth tells of a bright little boy in Maine who said, with more than a touch of irony, "Giftedness is hereditary; you get it from your children." Many parents who read *Guiding the Gifted Child*, a book co-authored by Meckstroth, have told her that they discovered their own abilities as gifted individuals while reading that book.[134] This is something that frequently happens to parents when they are in Supporting Emotional Needs of the Gifted

(SENG)–sponsored parent support groups,[135] initially built on the chapters of *Guiding the Gifted Child*.

Waypoints and Strategies for Voyagers

Voyagers finding their way through this stage of life encounter some common concerns. The following issues are waypoints that mark their journey:

1. The complexity of identity
2. Career decisions and career moves
3. Advanced training
4. Mentors
5. Relationships
6. Parenting.

Some ideas to help Voyagers successfully navigate the challenges that they can expect during this part of their journey are discussed in the following sections. You can use any of these approaches alone, modify them to suit your needs, or combine several of them. Or you can use them as a springboard to spark your own thinking and create your own strategies.

The complexity of identity

"Who am I?" seems like such a simple question that bright, intense Voyagers may find themselves asking on a conscious level, but this question often reflects an undercurrent of complex concepts just below the surface of their lives. They may grapple with answers to questions about their true identity a dozen times a day or, at least, a dozen times a week. Because of their sensitivity, intensity, and multiple roles, and because of their penchant for examining facets and ramifications of their actions, they seek answers to questions about who they are and what that means for their identity.[136] Here are some strategies for Voyagers contemplating those questions:

○ Think about occasions when you are not sure of your role in life. See if you can pinpoint patterns related to times when you do not feel as if you know the "real you" and experiment with changing those patterns.

○ Initiate or reinstate the habit of keeping a journal to sort out your thoughts and feelings about the various roles you play in your life and how they do, or do not, reflect your true identity.[137]

○ Use your computer, tablet, or smartphone to compile a running list of responses to the question "Who am I?" See what the list tells you about the different roles that you play at different times in different situations or with different people in your life. Keep this list handy and add to it as more ideas occur to you.

○ Join a group that is related to the part of your Self that you want to develop further—e.g., social group, support group, faith-based group, continuing education class, athletic team, or a group practicing a physical activity such as tai chi or yoga.

○ Explore self-help books and workbooks, or find a friend who is committed to the same path of growth and share your experiences along the way.

○ Write a one-act play depicting a dialogue between the various aspects of your Self. What would your "workplace self" say to your "family self," and what would both of them say to your "private self" (the parts of yourself that you do not let anyone see)?

○ Create a collage or other artwork that reflects the multifaceted aspects of your identity. See which aspects are easiest for you to claim and which you want to keep hidden from view. Use this to celebrate everything that makes you "you."

Alicia, a talented middle school teacher, is continually called on to share her innovative ideas for practical improvements for curriculum implementation at her school. She is also a busy single mom with school-aged children and is involved in creating after-school and summer activities for her local community so that her own bright children have meaningful things to do. She often feels overwhelmed. One Saturday, when her children were on a field trip that she had helped set up, Alicia had lunch with Maggie, a close friend from her college days. Maggie made an offhand comment pointing out how adept Alicia had always been at getting along with all kinds of people. This started a chain reaction for Alicia who became increasingly aware of how much of a "people-pleaser" she had become and how differently she behaved in different situations.

Because Alicia is a highly intense and introspective person, this all led to her tossing and turning at night wondering whether what Maggie said was true and, if so, was it a good thing or not. Alicia decided to keep a running list of all of the different roles that she plays in her life, reflecting on how they affect how she interacts with other people. From time to time, she transferred the list to a special file on her computer labeled "Who Am I?" and typed out her thoughts and feelings about each of the various aspects of her life to get greater perspective on how the pieces fit together to form her identity. She has begun to understand how she can be more authentic more of the time and has made it a goal to continue working on that.

Career decisions and career moves

The emotional intensity and visionary thinking of bright adults, along with their yearning to find meaningful challenges and a sense of belonging during their workday, often lead them to agonize about their career paths. They wonder whether they have made the *right* decisions in the past—e.g., about their college major, about the jobs that were available to them when they finished their degree, or about whether their current position offers enough opportunities for stimulation and growth. They ruminate about whether they should seek other options within their current field or if maybe they should go in an altogether new direction. They may find themselves feeling isolated and as if no one else at work is on their wavelength. Boredom sets in far too often, leading to a sense of dissatisfaction and moving them toward boreout if they do not find ways to alleviate the deadly drudgery in the workplace.

The following suggestions may help:

○ Create a chart or graphic or make a list that depicts your thoughts and feelings about what has been good about the decisions you have made in the past.

○ Gather data about your experience that demonstrates your abilities (including both paid and volunteer work); be prepared to share this information at work or when considering new career decisions.

○ Engage the services of a life coach or career counselor who works with gifted individuals—someone who especially understands the characteristics and needs of bright adults.

○ Explore online resources, such as O*Net,[138] the Occupational Outlook Handbook (OOH),[139] and state-specific job search and training sites.[140]

○ Review ideas and suggestions about decision-making offered in the previous chapter, including the use of the CPS (Creative Problem Solving) Model or the University of Massachusetts decision-making processes.[141]

○ Browse the library or bookstores for resources on various strategies for decision-making to see what information you can glean.

○ Search online for other decision-making tools or create your own, combining features that most appeal to you from the processes that you find.

○ Use social media sites like LinkedIn[142] to examine and explore opportunities for career growth; join online groups related to your areas of interest.

○ Brainstorm a list of options that you currently use or have used in the past to prevent boredom. Put a checkmark next to the ones that work well for you and strike through those that you think should be avoided now.

○ Enhance your sense of belonging by connecting with others who share your intensity and one or more of your passions—either at work or beyond.

○ Seek out and collaborate with others who are concerned about making the world a better place and have ideas about how to do that. Check out volunteer opportunities for an organization that relates to what you care about.

For the past five years, Tyler had been working at a job that seemed ideal to him when he first graduated from college. But, little by little, his enthusiasm had waned. It all seemed so dull and routine to him now. He had conquered everything that had been challenging at first, and he really did not see much opportunity for growth or even for variety in the assignments that were given to him. He started feeling alone and did not feel comfortable talking with anyone else about this. His co-workers and others close to him outside of work thought he had the ideal job situation, so he put on a good show and acted as if everything was fine. Meanwhile, he felt lonely and hollow inside. Something had to be done.

Since he had heard about people who had benefited from seeing a "life coach," he started asking around about what that process was like. Meanwhile, he decided to make a list of all of the experience he had already accumulated. Then he looked at O*Net online,[143] using the "Advanced Tools" to compile a list of other jobs that really interested him and suited his skills and knowledge. He found several do-it-yourself life coaching programs available online,[144] so he decided to try one or more of those first, since he was not sure whether anyone was available in his area who would understand bright, intense adults like him. He also considered suggestions he found online for choosing a life coach, and he eventually interviewed several coaches until, after several false starts when he was ready to give up, he found someone who seemed to "get" him. This helped him reflect on the decisions he wanted to make to gain more satisfaction from his life. He has decided to change career paths and is talking with a trusted friend about collaborating to start their own business on the side and make use of some of their strongest skills and interests.

Advanced training — I need mentors, not grad school

At this stage of life, many Voyagers consider going on for further training. For some, it is simply the next logical step in their well-established career path. They realize that the only way to get where they want to go in their profession is to obtain advanced training, even if they had thought that their previous schooling would be sufficient. Others have become totally bored with what they have been doing and have decided on new directions for their careers. Here are some suggestions that might help:

○ Use online resources, such as My Next Move,[145] to collect detailed information about your next career steps, including determining what qualifications you need.

○ Visualize what you think your life might be like if you pursue advanced training; use a T-chart to map out your thoughts and feelings about the pros and cons of getting and having advanced training.

○ To ascertain what the next step on your career path might really be like, use job shadowing by going along to work with someone who has the kind of advanced training that you are considering.

○ Volunteer in places that hire people who have similar advanced training in order to get a broader sense of how it could have an impact on your career.

○ Talk with professionals in your field who already have the kind of training that you think you might need; consider the relevance of their comments to your own career goals and personal characteristics.

○ Contact recent graduates of the programs you are considering; ask them to share their experiences and insights and reflect on whether their programs would or would not be a good fit for you.

○ Imagine that a reporter is interviewing you about what is essential in a program that you might enroll in to further your career. Record your answers to the questions about what you are looking for—cost, convenient location, online or not, working with a mentor, prestige, etc.

○ Narrow your options for programs that seem to fit your criteria and gather data about what is required for admission.

○ If others will be affected by your decision to seek advanced training (e.g., your spouse or significant other), periodically share with them your thoughts and feelings about doing so as well as the information you have gathered.

For the five years since her youngest child entered elementary school, Renee had worked as a staff climate analyst. She was passionate about issues of global climate change and wanted to be able to do more; she saw that she could have a much greater impact if she earned a master's degree or higher. She talked with people who were senior climate scientists with her company about what their jobs were like and asked their advice about what advanced training they thought would be good for her to pursue. Since she still was not sure which direction she wanted to follow, she used some vacation days to volunteer in places that hired environmental scientists and found that her real passion was for environmental chemistry.

Renee searched for master's degree programs that might meet her needs. She found online options for advanced training in environmental chemistry, which she realized might be a good fit with her busy work and family commitments. She asked for contact information for recent graduates of those programs and connected with several via email as part of exploring her options. Since her family was pretty skeptical about how all of this might work out, she periodically shared her thoughts with them in order to convince them to support her efforts. It took a fair amount of juggling by everyone concerned, but Renee was able to finish her master's degree and went on to more meaningful work in her field of choice.

Mentors

Seeking, selecting, and interacting with mentors who understand their intensity and complexity are often vital parts of Voyagers' journeys through this stage of life. Sometimes a relationship with a mentor just happens—a logical outgrowth of educational or work experiences. Other times, Voyagers must search for appropriate mentors. Once a mentorship has been launched, Voyagers need to work to make their relationship as mutually beneficial as possible. Some of the following suggestions relate to finding a mentor; some are designed to help smooth the waters along the way.

- ○ Join professional associations related to your career, get involved by volunteering for committees or performing other needed tasks, and make connections with experienced professionals within the organization.

○ Attend conferences and talk with presenters after their sessions.

○ Network—at work, at conferences, in social situations, and online.

○ Contact people with expertise in your field whose work you admire; ask them directly if they would be willing to mentor you.

○ Listen to your mentor. Avoid the temptation to do too much talking, including pontificating about the "latest and greatest" innovations that you know about because your training is so much more recent.

○ Maintain good lines of communication with your mentor; reply promptly to emails or voice mail, no matter how busy you are.

○ Express your appreciation occasionally for the time that your mentor spends with you and for insights shared.

○ Ask good questions; listen thoughtfully to the answers and ask for clarification as needed. Avoid arguing.

○ If and when the relationship seems to have run its course, find tactful ways to discuss wrapping it up with your mentor.

Bart, a psychologist working in private practice in a Midwestern college town, felt that he would benefit from having a mentor to discuss cases with and to guide him in making the best professional decisions—not only for his clients but also for his own career. He already belonged to the American Psychological Association and noticed that they had a convention coming up soon that was not too far away from where he lived. Although concerned about how big the event was and whether he could make any good connections, he decided to go anyway. He looked over the list of presenters on the schedule and found several whose work he admired and wrote to them ahead of time, asking if they might arrange to meet with him sometime during the convention. One of them wrote back, which Bart found encouraging. So they arranged to meet, and they have begun a mentor relationship using email and Skype to communicate on a regular basis. They have started making plans to co-author an article based on Bart's current applications of his mentor's work.

Relationships

The complexity of relationships for Voyagers is compounded by the basic fact that these bright adults are not average. In other words, there are far fewer people with whom they can connect in meaningful ways. Social relationships and romantic relationships can be a source of satisfaction and joy, but sometimes they can be elusive or even disruptive. Maintaining them can often be challenging, especially given the intensity and sensitivity of bright adults that can create interpersonal conflict as well as inner turbulence and angst. Here are some suggestions to enhance personal relationships:

○ Make time to communicate and spend time regularly with people you care about regardless of how busy your life gets.

• Nurture relationships that are significant for you, and spend no more time than necessary on those that are not.

○ When looking for a meaningful relationship, seek out people at activities and events that relate to what you care deeply about. Exchange contact information, make plans to get together later, and follow up on those plans.

○ Take time to let social and romantic relationships develop somewhat slowly and to enjoy the process along the way. Avoid letting your intensity sweep you along so quickly that you are too entangled too soon.

○ Develop your understanding of personality types, especially the difference between introversion and extroversion. Learn about yourself and about how to relate to people whose personality type differs from yours.[146]

○ If you are an extrovert, be aware of your communication patterns, especially when interacting with introverts. Pay attention to how your actions (including your exuberance and enthusiasm) may overwhelm some of the people who are important to you. Make an effort to curb any inclination you have to interrupt.

○ If you are an introvert, be selective about how you spend your time and allow yourself enough "solo" time to recharge your batteries; avoid getting defensive about your need for time away from others.

○ Listen to your inner voice about your relationships, especially when it comes to deciding which people are enriching your life or challenging you in interesting ways. Focus your energies on spending time with those people, rather than just on anyone who comes your way.

○ Exert effort to be as authentic about your thoughts and feelings as possible, and listen thoughtfully when others do the same.

○ Avoid getting overly concerned, distraught, and discouraged when conflicts arise in relationships with anyone you care deeply about. Find meaningful ways of resolving conflicts that fit your intelligence, personality type, and communication style.[147]

Randi, a market research analyst, loves her job, which takes up huge chunks of her time and energy and leaves her little time for nurturing relationships that she might like to have. She studies market conditions and guides the company's executives in understanding what products people want, who will buy them, and at what price in order to make decisions based on potential sales. When she comes home at night, she has pretty much "run out of steam" and just wants to curl up with a good book.

Randi began to feel lonely and yearned for a close connection with someone who could appreciate quiet companionship and maybe even share her passion for fine literature. However, being an introvert, she just was not sure how to reach out and find anyone who might be a good match for her. The usual recommendations for meeting someone (e.g., going to parties, online dating, and asking friends or relatives to arrange dates) did not appeal to her.

After serious consideration, Randi recalled several in-depth discussions that she had with a man she often saw at book-signing events at the local bookstore. Because she had also seen him regularly at the public library, she quietly asked one of the librarians about him and learned that he was a widower. Taking her courage in hand, she struck up a conversation with him the next time their paths crossed. It took a while, but eventually he suggested that they go out for coffee together, and they began to see each other fairly regularly. Little by little, what began as a good friendship led them into a romantic relationship. Their lives have not been without conflict, but they are learning to give each other ample space and time to let their feelings cool off before coming to grips with the source of their difficulties.

Parenting

A whirlwind of questions swirl through the minds of Voyagers as they deal with issues related to parenting—questions related to having children and questions about dealing with children if or when they do have them. Because of their intensity, Voyagers typically spend hours pondering every aspect of every decision about becoming parents or raising children. The following suggestions can help them find their way.

For those who do not have children:

○ Examine the costs associated with raising a child and consider how that might affect changes in your lifestyle.

○ Discuss parenting styles with your spouse or significant other.

○ Get up-to-date information from reputable sources if you are thinking about deferring pregnancy. Get facts about the risks, as well as finding out about delivery methods, etc.

○ If challenged by infertility or considering adoption, find others who have relevant, specific information that can address your concerns.

○ Discuss all decisions about having children with your spouse or significant other; if none is in the picture, share your thinking with a trusted friend or family member.

For those with children:

○ Connect with others who share your perspective and values; discuss parenting approaches with them.

○ Enroll in parenting classes that are based on credible sources; learn from others who have been on the same path.

○ Make up your own mind about what is right for parenting your child. Listen politely to people who bombard you with advice that, in your heart of hearts, you do not think is best for you and your child, but don't waste time and energy debating with them.

○ Gain insights about parenting your bright child by reading about gifted children in books and online.[148]

○ Consider joining a local or regional group of parents of gifted children for mutual support and to gather information; collaborate with others to advocate for your children.

○ Take time to reflect about how what you learn about gifted children relates to what you recall about your own childhood.

Because they both had strong concerns about issues related to global population growth, Margo and Kent gave a great deal of thought to whether to start a family. Since they were both highly analytical, they had seemingly endless discussions and found that they needed to hash out all of their thoughts and feelings and even sort out how they could both manage having children on top of their involvements in their respective careers. They were raised in very different cultural traditions, so they also discovered the need to resolve differences in their viewpoints about parenting styles. After they decided that they wanted to have children, it took a while for their first child to arrive—a bright and intense little boy. He brought them a set of extra challenges because of the early signs of his giftedness, making both Margo and Kent feel almost as if they were starting second careers—learning about giftedness and about how to parent a gifted child.

Differences and Similarities

Some Voyagers are already in graduate school, medical school, law school, or pursuing other advanced training; or they are vigorously seeking career advancement; or they are thinking about it. Most of them have busy lives—at work and at play—either with a circle of friends, dating in search of soul mates, or within committed romantic relationships or marriages. Those with children are caught up in busy family activities while juggling everything else in their lives.

Other Voyagers do not follow traditional routes or live up to anyone's expectations of what a bright adult "should" be doing. They drop out of college, go to work and learn on the job, or do not go to college at all. They may have had little support from their family and friends, but persist anyway—taking a circuitous route through life. For instance, Marco dropped out of college and works as a waiter while he develops smartphone apps in his spare time. Lisa is one of many artistic types who work at low paying jobs or jobs they dislike so that they can survive while they pursue their love of the theater, writing poetry, composing music, or painting. Countless Voyagers do not conform to society's expectations and take alternate routes through life.

Many Voyagers who begin to acquire the trappings of success may feel overwhelmed. They may have bought a big home or made all kinds of purchases that they thought would bring them satisfaction, but it has not quite turned out that way. These Voyagers become disillusioned with the lifestyle they have pursued, and yet they are bound to it and find themselves asking, "Now what?" They wonder if they should chuck it all and pursue an alternative lifestyle. The lure of simplicity beckons, but it is difficult for them to extricate themselves from the comforts and accompanying debts they have accumulated. Discussions over these issues and considering possible solutions can last well into the wee hours of the morning. During this stage of life, these bright adults need to sort out their priorities and focus on what is most important to them so that they can make decisions accordingly. However, they may be hard pressed to find the time to do that.

This is a stage that includes a wide range of differences for Voyagers in everyday circumstances and life paths. However, the similarities among them include the ways in which they respond to life with intensity and depth of thinking and feeling. These characteristics and others that typify bright adults continue to affect how they react to the challenges they face and to the decisions that they make about their complex, multifaceted lives.

Ralph and Amy are two young gifted parents who need to combine work and parenthood. Despite being busy with their children, they find that parenthood is quite boring, especially during the years when their children are very young. The problem is that they do not have much intellectual stimulation at home. Even when they attempt to have a meaningful discussion with each other or any other adults, they get interrupted because they need to respond to their children. By the time the children are in bed at night, Ralph and Amy barely have time to take care of necessary tasks, including housework and getting things ready for the next day, before going to sleep exhausted.

Although they both have jobs, their work is not very challenging either, partially because they both chose jobs simply to supplement the family income and provide them with time for their children. The result is that they feel bored both at work and at home, but they also feel guilty about that. They wondered how to deal with all of this.

When one set of their children's grandparents invited the grand-children to visit for a weekend, Amy and Ralph decided to use that time to see how they might sort out these problems. They each sat down individually and wrote out their feelings and their ideas for solutions and then started talking. They found that both of them wanted to make some changes but didn't know how to approach the subject with each other. As they looked at what each had written about possibilities for changing things, they discovered creative ideas on both of their lists and began to make plans to alleviate their problems with boredom at home and in the workplace.

CHAPTER 6

The Explorers—Setting a Course

~ ~ ~

"The man who goes farthest is generally the one who is willing to do and dare. The sure-thing boat never gets far from shore."
—*Dale Carnegie*

Kate was on her way to work when her phone rang. Caller I.D. told her it was a good friend, so she answered right away. Before she could get a word out other than "Hi," her friend said, "I only have a minute to talk but just wanted to check in with you. Seems like it's been ages since we had a chance to catch up with each other."

That is the way it seems to go these days in the lives of bright, talented, and gifted adults between the ages of 35 and 50. Many of them barely have time for snatching a bit of conversation in the midst of busy, busy lives, and even then, it is usually on the run.

On a Journey of Self-Discovery

I have dubbed them Explorers because they are on a journey of exploration to develop lives that agree with the identity and priorities they discovered during their years as Seekers and Voyagers. By this stage of life, Explorers have a better idea of who they are and are becoming, and they are clearer about what they want out of life. Their search is more focused and directed than when they were Seekers or even when they were Voyagers. Now they are involved in making corrections to courses that they set out on when they were younger. They have started to feel a sense of urgency about how to make their current lives match the lives they really want to be living.

Many Explorers are deeply caught up with their careers and families, scrambling just to keep their heads (and their mortgages) above water. Those who have children find that they have become intensely involved in parenthood. As a result, the course they had planned to follow throughout their lives has been radically altered. If they are aware that they are gifted, they may begin to wonder about their children's abilities and how they can best nurture them. Others have found a way to co-parent and still stick to career goals. Some have found that their lofty goals for their own accomplishments and for making the world a better place have slipped from their grasp.

Not all bright adults choose to have children. In fact, when following up on Presidential Scholars years after they graduated, Kaufmann found that 73% of her respondents had no children—some indicated that their pursuit of higher education or careers was the reason, some decided not to have children because of political ideology, and some "had serious reservations about bringing a child of their own into the world" because "their own childhood had been so troubled."[149]

Scrambling, Scrambling

Some Explorers consider completely new directions for their lives, and this leads to more exploration—researching possibilities, personally and professionally, if and when they have a chance to think about whether they are satisfied with life as it is. However, time for reflection may only happen at odd moments at work or while dashing off to their kids' activities.

Many Explorers are totally immersed in pursuing goals and passions that began to crystallize during early adulthood. Life at this stage may look quite different for them than for others in the general population because of the characteristic intensity of these bright adults. While most people between the ages of 35 and 50 simply want to settle into a comfortable life with a good, solid job and enough money to pay bills each month, Explorers want more. They want lives with meaning, they want to have in-depth philosophical conversations, and they want to know they are not alone in caring about the world. Whatever experiences they encounter, they respond with multifaceted levels of thinking and feeling.[150] They often question everything, including the "reasons" why others behave in ways that they find baffling and illogical. As Streznewski found, "gifted adults exhibit an intensity, an insistence on the integrity to do the work at its best, as well as chronic impatience with shoddy work and slow thinkers."[151]

Intensity is a characteristic strength, but one that also can cause problems for the gifted Explorer, including problems in relationships. This was true for them as Seekers and Voyagers, but other people were more willing to overlook their intensity and impatience, saying, "They're just young; they'll outgrow this." Acceptance for their intensity is harder to come by when they are in the 35 to 50 age group.

Time is a significant concern for Explorers, and their frenetic lives routinely leave them few opportunities for reflection. Erikson suggested that people find satisfaction during the middle years through meaningful work and family involvements, and to some extent this holds true for bright adults, too.[152] However, it is not the same for them as it was for the middle-aged adults that Erikson described in the 1950s when he first developed his theory. People then led much more permanently established lives; most were settled in their careers and in homes they would keep throughout their lifetimes and perhaps even pass on to their children. Their families moved along in predictable ways in keeping with traditional expectations.

In the 21st century, fewer gifted adults have similarly settled lives. The average U.S. family moves once every five years.[153] Bright adults follow career opportunities. Electronic advances lead to being more connected with others, but also to a life that is superficial or heavily work-oriented. Relationships with family and friends, or even that with yourself, can easily go by the wayside. Typically, in their middle years, Explorers are dealing with day-to-day demands, focusing on the "here and now" except when plans get disrupted—like getting caught in an airport during layovers or because of weather delays. These occasional unexpected interruptions sometimes can provide Explorers rare opportunities for contemplation—that is, unless they spend that time on their smartphones or computers.

Time to Change Course?

When they do pause in the midst of all that is going on in their lives and take some time to reflect, many Explorers are not so sure that they want their lives to continue in the same way. While dashing through their busy days and nights, they have nagging thoughts about making changes. They may start questioning what they are doing and whether it is what they want to do for the rest of their lives.

The catalyst for this sometimes comes from external circumstances, such as what happened for one gifted professional whose company downsized and eliminated her position or for a spouse who is suddenly single through divorce or death. Other times, the pressure is internal—a yearning for greater fulfillment, like the feelings of a stay-at-home dad whose children's growing independence leads him to question whether they really need him the way they did when they were younger, as toddlers or elementary school students.[154] Jacobsen called catalyzing events such as these "Evolutionary Moments," saying:

> *At various points, whether by apparent whim or by design, we've made course corrections. Whether we received navigational aid from someone else or our own inner compass guides us, whether the winds blew us off course or we diverted to avoid a storm, when we're finally back on the ground we can all look back and see when those moments took place.*[155]

This time of searching for meaning can be turbulent for Explorers. Although some in this age group avoid thinking and seldom take time for contemplation of how life should be, that is not the case for others. Instead they find themselves reconsidering long-cherished patterns of thinking, behaving, and responding to others and then try to live lives that are a better fit for their emerging worldviews.

> *Sometimes this feels like wandering about in a deep, dense fog where all the formerly familiar landmarks have taken on a totally altered appearance. At other times, it seems more like being caught in a hurricane, with fragments of their previous ways of life flying at them from all directions. Or it may be a passage onto a different path that finally feels right.*[156]

During this time, some Explorers begin to feel a keen need to accomplish something significant and to live life as fully as possible. Their inner urgings for a better life—one more congruent with what they really care about—propel them forward. They start to consider making changes in their career paths or geographically or even in their marriage or other relationships with family and friends. They feel increasing rumblings of dissatisfaction that spur them toward exploring new ideas and new horizons with other alternatives for leading more satisfying, meaningful lives. Hollis said:

> *Sometimes, to our dismay, we find that we have been living someone else's life, that their values have and are directing our choices. While this life we are leading never feels quite right, it seems to be the only alternative. Even when we win the applause of others, we secretly feel fraudulent.*[157]

The frustration that Explorers had when they were Seekers about living up to others' expectations intensifies at this stage of life. They feel a growing urgency to live up to their own expectations of themselves and to make changes before it's too late—before they are permanently locked into living out their lives in ways that take them too far afield from what their hearts desire. Sheehy quoted a 48-year-old man as saying:

> *I was taught as a small boy to strive for financial success. To be a good provider for my family. Stand on your own two feet and make good. This was drummed into me at an early age, and this was the goal I had in mind—to have children, support my wife, have a nice house, send my kids to Yale like my father did, and be a success in business.*[158]

A Growing Urgency

An undercurrent of sadness for missed opportunities runs through the lives of many bright adults at this stage in life. These experiences are often glibly labeled a "Midlife Crisis"—an often bittersweet description of what goes on for many adults as they start feeling distress and dissatisfaction with the current state of their lives. Rather than describing these times of transition between stages of life as crises, Sheehy more gently designates them as "passages," suggesting that they are basically critical turning points in the life cycle—times that blend vulnerability with significant opportunities for growth.[159] Although many adults experience this passage at midlife, those who are especially bright feel this particularly intensely and, perhaps, as more of a crisis. They run the risk of becoming immobilized as they try to make decisions about their lives, endlessly contemplating a complexity of alternatives and the ramifications of each. It is not necessarily easy for anyone to extricate themselves from a life they do not want, but the potential for a better future can move them forward if they have a vision of what they want their lives to be.

For bright individuals, their best-laid plans may well seem to be falling apart. However, what seems like disintegration can often turn out to be exceptionally positive.[160] They end up feeling that, instead of falling apart, their lives are finally coming together—becoming reintegrated in positive ways. As one bright adult wrote, for example, the time in her life when everything actually turned out far better than it would have if things had not gone haywire for her.[161]

Pursuing Passions or Making Money

A key part of the problem for many Explorers is finding a good balance between pursuing a career they are idealistically passionate about and maintaining employment that provides adequate financial support. As clinical psychologist, researcher, and author Elaine Aron asked, "How can one make money and still follow a calling?"[162]

At this point, some Explorers walk (or run) away from their "day jobs" and head in totally new directions. A recent series of podcasts featured interviews with two men, who are clearly gifted adults, discussing how they identify themselves. One, Erik Hess, is a former pilot, now a web designer and illustrator who sometimes still flies jet fighter planes. His co-host, Gabe Weatherhead, is a blogger and "reformed scientist working as a project manager and systems engineer." Weatherhead describes himself as follows: "I've been everything from a mechanic's helper monkey to a research scientist. I've been in school for over half of my life, which has led to a Ph.D. that I no longer use."[163]

In their search, some Explorers go into business for themselves. Some launch their own technology companies, developing websites and blogs that reflect their vision and their desire to put their long-standing fascination with technology into action. They create new products, live their dreams, and find ways to make their passion and innovative ideas become the source of their income. They often work at home, and their lives take them in drastically different directions from their original career paths. Radically changing careers is not unusual for gifted adults who may steer far from the course they had set when they were young—e.g., an actor who used to be in midlevel management in the corporate world, a teacher who decided to become a dairy farmer, or one bright young man who changed from law to medicine after finishing his law degree and passing the bar exam.

Others multitask and continue to work at their day jobs, carving out time to pursue their inner vision after work and on weekends during whatever hours they can spare. Wendy, a nurse and single mom in her early 40s, has two school-aged children and a full-time job in a doctor's office. With her passion for advocating for older adults, she decided to go back to school for a master's degree in conflict resolution. Even though she continues to work for the doctor for now, she is well on her way to becoming a mediator specializing in helping families interact respectfully and peacefully as they grapple with issues of caring for elderly family members. She plans to make this her career and is contemplating how she can launch her own company to do so.

Explorers often want to make a difference in the world. Some do this by working directly with people, as Wendy is doing. Others aim for a more global impact. Brighter adults at this stage of life are beginning to feel an inner drive toward generativity, a term originally coined by Erikson, meaning "a concern for people besides self and family that usually develops during middle age; especially a need to nurture and guide younger people and contribute to the next generation."[164] These are existential issues—related to our place in the universe and the desire for our lives to have some meaning.

Undercurrents of Frustration

For some, an undercurrent of frustration permeates their busy days; it comes from feeling that there is not much that they, as one individual, can do to make things better, especially during a time in their lives when they are so wrapped up in their careers and family responsibilities. Some, who are disillusioned about their ability to make a difference, shrug their shoulders and say, "Someday…," deferring action on their thoughts and concerns until the future when day-to-day issues are less demanding. Others sink into depression or become angry and cynical and may need outside help to dig their way out of the depths of despair. Webb suggests that disillusionment is a frequent state that these bright adults must learn to deal with, finding an evolving understanding of the world and their place in it by making personal choices and developing successful coping strategies to find a reasonable degree of peace of mind.[165] Most, however, seem to decide to do what they can now, even if it is as little as signing petitions online or, at the very least, learning about, donating to, and voting for political candidates whose campaign speeches give them hope that something may change for the better.

Some successfully find a niche that clearly has a significant impact on the world. Michael is an explorer who developed global concerns during his college years and has taken them to new levels of active involvement professionally. At age 37, he directed the Global Poverty Project for the United States; recently serving as executive producer and creative director of the Global Citizens Festival in Central Park in New York City, he developed and demonstrated an innovative approach to digital fund-raising to support significant causes—in this case, multifaceted efforts to reverse the course of extreme poverty in the world.[166] He and many others in this age bracket are not limited by geography, nor are they necessarily tied down with responsibilities and compelling obligations to spouses and families. Others do all they can to make a difference in the world while sustaining marriages and involvements with growing children.

Whether on a large or small scale, many Explorers find that it is time to make changes in the core components of their lives. At this stage, in the midst of day-to-day demands and their concerns about the state of their world, their nation, and their communities, they stop and reevaluate.

The sense of "now or never," of a pressing need to make the rest of their years as meaningful as possible, may begin with Explorers' reconsideration of their careers and dealings with others. It may start with dissatisfaction with their marriages or other relationships or involvements, or it may come after experiencing a life-threatening illness, the death of someone close to them, or some other traumatic event in their lives. As Cohen suggested, "Middle age, for most of us, is the first time that we seriously consider our own mortality."[167]

Marriages and Close Relationships

Many Explorers find that they and their spouses have moved beyond the initial hopes and dreams of "happily ever after" that led them to marry. Some leave "starter marriages" behind, often by mutual consent, allowing both spouses to pursue new directions either with new partners or by going solo.

As mentioned in the previous chapter, the concept of an intellectual "zone of tolerance" comes into play here. Webb described the importance of similar intelligence for those in relationships, the optimum falling within 20 IQ points of each other. "Outside of that zone, there will be significant differences in thinking speed and depth or span of interests, which likely will lead to impatience, dissatisfaction, frustration, and tension." As Webb commented, "This can make it difficult for gifted idealists to find others with whom they can share their lives."[168]

The Saga of the Bird & the Fish—A Parable with a Point [169]

One couples' counselor helped two bright adults sort out what was happening for them by telling them an old Jewish proverb that turned into a little story to help people in conflict understand the underlying issues embedded in their differing points of view.

Once upon a time in a far-distant land across the far-distant seas, a bird and a fish decided to join their lives together. But, as time passed by, things came to pass between them that caused storms to disturb their otherwise tranquil waters.

The fish said to the bird, "Why are you always flying off to the far corners of the world? Why don't you come down here and dive to the depths with me? You are MY bird, and what's right is right!" But the bird said to the fish, "I can't do that. I can't breathe down there. I'll die. What's right for you isn't necessarily right for me."

At about the same time, as time went on, the bird said to the fish, "Why do you spend all your time in the depths? Why don't you come up here and fly with me? You are MY fish, and what's right is right!" But the fish said to the bird, "I can't do that. I can't breathe up there. I'll die. What's right for you isn't necessarily right for me."

*This went on and on, and the waters of their world were
not peaceful for either of them. But then, one day when the
sun shone clear and bright, the bird and the fish said to each
other, "This isn't fun anymore. Maybe there is another way
of looking at this."*

*Then the fish said to the bird, "Tell me what you see from
way up there in the sky and what you see when you fly to the
far corners of the world." And the bird said to the fish, "Tell
me what you see when you dive to the depths and tell me what
it looks like when you look up from down there." And they
both said, "Maybe we need to stop storming about, struggling
over what's right or wrong, regardless of how strongly each of
us believe that we are right."*

*So the bird and the fish agreed to meet at the surface of
the sea and to listen to what each other had to say. They made
a real commitment to hear each other's point of view and try
to understand it. Because of this, their world was filled with
more light and peace than they'd ever known before, and their
lives were richer for it.*

For such couples, the process of considering dissolution of their
marriage is painful. However, in the long run, it can become another
instance of positive disintegration leading to hard-won personal
growth and development.

Some couples stay in their marriages and discover newly relevant
ways to relate to each other and reimagine and reconfigure their ongoing
relationship. They develop deeper intimacy as they both create a
more meaningful life together—balancing shared goals with individual
efforts to make their own distinct contributions to the world. Others
stay in marriages that are unsatisfactory and even hurtful because
change is too scary or too inconvenient.

Now that traditional family structures are a minority, many
Explorers find it increasingly acceptable to live nontraditional lifestyles
that may work better for them. These nontraditional or neotraditional
family structures include the following:

○ Married couples who choose to remain childless
○ Divorced/single parent
○ Divorced/joint custody

- O Widowed parent with children
- O Separated families
- O Cohabiting parents (not married)
- O Same-sex partners and families
- O Multigenerational families
- O Grandparents raising grandchildren
- O Military families in wartime
- O Families with donors as parents
- O Families with open adoption.[170]

Alternative family arrangements are more common in the 21st century than ever before and even include long-distance marriages in which spouses live apart, maintaining different homes in different states, on different coasts, or even in different countries. In addition to phone contact, they use email, texting, instant messaging, social media sites, and video chatting to keep in touch.

Bright individuals have long been known for androgyny—not in appearance, but in living lives less bound by gender roles.[171] As Kerr and McKay reported, "There is increasing evidence that accomplished women create their own models of marriage, family, and mothering that are independent of societal ideals and stereotypes."[172] Bright men are confronting these challenges, too, not only for themselves but also as they learn to relate to women who are more androgynous and less bound by traditional gender roles. Research studies and the literature suggest that gifted males have to deal with the dilemma of being both gifted and masculine—a combination that is often in conflict with "Sturdy Oak: stoic, stable, and independent…never to show weakness" behaviors left over from childhood.[173]

Traditional gender roles are breaking down more often now. A highly capable business executive, well along the fast track toward the top echelons of his corporation, found himself teaching business courses part-time at a local community college. He subsequently left the corporation and his 70+ hour work weeks and took on the majority of the family responsibilities that his homemaker wife had previously managed. She was able to go back to pursuing her career full-time as a television producer with one of the major networks.

Another bright couple who met after they had each been through several marriages and divorces decided that it worked better for them to live together without being married. They share custody of their children with their former spouses and have been able to establish amicable relationships with the latter. They report that being in a long-term committed relationship without marrying has freed them from traditional expectations of what husbands and wives should do so that they can invent their life together the way they want it to be.

Exploring New Territory

Explorers who head off in their own direction, particularly if it is a nontraditional one, often find that doing so creates tensions in their interactions with others. Because these Explorers are usually more established, they are less likely to be as concerned about whether their nontraditional behaviors cause discomfort for other people. Explorers have a broader life perspective, know themselves better, and often have created a reasonably solid base of at least a few close friends as well as financial stability. This makes it easier for them to chart their own course.

In the midst of compelling demands on their lives, gifted adults face the challenge of exploring new lifestyles and finding ways to be as authentic as possible—to be themselves in a world that gives them so many messages about conforming and performing in sync with the collective vision of what "success" should be. Their quest isn't necessarily an easy one as they search for how to let their lives speak volumes about who they are and what they care the most about. As author, educator, and activist Parker Palmer observed, "How much dissolving and shaking of ego we must endure before we discover our deep identity—the true self within every human being."[174]

Waypoints and Strategies for Explorers

Issues that frequently dominate the lives of gifted Explorers include:

1. Coping with hectic lives
2. Dealing with higher standards than others
3. Questioning everything about their lives
4. Reevaluating patterns of thinking, behaving, and responding to others
5. Developing lives that fit their emerging worldviews
6. Dealing with major life events.

The following sections offer some strategies to go along with each of these waypoints for Explorers.

Coping with hectic lives

Explorers often find themselves immersed in a busy, "here and now" frenetic pace of life. Under these conditions, there are limited opportunities for reflection or even for simple activities like recreational reading. Most Explorers are caught up in their careers and doing all they can while sustaining marriages and parenting growing children. They try to catch meaningful minutes while on the run, and they make efforts to grab occasional opportunities for contemplating life's journey. Ironically, they are often asking themselves whether they are doing enough. Here are some strategies to help Explorers cope with their hectic lives:

- ○ Turn off the television, computer, and other electronic devices at home; be aware of when "zone-out" activities are devouring time and energy.

- ○ Go outdoors, even if only for a 10-minute walk after lunch or supper.

- ○ Be prepared to make the most of "downtime" (e.g., waiting in airports or doctors' offices) either by bringing along your laptop, iPad, or an intriguing book that you have been wanting to read or by using the time for reflection and contemplation.

- ○ Set aside time for regular exercise; find where and when you can squeeze in whatever form of exercise works best and energizes you.

- ○ Participate in activities with colleagues and family members that include movement and getting out in nature.

- ○ Encourage implementation of "walk-and-talk meetings" at work, rather than sit-down meetings in a conference room.

- ○ Make time for journaling your thoughts and feelings about life, either handwritten, typed on a computer, or through the dictation feature on your smartphone.

Dave regularly downloaded articles to his iPad that he wanted to read and made sure he always had it along with him. These included materials providing the latest information in his professional field as well as thought-provoking personal growth articles. He created two separate files on his iPad for making notes and journaling about each of these different types of reading material.

Dealing with higher standards than others

Those who take pride in themselves set high standards; they emphasize detail that others sometimes neglect. Bright adults may find themselves caught in conflicts with other people when they expect the same high standards from those people that they demand of themselves. These Explorers are frustrated when confronted with slipshod work and superficial thinkers, and they are often perceived as arrogant and abrasive by others who do not share their vision. The following are some strategies that may help:

○ Develop good listening skills and negotiation tactics.

○ Consider specific aspects of projects you are working on and prioritize the importance of each component so that you can spend your time and energy on those aspects that matter the most to you.

○ Offer to take the lead on joint projects or to take sole responsibility for the aspects of the project that you care the most about.

○ Implement your own projects outside of the workplace where you can exercise your own creativity and do things in ways that are gratifying to you.

○ Become self-employed; start your own business.

Elena developed a low-tech strategy for prioritizing the multiple facets of any major project she was working on by using colored 3 × 5 index cards, a different color for each project. She categorized each task on a separate index card and marked each card as high, medium, or low. Stacking them in descending order of their priority, she spent the bulk of her time and energy on those that were most important, sometimes changing the order of her cards at the end of the workday based on where she wanted to begin the next time she got back to the project. As soon as each task was done, she filed her cards away. When she was a project manager working with other people, she instituted a similar system. She encouraged all of the members of the team to claim tasks that were most compelling to each of them, followed by dividing the less interesting ones among the team.

Questioning everything about their lives

Explorers often question the way their lives are going and contemplate whether they want to continue in the same direction or set off on a new heading. They have second thoughts about what they are doing and ask themselves questions like, "Do I want to keep on in this career for the rest of my life?" "Is this where I really want to live?" "What about my relationship with my spouse or other family members?" "What about the other people in my life?" They begin contemplating new directions, exploring various possibilities personally and professionally, and envisioning new horizons and considering new alternatives, and they often feel a growing urgency to make changes before it is too late. Here are some strategies for those who question everything about their lives:

○ Take one area of your life about which you feel a sense of dissatisfaction and list the good things about it; repeat this with other areas of dissatisfaction and see what the lists reveal to you.

○ Complete a "Self-Assessment Wheel" to look at your current level of satisfaction in various areas of your life. See the instructions in Appendix 7.

○ Visualize what an ideal day and an ideal life might be like for you, journaling your ideas about them and determining if any part of what you have written might be incorporated into your life as it is now.

○ Discuss your feelings with your spouse, significant other, a trusted friend, or a counselor—someone who is a good listener, who will not be overly judgmental or upset about what you are saying, and who can resist telling you what you should do.

○ Do research on anything you might like to change about your life—changing your career, relocating, making modifications in one or more of your relationships, or using your leisure time differently.

○ Either decide not to decide—i.e., to sit with your thoughts and feelings for a while—or decide to move forward to make one or more changes in your life.

Raj, a bright Explorer who was feeling an undercurrent of dissatisfaction about his life, had been hearing a lot about creative visualization. So, on his way home from work one day, he stopped at a bookstore and purchased a couple of CDs designed to assist with guided imagery. After listening to them, he tried using a generic technique of visualizing what he thought an ideal life might be like. After a few false starts, he became more adept at visualization and found that he already had parts of his vision in his life. Further, he discovered that some parts of his life could be improved with just a few minor changes, while others needed more long-term contemplation. He established a regular practice of creative visualization along with journaling to help him sort out his thoughts and feelings instead of just allowing them to rattle around in his head.

Reevaluating patterns of thinking, behaving, and responding to others

Even in the midst of everything that they are involved in, bright Explorers become acutely aware of how their priorities have changed. At this stage of life, they want to match their lives to the identity and the primary concerns that they discovered when they were Seekers and refined when they were Voyagers. Explorers want to pursue goals and passions that started to crystallize for them during early adulthood, finding themselves on a quest to figure out how to do that. Although they are quite conscious of their responsibility to make a living, what they really want to do is make a life—the "if only" kind of life that they can envision for themselves. They search for ways to take charge without allowing others to steer them in alternate directions. Here are some strategies for changing patterns:

○ Carve out time for solitude and stillness—take a walk outside with your cell phone off, spend time just "being" as you drive

instead of turning the radio on, learn simple meditation practices and implement them for 10 to 15 minutes per day, etc.[175]

○ Identify the expectations of others regarding your career and
family; think about how you feel about those and how they
compare to the expectations you have of yourself now.[176]

○ Make a two-column list with the left side being "I used to…"
and the right side being "But now I…"

○ Use your creativity to explore your goals and passions—
poetry, music, art, etc.

○ Consider suggestions offered in self-help books on blending
your passions with earning enough money to provide financial support.[177]

Melanie realized she had gotten into a sort of "velvet rut"—com-
fortably following preprogrammed ways of thinking and living her life.
She decided she was ready to reassess her thoughts and feelings. She
began with turning off the TV at home and turning off the radio in
her car so that she could think or "be." Then she discovered that her
local library was offering free art classes given by a woman described
as having an "uncanny talent in finding that inner voice within each
of us ready, willing, and able to create."[178] These classes explored different media and were designed to meet the needs of people just like
her—including beginners. It sounded like just what she needed. She
used the art classes to explore her innermost feelings and to help her
sort out what changes she wanted to make in her life, especially in relation to other people's expectations. She has now made a five-year plan
for what she really wants to do, regardless of what anyone else might
think, and finds herself more energized than she has been in years.

Developing lives that fit their emerging worldviews

At this point in their lives, Explorers have an ever-growing
understanding of the interdependence of all people in the world. With
their increasing global perspective, Explorers may feel frustration,
wondering what they, as individuals, can do to make things better.
Here are some strategies that fit their emerging worldview:

○ Identify your most pressing global concerns and participate in organizations that focus on those issues.

○ Sign petitions, send letters or emails, or make phone calls to decision makers who can influence solutions to world problems that you care deeply about.

○ Join a local chapter of an organization that takes action on issues that concern you; support them financially even if you do not have time to get more involved right now.

○ Consider a variety of opportunities for volunteer work or for new career possibilities that reflect your yearning to make a difference in the world.

○ Find appropriate ways to speak your truth about issues you care about (global climate change, endangered species, world hunger, poverty, etc.) when you are with people whose viewpoints differ from yours.

Over time, Marty became more and more concerned about what was happening to the planet due to what he considered to be so many people's wanton, environmentally destructive behaviors. Although he didn't have time immediately to get heavily involved, he signed online petitions, set up regular donations to organizations that he felt were doing meaningful work, and joined a local group affiliated with the Sierra Club. When he could, he also participated in the Second Saturday events run by his state's chapter of The Land Conservancy and worked with other nature lovers to help maintain some of the undisturbed land in his area.[179]

Dealing with major life events

Cataclysmic events in the lives of bright adults often prompt Explorers to reevaluate, reassess, and rethink what their intent was earlier in life. Divorce, a death in the family, job loss, an accident or serious illness, or even a date that has special significance—any of these kinds of catalysts can throw people off course from their original direction even when they were perfectly happy with their lives. When these events occur, it is important to try to integrate everything they have learned previously about themselves—including when they faced significant issues or life changes in the past. Here are some strategies for dealing with major life events:

○ Take a reasonable amount of time to grieve over a loss in whatever way is meaningful for you.

○ Connect with others who have experienced similar losses; after commiserating, move on to share positive approaches.

○ List everything you gained from the previous time in your life up until this happened.

○ Reconsider your initial goals for your life and decide whether they are still valid.

○ Consider the possible alternatives for where you might go from here, write them down, and then rate them on a scale of 1 to 10 based on how you feel about them.

○ Write a "future scenario"—a description of where you want to be 5 or 10 years from now in terms of career, geography, lifestyle, and relationships—followed by what you might need to do (e.g., financially or educationally) to get there.

○ Begin to implement the ideas that seem best for establishing a new direction for your life.

Explorers often encounter storms along the way that blow them off course and send them in new directions. These are times when they must reassess their earlier intent and decide whether their goals are still valid based on all they have learned about themselves up to this point in time. Explorations during this stage of life may lead them either to smooth sailing or into rough waters as they journey onward through the lifespan. Sometimes it's a little of both.

Madeline had put her heart and soul into her work for a large architectural firm, designing houses for the 55+ market in a resort community on the Great Lakes. Then she was told that her company was downsizing because all the older people were moving south to escape the cold and snow and "the market was dying." She was devastated. After ranting and raving to her best friend, she made a list of everything she had gained from her years of working as an architect for that firm. Next she sat down at her computer and listed all of her other options and decided that if the business was all in the south, she would move south, too. She went online, started a job search, and found a new position and a new life on the Gulf Coast and says she's never been happier.

A Kaleidoscopic Life

In the midst of their journeys, this phase of life for Explorers might be aptly described as being like a kaleidoscope. The brightly colored fragments of their lives swirl into place and recombine into new patterns. Previous thoughts, feelings, experiences, and interests from earlier times intermingle with bits and pieces of what is going on for them now.

New insights get added to the mix virtually every day. Those "light bulb moments" sometimes come when least expected—in the shower, driving on the freeway, or waiting for a train. Suddenly, your current situation is seen in a new light, as if all those pieces in the kaleidoscope of your life just fall together into a different pattern that is lighted from within—one that makes more sense now than it ever did. Sometimes it is something as simple as a snippet of Shakespeare that your high school English teacher required you to memorize that you finally understand. Or maybe when you look back on your life from this vantage point, you begin to see how events that seemed so awful when they occurred make sense now as a part of your overall journey.

CHAPTER 7

The Navigators—Smooth Sailing or Stormy Seas

~ ~ ~

"No aspect of the sailor's world is more mysterious to the landsman than the practice of navigation. To find a precise point in a trackless waste seems neither art nor science, but magic."

—*Carleton Mitchell*

It was one of those mile-marker reunions. Even though Willard had never gone to any of them before, four decades had passed since high school graduation, so he decided to attend his 40th reunion and see what his former classmates had been doing. He suspected that they all had led more conventional lives than he had, so he was not sure if he really wanted to let them know how circuitous his life's path had been.

Identity and Direction

Whether or not their journeys take them on a direct route, bright adults between the ages of 50 and 65 typically have increased clarity about their personal goals and values. These serve them well as an internal compass to help them find their way. I call them Navigators. They use their goals, values, and abilities to guide them during this stage much like those who use their skills in navigation to find their way on land or sea or in the air. These bright adults have moved beyond seeking their place in the world or exploring myriad possibilities. They now have a much better idea of where they want to go with their lives.

By the time they reach their 50s, their quest has generally brought them greater perspective on who they are and what they want from life. Their prior knowledge, including self-knowledge, is usually extensive and helps them along the way.

Navigators possess a good understanding of their true identity and passions, well beyond what they might have found at earlier times in their lives. As Jacobsen said, "At this stage of our development we know who we are, why we are different, and why we are intended to deliver our exceptional gifts in the service of something greater than ego, broader than individual accomplishment, and deeper than external approval."[180]

Although not all Navigators find smooth sailing, most do. Even if they head into rough seas occasionally, they do well. They finally feel that their direction in life is clear, and they can enthusiastically enjoy their well-established careers, ongoing community involvements, and relationships with friends and family. They launch themselves wholeheartedly into finding ways to increase their knowledge and their involvement in meaningful work.

These Navigators are a good match for the way historian and memorabilia collector Marc Newman portrayed this age group. He described them as generally: 1) *goal oriented*, having had educational and financial opportunities and continually striving to make a difference in the world; 2) *competitive*, tending to be clever and resourceful in their quest to get ahead in life; and 3) *independent*, frequently questioning authority and challenging past practice.[181]

Weathering the Storms

These particular Navigators tend to weather life's occasional storms well, taking change in stride and even celebrating whatever life has brought to them. They tell other people, "Even though this isn't at all what I thought my life would be like, things actually have turned out better than I could ever have imagined." Although becoming map makers isn't necessarily the purpose of these bright adults, they may find themselves charting courses that others can follow.

However, there are gifted adults in this age group who continue to be plagued by self-doubt and a nagging awareness of how much they still want and need to learn. Some are dissatisfied and unhappy but still have not figured out why or what to do about it, and these Navigators regularly find themselves traveling through stormy seas. Although they may have a vision of the kind of life they want to lead, they frequently wonder if they will ever be able to get there. At times, they will be overly self-absorbed and oblivious to those around them. However, their behavior may really be more about increasing introspectiveness—a time of reflecting on life's journey. Nonetheless, some of them are truly narcissistic.

As described in the previous chapter, something similar can happen to the Explorers, but it is even more common during the years between 50 and 65. The catalyst for Navigators' time of reflection is usually a major event—one of those "Evolutionary Moments" like losing a job, experiencing a loss or serious illness in the family, the onset of health issues, a serious accident, or a milestone birthday or year with special personal significance.[182] These Navigators grasp onto the hope that their ruminations and reflections will lead them to more satisfying, meaningful lives, since they often have an even more intense feeling than the Explorers do—a strong sense that time is running out for them.

Out of Sync?

Some Navigators are locked into professions where they have worked diligently to succeed, only to find themselves feeling as if they have outgrown most of the opportunities that were available to them or that the work no longer holds any fascination for them. Because of their growing dissatisfaction, they feel out of sync with others in the workplace. Not only are they unhappy, but as Streznewski noted, "Those who find themselves, for whatever reasons, trapped in the mainstream of unchallenging jobs are a source of frustration to the people who must work with them."[183]

Their dissatisfaction spills over into their personal lives as well. Their friends and family become weary of listening to a litany of complaints about what is wrong with their jobs, their colleagues, the structure of the organizations where they work, or the world in general. Being cast adrift in midlife either by some activating event or by their own choice may turn out to be a mixed blessing; though initially turbulent, it might even be a relief for all concerned.

Those whose impetus is strictly an internal yearning to move on find that they are much clearer about what is really important to them. They want to do more with their lives. At this stage, middle-aged adults often fear inactivity and meaninglessness. There is an urgency to accomplish something worthwhile or, at the very least, to live life as fully as possible in the years that remain.[184] They sense a growing pressure to use all they have learned so far to fulfill their mission in life. They consider the possibilities of what they want to do next and think, "Maybe then, I'll finally be happy!"

The topic of happiness has increasingly become the subject of studies by psychologists as part of the positive psychology movement.[185] The ways people interpret occurrences in their world determine their happiness, and major factors for happiness are feeling connected with others and having a sense of meaning and purpose in life.[186]

Making Connections

It is not always easy for bright adults to find and connect with kindred spirits who share their intense interests as well as their dedication to making things better in the world in whatever ways they can. However, as Tolan stated, "Those who have chosen a career path that puts them into contact with other gifted adults may regularly experience the joy and excitement of the intellectual synergy that occurs in such a group."[187]

Nonetheless, some bright adults fail to find this because they have settled into comfortable and lucrative positions at work that provide the outer trappings of success without the satisfaction of meaningful interactions with other gifted adults. They trudge through life, stifling their enthusiasm and simplifying their vocabulary in order just to get along with others day to day, feeling disillusioned and disappointed but uncertain what to do about it. They even may go on assuming that there is something wrong with themselves, that they never developed social skills, or that they are just too different from others to make meaningful connections with them.

Uncharted Territory

The routes that disillusioned gifted adults take at this stage of life may bring them into uncharted territory, and as they head in this new direction, they may be saying to themselves, "Here we go again!" It feels to them like a flashback to the days of being Seekers or Voyagers. The significant difference, however, is that Navigators' perspectives on what is happening and how to handle changes in their lives are fueled by greater self-understanding. Bateson described the similarities and differences between this stage of life and those experienced earlier by saying:

> *The challenges that lie ahead at 50 and 60 are those that we encountered at 16 and 25: discovering who, finally, I am, who and what I am able to commit to, how to sustain that commitment, and how to invest my energy and my caring. Wondering whether I am still the person I have spent 60 years becoming and whether that is the person I want to be. Amazingly, after the passions and commitments of a lifetime, we have reached another threshold that calls for new or reaffirmed commitments, a new and more contingent sense of self.*[188]

One coordinator of gifted services for a regional educational center put her greater self-understanding to use when organizational changes eliminated her position. Thanks to her optimistic explanatory style, she was able to take a philosophical attitude toward her future.[189] Aware of the upcoming changes, a school district administrator in her region asked her if she was upset by the turn of events. She shrugged cheerfully and smiled, saying to him, "I'll be wherever I'm supposed to be." A year later she saw him at a conference after she had already found an excellent new position in her field, and they laughed about that previous conversation. He told her, "You were right; you said you'd be exactly where you're supposed to be!" Clearly, in telling herself and others that everything would be okay, she was able to weather the storms in her life and find her way into calm waters.

Asynchrony Strikes Again

Sociologist, author, professor, and scholar Sara Lawrence-Lightfoot commented on what traveling through this stage of life is like for both women and men, stating, "the process of learning something new feels both familiar and strange, exciting and terrifying, mature and childlike, both in character and out of body, like returning home and setting out on an adventure to an unknown destination."[190] These conflicting feelings are typical of the asynchronous development seen in gifted adults. The asynchrony of bright adults adds to the complexity of their lives; they experience aspects of their surroundings with childlike delight while simultaneously feeling concern over serious issues, such as climate change, poverty, and peace.[191] Tolan suggested that asynchronous development in adults is more a matter of individual personal growth and choices rather than being closely related to physiological development such as is the case with children. She intimated that, "We expect adults to be able to use abstract reasoning; we are not as likely to notice one whose reasoning takes him into complex realms where most other adults could not follow, as we are to notice a child who uses abstract reasoning long before other children can."[192] We expect adults to be doing more complex, abstract reasoning, figuring that it just comes naturally with maturity.

Asynchrony does not go away any more than giftedness does. These lifelong characteristics and emotions may be confusing to others who do not experience them and may throw bright adults and those close to them into a fair amount of turmoil. Finding equilibrium in their lives is a major task for Navigators.

Some multitalented adults whose creative interests spanned the earlier years of their lifespan find balance later through multiple diverse outlets for their abilities. At age 60, Rick is a good example of a multitasking Navigator. He recently took early retirement from teaching in a major metropolitan school district in the Midwest and relocated permanently to South Florida with his life partner. He negotiated the remodeling details for a house they are purchasing, and also manages a rental property that they own. He edits a Chicago-based lifestyle magazine for LGBTQ 20-year-olds who enjoy health and fitness, fashion, dining out, travel, etc.[193] He also has three other LGBTQ publications for which he writes restaurant, travel, and fashion reviews; has written shows for children's theater; and just revised the libretto for his fourth full-fledged musical. He was inducted into Chicago's Gay & Lesbian Hall of Fame for his five decades of writing for the LGBTQ press and for his charitable work. Besides all of these involvements, Rick has maintained a close personal relationship with his son who is dealing with a life-threatening illness.[194]

Midlife Quest

A great many adults in this age group find themselves yearning to make a difference in the world while there is still time. Cohen reported that the idea that everyone experiences a "crisis" in midlife is really a misconception, stating, "I have found instead that most adults experience a sense of quest in midlife. The insightful reflections that are common in this phase can provoke a powerful desire to find meaning in life, to begin new works, or to take existing works in new directions."[195]

Navigators' inner drive toward generativity typically begins to accelerate at this stage of life. This may take the form of providing guidance for their own children and other young people, of having a positive impact on the fields in which they work, or of making a difference through volunteering in various organizations. Middle-aged adults are likely to take a long-range perspective—to consider societal objectives, to contemplate their own long-term goals, and to think about how they might possibly improve the world.[196]

However, Navigators find themselves caught in another paradox. Their longing to positively influence the world clashes with their yearning for the fulfillment of needs, wants, and desires, which has been postponed for most of their adult lives. Despite their struggle, many ultimately succeed in finding ways to resolve these seemingly conflicting demands. As Aron suggested in writing about highly sensitive persons, their jobs are just a way to make money; their true vocations are what they dedicate themselves to in their spare time.[197]

Some Navigators turn lifelong passions into full-time vocations at this point in their lives, while simultaneously finding ways to fulfill their urgings toward generativity. One artist, who had worked in the printing industry for all his life to support his family, painted whenever he could, after work and on weekends. At age 55, however, he found a way to pursue his art full-time, as well as to extend positive efforts on behalf of others. He produced a growing body of work, became involved with a local artists' coalition that he helped found, and created a way that upcoming artists could connect with galleries and find appropriate outlets for their work.[198] All five of his children were grown and on their own, his house was paid for, and his wife had a tenured university position, making her able to support them once it was just the two of them.

Navigators who deferred the dreams and desires for public service that they had when they were younger may decide to reactivate those early longings. A librarian who had always wished that she had joined the Peace Corps back in the 1960s when it was first established decided she finally had the time and the freedom to do just that at the age of 63. She knew that she was enthusiastic about travel and spending time in other countries, comfortable living in very basic environments, and able to adapt to diverse circumstances, and her global concerns had never waned. Upon investigating, she learned that her experience and background made her particularly well suited as a Peace Corps Response Volunteer and that she could sign up for a 3- to 12-month assignment where her skills were critically needed.[199] She retired from her position with a regional library and joined the 8% of Peace Corps volunteers who are over the age of 50 so that she could put her gifts and talents to use helping others.[200] Currently working on library development in her host country, she helps incorporate technology into a local community resource center. In her frequent emails to friends and family, she reports that she is happier than ever and is considering signing up for a two-year term to serve somewhere else abroad when her current assignment as a Response Volunteer is over.

Waypoints and Strategies for Navigators

Six waypoints mark the journey of Navigators and represent issues that bright adults usually deal with during this time in their lives:

1. Coping with conflicting feelings and asynchronous development
2. Using prior knowledge, including self-knowledge
3. Responding to an urgency to accomplish something worthwhile
4. Dealing with dissatisfaction
5. Balancing everything in their lives
6. Setting a new course in life.

Navigators can benefit from implementing suggestions related to each of these waypoints. Determine which you would like to start with, maybe even combining several that appeal to you.

Coping with conflicting feelings and asynchronous development

Because Navigators are still living with asynchronous development—being multiple ages simultaneously—they often become increasingly introspective, are plagued by self-doubt, and are once more trying to get their bearings and see where true north is for them. They have a nagging awareness of how much they still want and need to learn and wonder if they will ever be able to get to the destination they envision. Here are some suggestions:

○ Learn more about asynchronous development and how it plays out for other people like you.[201]

○ Use whatever forms of creative expression suit you best for expressing your thoughts and feelings, either privately or publicly—photography, poetry, dance, music, etc.

○ Seek out and spend time with others like you; discuss your thoughts and feelings—either face-to-face, online, or on the phone.

○ Take action on your deeply felt concerns.

○ Celebrate your zest for life and avoid apologizing for your childlike enthusiasm.

Cassandra had always wanted to learn ballroom dancing but had only danced in her dreams or with an imaginary partner in the privacy of her home. She always thought it was childish to want to get involved in ballroom dancing "at her age" and that she would look foolish if she tried. Finally, she decided that, at this point in her life, it made no sense to care so much about what other people might think, and she went in search of classes. At the dance studio, she discovered people of all ages who were learning to dance—some, like her, were just beginners; others were proficient. She found plenty of the people there were significantly older than she was, and they shared that they had only gotten into ballroom dancing in the past couple of years. After taking ballroom dance classes for a while, she joined a local club that organized monthly dances where it did not matter whether or not you came with a dance partner. There were always people to dance with, and she found that she had a fair amount of talent for ballroom dancing. At the club's monthly dances, she made new friends, talking about dancing and all kinds of other topics of interest.

Using prior knowledge, including self-knowledge

Bright adults need opportunities to use all that they have learned in their lives, like sailors who rely on familiar charts that they have used regularly. Navigators with rich and diverse backgrounds have a full panoply of fascinating life experiences and knowledge to draw upon and share. Because of their characteristic reflectiveness, they have gained a great deal of self-knowledge—understanding who they are, what they care about most, and what they are not willing to accept in their lives any longer. Here are some strategies to help Navigators use prior knowledge, including self-knowledge:

○ Share your knowledge and experience with friends and family, as well as with colleagues and younger employees in the workplace.

○ Mentor others at work or in the community.

○ Keep a portfolio or other organized collection of archival materials about yourself and your areas of expertise—either hard copies or digital versions.

○ Find effective ways to question authority and challenge past practices.

○ Write for publications. Start a blog.

○ Speak at conferences or other gatherings related to your career, relevant fields of interest, or avocations.

○ Be a guest lecturer at adult learning centers or in college classes; teach continuing education courses—face-to-face, online, or hybrid.

Karl, a family practice physician in a rural area for more than 20 years, had kept copious notes on all of his patients. He decided to organize a collection of the more interesting cases from over the years. He really enjoyed looking back and remembering the people involved. He put together a notebook that, little by little, started to become something he wanted to share, with identifying details removed of course. When a nearby college asked him if he would be a guest lecturer in a class for beginning premed students, he said *yes* and used some examples from his collection of cases to bring his presentation to life so that the students could see how interesting family practice could be. The students enjoyed his lecture so much that he was asked to do regular lectures at the college. Then he started writing a book about his life as a country doctor. Later on, one of the students who had heard him speak asked to do a residency with him, and he found great satisfaction in mentoring that student and other young people while continuing to practice medicine in the small town where he lived.

Responding to an urgency to accomplish something worthwhile

At this stage, bright adults characteristically get as fully involved as possible, immersing themselves intensely into careers, community service, and relationships. They steadfastly pursue their goals, using all they know and can do. Navigators often have an aversion to inactivity and strongly resist having a meaningless life; they want to live their lives as fully as possible, using their knowledge and experience to pursue their life's mission. Here are some suggestions:

○ Celebrate all that you do in your career, community activities, and relationships with friends and family; avoid apologizing for your high levels of involvement.

○ List your activities and prioritize the items on your list; find ways to extricate yourself from things that are no longer satisfying or meaningful for you.

○ Practice saying *no* to requests for new commitments that only peripherally interest you. Try saying "I'm sorry, I just can't," without explaining why and inviting a barrage of cajoling.

○ Identify your current goals related to each aspect of your career, community involvements, and relationships; write them down and make time for journaling about them in relation to your mission in life.

○ Reflect on goal-setting strategies that have worked well for you in the past and apply them to the goals you are establishing now.

Becca always enjoyed her career as a realtor, but she also loved performing in community theater productions and was asked to direct her local theater's next performance. For years, she had organized children's drama programs for the park district. She also took care of her grandchildren twice a week. Because she was so good at getting things done, her name was the first one mentioned when anything needed to be accomplished, whether it was at the real estate office, in the community, or in her large, extended family. However, when her dentist found a lump on her parotid gland during a routine examination and had her admitted to the hospital for a biopsy, she used the time to reconsider everything she was doing. While waiting for the biopsy results, she listed all her activities and prioritized the items on her list. When the results of the biopsy showed the lump was benign, she was ready. She became more selective about her activities, gradually extricating herself from ones that were not all that important to her. She learned to say *no* to new requests and found that this freed up time for considering what her mission in life really is.

Dealing with dissatisfaction

Some Navigators find themselves coping with disillusionment and disappointment, reconsidering the course they have taken in their lives and wondering whether they should keep heading in the same direction, hoping to recapture their enthusiasm. They may feel locked into their professions or may think they have outgrown what they are doing. Some of them feel out of sync with other people in the workplace and may be unhappy at home. Their dissatisfaction at work often spills over into their personal lives or vice versa.

To add to the complexity of all that they are already involved with, Navigators routinely feel an increasing inner drive toward generativity. This paradoxical time in their lives can be difficult—they often find that they are not sure whether to try to make a difference in the world or to allow themselves to pursue their own desires at last. Here are some strategies to deal with dissatisfaction:

○ Organize a getaway with your spouse or significant other and spend meaningful time getting to know each other again.

○ Take a hiatus from electronic gadgets at home; use the newly gained time for reading or conversation or getting out in nature.

○ Acknowledge all of your feelings, including relief, when significant events happen in your life.

○ See what changes you might make at work, such as taking on a new project or working with some other facet of your organization or with people you have not been involved with before.

○ Tackle a new challenge professionally—something that represents a real "stretch" for you.

○ Create a new program at work that will benefit colleagues or employees; collaborate with others who are interested.

○ Fulfill urges toward generativity by mentoring younger people in your profession.

○ Reactivate earlier longings of your heart, pursuing lifelong passions either as an avocation or by turning them into a full-time vocation.

○ Do volunteer work related to causes you care about that can make a difference in the world and allow you to productively use your knowledge and experience.

○ Make decisions about the actions you want to take to increase your satisfaction in life.

Ron was increasingly alarmed at how much obesity he saw all around him, including in his colleagues at work who clearly had sedentary lives. He and his wife had studied exercise and health and common misconceptions about food as well as the emotional aspects underlying overeating. One weekend, after Ron and his wife went away to spend some quality time together, they hatched a plan. He proposed a program of "Wellness at Work" to the director of his department who said he could give it a try. It was designed to provide education and support for healthy eating and exercise habits. Three or four other people were interested in launching it, and they had great success in implementing it for a six-month trial period. With this and a summary of the research from the Internet about the value of such programs, Ron and his wife began providing consultation services to other organizations to set up similar programs.[202] They created a website that evolved into a successful full-time business for her while Ron stayed in his current position at work and continued his involvement with the "Wellness at Work" program there.

Balancing everything in their lives

Bright adults need multiple outlets for their abilities, but this may result in feeling as if they want to go in six directions at once. Even though multipotentiality is a hallmark of many bright adults, Navigators often find that they have focused their attention on only one or two of their abilities in order to be successful in their careers. They may want to incorporate more of their interests into their lives now and put more of their gifts and talents to use. But it can be challenging to do that without getting out of balance, given everything else they are involved in. Here are some recommendations:

○ Use the "Self-Assessment Wheel" in Appendix 7 to review your current level of satisfaction in various areas of your present life to determine where your life might be out of balance.

○ Inventory your gifts and talents; consider those that you have not been using in your profession but always wanted to develop further.

○ Be selective about interesting activities and projects to enjoy during leisure hours—especially ones that capitalize on abilities that are different from those you use at work.

○ Divide your activities and projects into those that you find energizing and those that are less so; eliminate (or at least postpone) some that are draining your energy.

○ Determine if flextime or telecommuting are options in your career.

○ Multitask, including using travel time for reflecting about how to create more balance in your life.

Although Maria had always loved reading mysteries and thrillers, she never had time for recreational reading because of her busy professional life, and she really felt it was a loss. Even during her leisure hours, she was so caught up in reading professional journals and books, preparing presentations for professional conferences, and downloading the latest research in her field that there just never seemed to be any time left over. She could see that her life had gotten way out of balance. After some thought, she decided that each night she would allocate the last hour of the day to recreational reading. She picked up some used paperbacks by authors who used to be her favorites and began reading their books again. When she heard that several of them were appearing at a book fair in the next city, she decided to go there to meet them, even though she had some other pressing projects on the "front burner." She thoroughly enjoyed her day at the book fair. When she returned home, she plunged back into her pressing projects with renewed energy and enthusiasm, finishing them in record time.

Setting a new course in life

Whatever the catalyst is for moving on and heading in a new direction, many Navigators essentially find that they do not have a choice. They need to reconfigure their lives and set a new course for the next part of their life journey, the next anchorage, or the next port of call. Facing the need to change directions radically at this stage of life can be daunting. Unlike Explorers, the Navigators often feel they have fewer options for changing course at this time in their lives, fearing that their age will be a limiting factor. They worry that they are not as employable as when they were younger. Besides considering new ways to deal with core components of their lives, such as career and family, Navigators also typically yearn to blend their own needs and wants with their growing desire to use their gifts and talents to make the world a better place.

Many of the strategies suggested for Explorers can work for Navigators as well. Variations of some of those will be helpful for Navigators, too, so you will find some of them included here:

- ○ Consider the possible alternatives for what you might do from here on; write them down and then rate them as *plus, minus,* or merely *neutral* or *interesting* based on how you feel about them.[203] Pursue your *pluses.*

- ○ Contemplate how you might downsize so that you can have a satisfying lifestyle (or possibly one that is even more than satisfying).

○ Write a "future scenario"—a description of where you want to be next in terms of career, geography, lifestyle, and relationships—followed by what you might need to do (e.g., financially or educationally) to get there.

○ Make three lists—one for needs (essentials for your life), one for wants (preferences), and one for desires (what your heart longs for); imagine what your life might be like with some or all of these elements in it.

○ Think about the issues on the planet of greatest interest to you and consider how you might get involved with other committed individuals or organizations to do something that might be meaningful (both for you directly and for making a difference in the world).

○ If you are still not sure about what you want to do, decide to review your thoughts about your options after a specific amount of time (a day, a week, or more) and put that on your calendar. When it is time, take out everything you have written, look at it again, and incorporate what you have learned into the decisions you make next.

Steven, a scientist whose company was downsizing, received notice that his position was being outsourced to another country. He had three months to determine what he was going to do before he would be unemployed. After a lot of discussion with his wife, who had previously worked in a field similar to his, the two of them decided that if the company was downsizing, they could take what amounted to an early retirement and downsize, too. They each took time separately to make lists of needs, wants, and desires and then compared their lists to figure out what they could do to attain as many of the items on both of their lists as possible. They decided to sell their house, since it was much bigger than they needed; they gave their grown children a chance to claim any household things they wanted and then sold or donated the rest to charity. They moved into a townhouse in a warmer climate, and they each became involved in organizations that were dedicated to causes they cared about or related to their respective areas of expertise. Although they did not have all of these elements in place before the three months were up, it only took a couple more months before everything was set for them to move on to this next chapter of their lives. Eventually, they both volunteered in the local school system in their new location where they thoroughly enjoyed sharing their passion for science with middle and high school students.

Joy or Turmoil

Many Navigators find that the joy is in the journey, although some of them see that only in retrospect. For those who have had smooth sailing, their enthusiasm about their life experiences comes easily. Though they may have hit some rough waters in the past, these bright adults have happily found their niche in activities that provide them with continual challenges. They have found people on their wavelength to connect with, and they have developed meaningful relationships with friends and family. They are active in their work and communities and are able to pursue other interests during their spare time.

Other bright adults continue to live in turmoil at this stage and try one alternative after another to ease their discomfort. Sometimes this provides temporary relief, and sometimes they have to continue searching for a while before they find a way to chart a new course that is more satisfying and meaningful. In the midst of all the chaos, they may not find this stage of their lives to be particularly joyful. It may take hindsight for them to see the value of all that has gone before. Only then can they start to feel satisfied with where they are at this point and all that they have learned along the way.

CHAPTER 8

The Actualizers—Making a Difference

~ ~ ~

"Ideals are like stars: you will not succeed in touching them with your hands, but like the seafaring man on the ocean desert of waters, you choose them as your guides, and following them, you reach your destiny."

—*Carl Schurz*

"So you're retiring. Congratulations!" On hearing these words for what seemed like the umpteenth time, one bright retiree finally said to this well-meaning friend, "Well, yes, that's sort of true. I am retiring from my job, but I'm not going to stop working. I have all kinds of plans to keep going, just not at the same place or in the same way!" She was baffled by being congratulated about this waypoint in her life, as if it were the culmination of her accomplishments and she should now gracefully do "retirement things" and more or less fade into the sunset. The truth was that she had no intention of doing anything like that.

Retirement or "Unretirement"?

Bright adults between the ages of 65 and 80 are seldom like the images we once held of "senior citizens"—Granny and Gramps sitting in their rocking chairs steeped in nostalgia and contemplating the final days of their lives. The rocking chair image just doesn't jibe with what life is like in the 21st century. These days, we see active older adults working tirelessly to use their knowledge, skills, gifts, and talents in significant ways to make meaningful contributions to the world. More likely, we will find them running a home-based business, taking art classes, going back to school for fun or for another degree, volunteering with a favorite organization, becoming active in politics, and traveling to places they have always wanted to go.[204] They continue to pursue interests and passions that are an extension of their years as Seekers, Voyagers, Explorers, and Navigators. Although other adults in this age group also lead busy lives, the intensity of these gifted Actualizers is more likely to lead them to in-depth participation that is especially intellectually and creatively challenging, often with valuable implications for future generations.

I call gifted adults at this stage of life Actualizers for two reasons. First, many of them function in ways that fit with Abraham Maslow's description of self-actualization as an ongoing process.[205] They use their capabilities fully, creatively, and joyfully as a part of self-actualization. Second, so many of these bright adults play an active role as catalysts for other people to actualize their own goals and dreams, much the way a lighthouse shines a beacon to help sailors find their way. Both of these perspectives relate to the ways Actualizers make things happen for themselves and for others.[206]

Actualizing is a growing part of these bright adults' efforts toward generativity—making a difference in the world and passing along their knowledge, experience, and wisdom to others in order to help the latter in their own quest. As Streznewski said, "These people do not behave in terms of endings. What they seem to do at a certain point is simply start on another lifetime."[207]

Many Actualizers continue with dynamic work in fields that they have been actively involved in throughout their careers. They keep on putting their gifts and talents to use in these areas—choosing involvements that remain meaningful to them. Some do not retire at all; they just keep on working in their professions, often finding ways to launch new projects that incorporate their interests and insights. One pediatrician continued her private practice well beyond the age of 70 and then established a center for the prevention of child abuse in conjunction with her local community mental health center. She developed a team approach in which she provided medical services, collaborating with a psychiatrist and a psychiatric social worker to keep families together while working to reverse their long-established patterns of abuse.

Some Actualizers take their retirement one step at a time, gradually shifting to working part-time so that they can keep their hand in without the time-consuming commitment and responsibilities of full-time managers or directors. Others retire from their "day jobs" but choose not to abandon the careers that have been the focus of their professional lives. They serve as consultants, teach courses in their areas of expertise, do presentations at conferences, and write for publication. Cohen reported on the preliminary results of his study on 21st century retirement, stating that "not having to work full-time or not having children to look after on a daily basis allows them time to take stock of their lives in a way they've never experienced before."[208]

In this stage of life, some bright adults launch completely new careers—often ones that are an outgrowth of interests that had always intrigued them but had not been their emphasis during earlier stages of their lives. One special education professor took courses in counseling psychology at her university while she was still teaching there. Since the counseling department had an accredited program, she obtained her license and then went into private practice as a therapist when she retired from university teaching.

For some Actualizers, retirement allows them to develop creative interests (e.g., art or photography) that they had never been able to pursue in much depth before. Authors Zalman Schacter-Shalomi and Ronald Miller describe this as resurrecting unlived lives, commenting about how many people had censored the voices of their authentic selves earlier in life and only later found that those voices started to clamor to be expressed in the world.[209]

Some Actualizers pick up an old musical instrument and refresh their skills. They play in regional orchestras with others who find they also have time now for regular rehearsals and periodic performances. Their interactions are energized by their mutual love of music and by having opportunities to participate and perform with other musicians.

Many bright adults at this stage of life are seeking connections with like-minded others while simultaneously finding ongoing opportunities to expand their knowledge. Actualizers actively seek interesting people to share ideas and experiences with—particularly those whose lifelong passions or hobbies overlap with theirs. Additionally, though, these bright adults are much more able to acknowledge that not everyone they come in contact with will be like they are. Some Actualizers choose to be increasingly selective about who they are willing to be around; they do not want to waste their time in nonmeaningful activities or pastimes. Others develop a philosophical attitude and tolerance but still make conscious choices about how much time they want to spend with people who are not on their wavelength.

A growing number of colleges and universities have created academies for lifelong learning where older adults can sign up for courses and connect with other people who share their interests. One large Florida community for active older adults even has its own independent, stand-alone lifelong learning college and reported nearly 19,000 participants during a recent calendar year.[210] These organizations, which provide ongoing educational opportunities for Actualizers, offer a great resource for intellectual stimulation through lectures, intriguing discussions, a wide variety of options for learning experiences, and regular interaction with other bright adults.

However, not all Actualizers have a chance to do what they would really like for themselves, including getting out to participate in these kinds of experiences. Some Actualizers have responsibilities other than pursuing their own personal dreams and desires, such as raising their grandchildren if their own children are unable to do so. Some of those who find themselves in this boat just decide to ride it out until their other responsibilities ease up, thinking, "This, too, shall pass." They figure that the day will come when they will have time for themselves again. Others realize that they need to take care of their own needs now, too. They carve out time from their responsibilities by getting coverage so that they can get away regularly. If they are caregivers for elderly parents or a disabled spouse, they seek respite care for themselves. If they are taking care of their grandchildren, they find child care alternatives so that they can get away from time to time to follow their own interests.

With their years of experience and maturity, Actualizers sometimes surprise themselves and others by their increased willingness to speak their minds regardless of circumstances. Cohen described this as "the liberation phase: a time when we feel a desire to experiment, innovate, and free ourselves from earlier inhibitions or limitations."[211] The clarity they have about their identity at this time in their lives results in a certain indifference to what other people will think. They sense a freedom and emancipation from restrictions that previously held them back.[212] Furthermore, as Webb indicated, "Many adults, as they get older, discover that they have a broader view of time, existence, generations, and life meaning than they did when they were younger."[213] Their experiences have led them to a more in-depth understanding of themselves and a significantly increased comfort level with who they have become.

Self-Awareness/Self-Acceptance

Despite all of this, most bright adults do not acknowledge gift-edness as being part and parcel of who they are. They brush off any suggestions that they are gifted or talented even though their abilities are quite easy for others to see. Very few actually think of themselves as gifted and scoff if you mention the possibility to them, although some might acknowledge the idea that they have abilities, talents, or perhaps some skills they have developed over the years. They typically point out someone else in their life—a spouse, a sibling, a parent, or a child—saying *that* person is gifted but they themselves really are not. As Tolan said, "The gifted frequently take their own capacities for granted, believing that it is people with different abilities from theirs who are the really bright ones."[214]

Nonetheless, even though giftedness is not on their radar screens, by this stage of life, most Actualizers have accepted themselves for who they are and acknowledge that not everyone will be like they are in intellect, interests, or intensity. They don't feel any particular need to impress anyone, and they don't care a whole lot about how other people see them. They are "comfortable in their own skin."[215]

Keeping On or Moving On

Most Actualizers have developed a philosophical attitude and tolerance for differences and have decided not to waste much energy on expecting anyone else to function the way they do. However, getting to this point may have taken them through tumultuous times. As Jacobsen indicated, "The journey of self-actualization is never an easy one. It is a long, unpredictable, and arduous trek, not a simple trip to the corner wisdom store, and certainly not a destination with reserved seating."[216]

The emphasis of self-actualization is the *self* and on continuing to discover how to live as meaningful a life as possible, regardless of age. For Actualizers, specifically, it really involves looking within and setting a course that will be the most satisfying to them, and as Jacobsen said, "Recovering the vitality of the true self motivates us like nothing else."[217]

The focus for Actualizers isn't just on themselves, however. They look beyond themselves. Jane Fonda labeled this stage of life the "Third Act" and said, "Just as the Third Act is the time for journeying inward to allow the flowering of consciousness and growth, it is also the time to radiate that consciousness outward as a resource not only for our own self-fulfillment but for the world, as well."[218]

Because many Actualizers feel so comfortable in speaking their minds, they often get into heated discussions about significant issues with others whose viewpoints differ radically from their own. Some may try to resolve disagreements peacefully, even though this may be challenging especially when they are embroiled in a debate with another bright adult who sees things differently. Some Actualizers are open to compromising and generally look for common ground. Others simply decide that the best they can do is "agree to disagree." Some walk away, shaking their heads, doubtful about whether the other person will ever understand the points they are so convinced are "right."

Making a Difference

Actualizers characteristically display an ever-growing desire to make some sort of lasting contribution to the world, and at this time in their lives, they are more likely than ever to act on this desire— something that is more pressing for them now. Though in earlier stages they yearned to do something to make a difference in the world, they seldom had the time to do so then because of heavy commitments to their careers and their families.

Actualizers actively look to find ways to share their knowledge directly with younger people or they work with organizations that seem likely to have a positive impact in the world, or both. Their legacy is more important than ever to a great many bright adults at this stage of life. As Bateson said, "The future is built from what we are able to pass on, whether in words spoken or words on paper, actions taken or gestures made."[219]

This generativity includes encouraging others to move toward their heart's desire, while the Actualizers pursue their own—both experiences characteristically interact in the lives of Actualizers and usually play an increasing role in their lives. It becomes especially important when they find themselves contemplating how many, or how few, years they may have left on the planet. The concept of generativity, originally described by Erikson, often overlaps with self-actualization; the satisfaction from making a difference in the world helps bright adults live more satisfying, meaningful lives.

Mentoring Others

Mentoring is a key way Actualizers uniquely contribute to the next generation and the continuation of their life's work. In Chapters 4 and 5, on Seekers and Voyagers, respectively, we looked at mentors from the perspective of the mentee. It is also important to look at mentoring from the point of view of the mentors and consider what it's all about for them.

For some, this was always part of what they did. Teachers, teacher educators, counselors, psychologists, and social workers are among those whose work has always involved guiding others. This is also true of professors, coaches, editors, and anyone in a supervisory position who focuses on helping others make their own unique contributions through their work. For some Actualizers who achieved status and credibility at high levels in their organizations, mentoring always was a natural outgrowth of their positions as they provided leadership for others.

Mentoring is often seen as a one-way street—where older, wiser persons impart their abundant knowledge to younger, less-experienced practitioners. However, meaningful mentorships are more reciprocal than that. The possibilities for synergy are virtually unlimited and can lead to extremely involved and complex relationships. Actualizers, more than younger gifted adults, need to respect their own energy levels, however, because the effort to be compassionate and caring can become exhausting; they need to find ways to extricate themselves from overly intense involvements that can generate "compassion fatigue."[220]

In Chapter 4, I talked about the value of mentors serving as "polestars" for bright young Seekers. The benefits for mentors are equally significant, including the joy of interacting with others who share their passions. The pleasure of brainstorming ideas and sharing experiences brings delight to mentors as they discover new perspectives and insights from the relationship. As Webb said, "mentoring and teaching can foster authentic relationships."[221] Of course, some Actualizers who try to mentor others get frustrated when their suggestions are dismissed out of hand or their ideas treated as outdated, as if they are too out of touch with the way the world is now. Sometimes they are; sometimes they are not. Fortunately, most Actualizers have lived long enough that they now have perspective on the impatience (and occasional impertinence) of youth.

Actualizers who are mentors are sometimes praised as "role models," but many Actualizers bristle at the idea of being a role model for anyone. Most of them are just being themselves, offering any wisdom and knowledge they can for whatever use it might be. The idea of being a role model is anathema to them, and they understand the Robert Browning poem that says, "'Tis an awkward thing to play with men's souls, and matter enough to save one's own…"[222] Being an idolized role model feels like a burden—one they do not want to bear.

Regardless of how they feel about being considered a role model, some Actualizers do become overly embroiled in their efforts to maintain programs or businesses that they have founded and develop what some have called "Founderitis." They have difficulty stepping aside and letting others run things their way, even if they have been mentoring others to step into leadership positions. They do not want to lose control and see things change from what their original vision was and still is.

The best mentors want their mentees to be independent and true to themselves, not to become clones of anyone else. These mentors "are putting what they have learned into the hands of a new generation they respect but cannot and should not control."[223]

Branching Out

Actualizers routinely get involved in political activism, environmental efforts, health care, education, labor concerns, poverty programs, international relations, government-sponsored initiatives, and more. Bright older adults frequently work in nonprofit organizations, community groups, educational settings, and the like. Mentorships are sometimes an extension of these activities within the context of organizations whose emphasis is making a difference in the world. The tricky part is finding places where these bright older adults will be valued for all they can contribute. This is not necessarily a given in today's world, especially in the United States and other countries that focus heavily on a youth culture.

A growing number of organizations focus on meaningful ways for post-midlife adults to make good use of their gifts, talents, goals, and values. Encore.org is one example. It focuses on "encore careers"— ways to "combine personal fulfillment, social impact, and continued income, enabling people to put their passion to work for the greater good."[224] Marc Freedman, of Encore.org, clarified the focus in *The Harvard Business Review* of "social innovators in the second half of life." Objecting to suggestions that mature adults are "reinventing" themselves, he stated, "…the most powerful pattern that emerges from their stories can be described as reintegration, not reinvention. These successful late-blooming entrepreneurs weave together accumulated knowledge with creativity, while balancing continuity with change, in crafting a new idea that's almost always deeply rooted in earlier chapters and activities."[225]

Making Connections

Actualizers are typically clear about the importance of spending time with others who share their passions and commitment to the future of the world. Some find this through mentoring; others find kindred spirits in organizations that reflect their interests and concerns.

Some Actualizers follow these pursuits with spouses or life partners whom they found during their earlier days. Others are "solo sailors," doing what they do individually and bringing their enthusiasm back home or someplace else where they can share their excitement. Whether solo or with others, the ongoing urge for suitable activity and their insatiable curiosity go on and on throughout their lives. As Streznewski said, "Always, there are new things to learn."[226]

A few Actualizers at this point, however, choose to put their previous approach to life behind them rather than being heavily involved in the world at large. Some are people who had always seemed like they were living multiple lives simultaneously. They were the multitaskers—involved in so many activities at the same time that they always seemed to be dashing from one thing to another, while always thinking about everything else they had to do. Self-actualization for this group relates more to finding inner peace and creating a life that gives them serenity and satisfaction. They may care for their grandchildren, tend their homes and their gardens, go to lunch with their friends, read for their own pleasure, and relax into a more simplified, reflective lifestyle.[227] It may be that this group of Actualizers had lived so intensely up until this point that they are merely ready for a much quieter, gentler, easygoing lifestyle. When asked if she missed her previous involvement in her career, one woman smilingly answered, "Do you miss junior high school? Don't you want to go back and do that again? No? Well, I don't want to go back to my profession anymore, either. That was then, and this is now."

Waypoints and Strategies for Actualizers

Let's look first at the *inner* voyages of bright adults and how they can make meaningful use of their knowledge, skills, gifts, and talents to move ahead into self-actualization—an ongoing process for gifted adults. Then we will pay attention to actualization as an *outer* journey—being a positive force to help other people actualize their own goals and dreams.

This is a time for bright adults to determine what activities they really want to be involved in so that they can spend their time on their deepest interests and passions. For some, it may be a matter of slightly changing life emphasis. Others may feel that they are launching another lifetime rather than putting their lives into dry dock.[228]

The waypoints that typically mark the lives of Actualizers are:

1. Reflection
2. Enjoying greater clarity about their identity
3. Seeking ongoing opportunities to expand their knowledge
4. Connecting with others
5. Generativity.

Reflection

Actualizers characteristically find themselves taking stock of their lives in ways they have never experienced before. They want to set as satisfying a course for their lives as possible. As they look within, they enjoy feeling a much larger sense of freedom from prior restrictions. Their emphasis is on the self, reflecting on what they have learned along the way and considering where they want to go from here. Here are some suggestions to help make the most of reflection:

○ Develop dormant creative interests—art, photography, etc.— to discover how self-expression can enhance reflections on your life.

○ Create a timeline of your life to reflect on your journey to this point; then consider possible directions you might go in the future.

○ On a large sheet of newsprint, chart your past as an odyssey using any means of transportation you would like as a metaphor—cars, trains, boats, planes, or even a combination. Depict the surroundings at different times in your life in whatever ways might be relevant so that you can see how each of the legs of your journey was affected by where you were and what was going on around you.

○ Use mind-mapping computer software and create a mind map of your life.[229]

○ Write or draw your responses to the following questions: "What do I have an appetite for? What do I want to taste again and again, or for the first time? What do I not want to stomach any longer? What, for me, would be a healthy diet for living?"[230]

Al, who recently retired, had often used mind-mapping software to organize projects at work. So he made a mind map of what life was like for him prior to retirement, using it to contemplate different aspects of his life up until his last day at work. He created branches on his mind map for career, family, friends, recreation, health, and travel. Then he created a second mind map to show graphically how he would like his life to be from here on. Following this process, he decided to focus on specific things he had been postponing—more recreational reading, international travel, and going back to writing songs and playing his old guitar that he had not touched for years.

Enjoying greater clarity about their identity

Actualizers usually have a deeper understanding of themselves and their identity, and they often look back at the past with amazement at their life's journey up to this point, observing how the stops and starts along the way contributed to who they are now. Actualizers generally spend a lot less time concerned about what other people will think of them. They are more willing than ever to be authentic and speak out about whatever is on their minds without the kind of self-censorship they used to have when they were younger. Because they are more at peace with themselves, some even find that they are more open than ever to considering other people's points of view. Here are some approaches that may be helpful:

○ Write a letter to your "younger self" and tell the person you were then what he or she will be like at the age you are now.

○ Fold a paper in half (or create a two-column document on your computer). On the left side, list significant changes in your life up until now; on the right side, write ways that each change contributed to who you are now.

○ Draw a humorous cartoon of yourself as you see yourself now, tucking it away for later or sharing it with a trusted friend or family member.

○ Put together a playlist of music that you feel best reflects meaningful aspects of your identity now; listen to it often and add to it whenever you find more music that fits.

○ Start (or continue gathering) a collection of quotes that speak to you and your current perspectives on life and living.

○ Keep a log of times when you speak your mind about something you care about that you might have kept silent about in earlier years.

○ Find ways to resolve disagreements about significant issues peacefully or decide when it is best to "agree to disagree."

Glenda had always avoided arguments and used to say that her tongue was sore from biting it so often to opt for "peace at any price." However, as she moved into her late 60s, she began to speak up more often and realized that the ceiling didn't actually fall on her head and that people didn't really reject her because she disagreed with them. She started to keep a log of the times when she shared her thoughts— times when previously she would not have told others that she saw things differently. She learned that it was okay to say gently, "Well, I don't agree with you about that," and then tell them why, without getting upset about what they might think of her. Little by little, she began to realize that most people actually respected her more for sharing insights, ideas, and perspectives that they had not thought about. When others did not seem to feel that way, she found that she could just walk away and still feel good about herself for speaking up.

Seeking ongoing opportunities to expand their knowledge

Actualizers actively enjoy finding ways to experiment and innovate. Much less bothered by earlier inhibitions or limitations, they regularly find themselves responding to an ongoing urge to learn and do new things. Bright adults of all ages tend to have insatiable curiosity. There is so much they want to know about the world, and gaining new knowledge is so exhilarating—like that moment when the wind picks up, fills the sails, and suddenly propels the sailboat forward. Here are some suggestions Actualizers may find useful:

○ Search online or check local colleges and universities to find lifelong learning institutes (LLIs) or academies that offer classes nearby; sign up and participate in those that interest you.[231]

○ Audit college and university classes or take courses for credit in content areas you have always wanted to study.

○ Pursue an advanced degree "just for fun."

○ Read, listen to podcasts, watch TED Talks, and search out other informative sources about topics you would like to learn more about.

○ Take part in book clubs and other discussion groups where significant ideas are shared.

○ Attend free lectures and other sessions offered by local libraries.

○ Go to conferences and other gatherings where you can expand your knowledge about whatever interests you.

○ Volunteer to work with organizations where you can learn more about what they do and how they do it.

○ Listen to public radio and watch programs on public television that cover topics that you would like to know more about.

○ Participate in Road Scholar educational travel where you have a choice of wide-ranging opportunities to learn from local and internationally known experts.[232]

A semiretired financial planner, who had always been interested in computers, learned all he could about technology in his spare time, even when he was still working full-time. He regularly bought the newest devices, kept up with the latest updates, listened to podcasts, and watched relevant TED Talks online. Whenever his friends had computer glitches, they called on him. He usually could troubleshoot their problems, and they even noticed that he seemed to know more than most of the tech support staff that they previously had relied on.

On one podcast, he heard about an upcoming computer conference and decided to attend for the first time when he was in his early 70s. He immersed himself in the exhibits, attended sessions, and heard lectures by "geeks" who were as passionate as he was for new developments in technology. At the conference, he learned specifics about how to develop "apps" for mobile devices and tablets. Since he had an idea that he thought would be especially user-friendly for people in his age group, he eagerly decided that this would be his next project, and he came home more energized than he had been for ages. He decided to attend this conference regularly and started salting away the funds so that he could go again the following year.

Connecting with others

Bright adults have always needed to make connections with others like them. Though this can be a challenge for them at any age, this plays out differently compared to earlier times in their lives. Finding kindred spirits between the ages of 65 and 80 is a challenge that is affected by changing circumstances—e.g., retirement, new jobs, or deaths of confidants. Where previously they had friends within their profession and spent hours on "shop talk," now these Actualizers desire connection with a broader range of people, often needing to develop new friendships. Here are some suggestions:

○ Draw a diagram with concentric circles and use it to depict the people you know based on how close you would like your relationship to be and how much time you might like to spend with them.[233]

○ Actively use the telephone, snail mail, email, video chat, or social networking sites to reconnect with friends you used to enjoy spending time with before losing touch when your lives became too busy.

○ Follow up on invitations from friends or former colleagues that sound worthwhile.

○ Reflect on your greatest interests; identify where you might find others who share your passions, go there, and get involved in meaningful activities where you can get to know other people like you.

○ Volunteer for causes you care about and meet others who share your concerns and want to take action (political activism, environmental cleanups, poverty programs, education initiatives, etc.).

○ Invite someone who seems to be on your wavelength for coffee or lunch or to go to some events of mutual interest.

Sarah, a retired high school science teacher, had a longstanding interest in amateur radio,[234] but she always was too busy to find time for it. After she had retired, she saw a newspaper story about an informational session of the local ham radio club at a nearby YMCA. She asked her bright 12-year-old grandson if he would be interested in going along with her, and he said *yes*. When she got there, she found people of all ages—men and women alike—who talked about the many different facets of amateur radio and all that ham radio operators do. She was especially intrigued when one speaker talked about providing emergency communications in areas struck by hurricanes, floods, tornados, and other natural disasters.

When the club members announced that they would be offering a series of classes for people interested in becoming ham radio operators, Sarah and her gifted grandson both signed up. (He was especially drawn to the idea of communicating with people in other parts of the world.) At the end of the classes, they both took the Federal Communications Commission tests and got their licenses. She became actively involved in ham radio and developed new friendships with interesting people from all over the world, and she was on call whenever ham radio operators were needed to provide communications in disaster areas.

Generativity

Because Actualizers usually have a broader view of time, generations, existence, and life meaning, generativity plays an increasing role in their lives. They typically find themselves looking well beyond themselves—looking outward with an eye toward how to be a resource for the world, as well as for their own self-fulfillment. They have an ever-growing desire to contribute and leave a legacy for the next generation. They find satisfaction in helping others, and they enjoy sharing what they have learned over the years. Here are some behaviors that can facilitate generativity:

○ Contribute the unique gifts and talents, wisdom, and insights you gained from prior experience through writing for publication, doing presentations, holding webinars, creating and maintaining a blog, developing a website, etc.

○ Establish a succession plan for projects or organizations you have worked with for years.

○ Mentor newer members of your profession to guide them and directly pass along your knowledge, experience, and wisdom; foster a reciprocal relationship with them.

○ Guide others who share your passions and commitment to causes that can make a difference in the world.

○ Work with organizations that you believe have potential to make the world a better place—as a volunteer or as a part-time or full-time paid employee.

○ Volunteer for organized efforts, such as Habitat for Humanity, RSVP's "Senior Corps," or AARP's "Create the Good" program.[235]

○ Donate goods and services to help others who can benefit from them.

○ Make whatever financial contributions are reasonable for you in order to support organizations that are doing what you consider to be worthwhile work.

Greg was a physical therapist who maintained his private practice while he expanded his efforts to write for the *Journal of the American Physical Therapy Association* (APTA) and *Perspectives Magazine,* APTA's publication for new professionals.[236] He started teaching physical therapy students and contributed his ideas about what the future of physical therapy should be via a blog on the APTA website. Using social media to communicate with other physical therapists in private practice, he established strong connections with several who were just starting out.

He then decided that it was time to create a "succession plan" for his own physical therapy business, and he mentored a promising physical therapist in his office to learn the ropes and subsequently take over his practice. They worked together on a five-year plan, with his giving increasing control to his successor. This freed him up to create a website for the business, as well as to coordinate efforts with social service agencies in his region to reduce paperwork and reorganize how services, such as physical therapy, are provided.

Out in the World or Peace Within?

Whether Actualizers take their interests and insights into the world to become involved in a wide range of activities or limit their involvements to quieter ways of finding inner peace, this stage of life has great potential to generate life satisfaction beyond what they might have envisioned during earlier times of their lives.

Actualizers face many practical questions about what they want to do at this point in their lives. Do they want to continue working well beyond the usual retirement age of 65? Do they want to switch to part-time work? Do they want to begin a new career path? Do they want to put their years of working behind them and focus on all the things they have wanted to do that they never had enough time for?

An undercurrent running beneath these basic issues involves what Actualizers want the years between ages 65 and 80 to be like for them. Do they want to take their concerns about what is wrong with the world out into the world to make a difference? Or do they want to spend their days in quiet contemplation, seeking peace within? How much involvement do they want with other people? Where do they want to spend their time and energy? What is most likely to bring them the greatest satisfaction and give meaning to their lives?

CHAPTER 9

The Cruisers—Sailing On

~ ~ ~

"The ideal cruise requires a good yacht, pleasant company,
and a strange coast with plenty of islands and rocks."
—Humphrey Barton

"Grandma, what's it like to have lived so many years?" When Emily answered her grandson, she said, laughing, "I can't say that I ever think much about that. Every day there's so much that's interesting to do and to think about. I just don't waste a lot of time thinking about the past or about everything I've seen in my lifetime. I don't pay much attention to how things have changed during the 80 plus years of my life either."

Most gifted adults at this last stage of life are still avidly intrigued with numerous topics and ideas. As Streznewski noted, "The high-powered brain/mind that drives a gifted person's life does not suddenly switch to low gear simply because the body ages or reaches a certain milestone age. The persistence of curiosity, the need for stimulation, and the drive to do things do not fade."[237]

Moving Along at Just the Right Speed

I describe them as Cruisers because this stage of life is a slow-paced but still vibrant journey, much like being on a cruise ship. Rather than just coasting, Cruisers move ahead at a speed that best reflects who they are now.

153

At this point in life, they are not likely to be setting a new course. Their values and interests provide them direction and serve as well-established ports for their journey. Their minds remain intensely active—especially compared with others their age of average intelligence or abilities. Even in the face of changes that affect what they are physically able to do, they fundamentally know who they are and what they want their remaining years to be like, and they continue to be dynamic.[238] Some travel to places they have always wanted to see. Some take their grandchildren on trips or participate in church groups or activities held at senior centers or retirement communities. Some volunteer with community organizations or schools; others serve on boards. Some get involved with music groups or take courses in subjects of interest. And, unfortunately, some live in nursing homes where they find little to stimulate their still active minds, something that is even more challenging for introverts who do not particularly like to socialize and especially do not want to spend time in superficial conversations or meaningless activities, such as crafts.

Taking Care of What's Important

Health challenges and physical problems associated with age are more of an issue for Cruisers. However, Cruisers regularly use their mental abilities to think through how they can best take care of their bodies, and for many of them, their efforts pay off in tangible ways.[239] They pay attention to exercise and diet and follow good advice for living a healthy life. They may take daily walks, swim, or attend Silver Sneaker classes at a gym. They may even do light weightlifting or take a yoga class. Most do what they are able to and then cope with arthritis or whatever else comes along as best as they can, perhaps walking with a cane. Cohen described this stage as the "encore phase," commenting that "despite illness or physical limitations, during this time of life people are still driven by powerful forces, such as the desires for love, companionship, self-determination, control, and giving back."[240]

In addition to the powerful forces that Cohen listed, Cruisers characteristically have an intense drive to continue to use their minds. In *Beyond Old Age,* Annemarie Roeper's book of essays published a year before her death at age 93, she urged all elders to keep their minds carefully trained and in continuous use. "Keeping a sharp mind becomes a way of preserving one's independence and control. Just as I consciously watch every step I take so that I can keep control of my body and won't fall, I watch every thought I think, so that I can keep control of my daily life."[241] Regrettably, opportunities for mental stimulation may gradually become more limited for many Cruisers, a tragic waste of their ability to lead satisfying and meaningful lives and to contribute their ideas and insights to others around them.

Some Cruisers have minds that remain as clear as ever, despite the ways that the aging process may affect their bodies. Others notice times when their minds are not as sharp as they used to be, and still other Cruisers are all too aware that their mental abilities have diminished significantly. They feel a poignant sense of loss for what had been one of their significant strengths and a source of satisfaction for them during their earlier years.

Responding to Ageism

Although some limitations faced by Cruisers may be due to physical changes, including vision, hearing, and personal mobility issues, there is more to the story. Rampant ageism in our society often results in elders being summarily dismissed as being "too old" to have anything worthwhile to contribute, and Cruisers frequently get frustrated with the many times they are ignored or overlooked.

I recall visiting Annemarie Roeper in northern California when she was in her early 90s and we went out to dinner at her favorite waterfront restaurant. After getting our menus, our server looked at me, asking, "What would she like to eat?" Annemarie replied to the server very pointedly, "*She* would like…" and proceeded to give her order, including regular (not decaf) coffee. The surprised server, who pigeon-holed Annemarie as a feeble "little old lady," was so sure that Annemarie wasn't capable of ordering for herself and positive that she would want decaf.

Despite some age-related physical challenges with hearing and mobility, Annemarie's mind was fine. She resented being dismissed as if she weren't still a capable person in her own right. She continued to use her wisdom and knowledge throughout her Cruiser years to influence her chosen field of gifted education. Even into her 90s, she continued to write and confer with the administration of the school she and her husband had founded, and she also collaborated with a group of professional colleagues to develop a training program so that others could learn her method of qualitative assessment for gifted children.

People in this stage of life are so different now than in previous generations, because modern science and medical breakthroughs have greatly improved life expectancy. Today's older adults are healthier than previous generations were, mentally and physically. Not only do people live longer in the 21st century, but their life quality has vastly improved. As Bateson commented:

> *I have been exploring the idea that our new longevity is not equivalent to an extension of old age, years added on at the end, but rather a period inserted in the life course after the era associated with full adult participation and generativity but before the decline of old age, a period characterized by the accumulated experience of adulthood but endowed with health and energy, so that wisdom is combined with activity and often with activism for the common good.*[242]

Despite some inevitable challenges, Cruisers can continue to have satisfying, meaningful lives at age 80 and beyond. Some, like Annemarie, just "keep on keeping on," doing what their life's work has always been. Others, particularly those whose intense and widespread involvement has continued on many fronts throughout their lives, become more selective and now prioritize how they choose to spend their time and energy. In his persona as "Mrs. Sundberg," Garrison Keillor wrote, "One of the beautiful things about growing older is that you gain the wisdom and insight to designate what is and is not important in your own productive, happy life."[243]

Keeping On with Keeping On

This time period is often an extension of the life these bright adults settled into when they were Actualizers. In his 80s, Walter is a knowledgeable musicologist even though he was not a professional musician nor had he ever been a high school or college music teacher. However, his lifelong love of classical music and expertise has made him so well respected during his retirement years that he is now paid to present a series of lectures on musicology at regional libraries. Walter regularly offers a 90-minute lecture every week for 10 weeks, focusing on a different composer in each session. His audience ordinarily includes other bright Cruisers, many of whom frequently also attend other lectures or classes in their community.

What else do you find Cruisers doing? They go to the theater or concerts, organize and participate in book clubs, and mentor younger people who are interested in what they have to say. Some keep on working for causes they believe in and are involved with organizations that value their contributions and pay little attention to their age.

In *The Life Cycle Completed,* the book she wrote to extend the work of her husband Erik, Joan Erikson expressed concern about how our country too often neglects to do enough to make things better for elders—how we fail to "recycle" their value and usefulness the way we recycle other old things rather than taking them to the dump. She questioned how the elder years might be made as meaningful, stimulating, and rich as possible, asking, "With what stories of successful aging do we alert and inform ourselves on our way?"[244]

The good news is that stories of successful aging are now increasingly available. Here are a few examples:

○ *Composing a Further Life: The Age of Active Wisdom* by Mary Catherine Bateson[245]

○ *The Blue Zones: 9 Lessons for Living Longer from the People Who've Lived the Longest* by Dan Buettner[246]

○ *The Longevity Prescription: The 8 Proven Keys to a Long, Healthy Life* by Robert N. Butler[247]

○ *The Mature Mind: The Positive Power of the Aging Brain* by Gene D. Cohen[248]

○ *If I Live to be 100: Lessons from the Centenarians* by Neenah Ellis[249]

○ *Prime Time* by Jane Fonda[250]

○ *Finding Meaning in the Second Half of Life* by James Hollis[251]

○ *The Third Chapter* by Sara Lawrence-Lightfoot[252]

○ *Your Life Calling: Reimagining the Rest of Your Life* by Jane Pauley[253]

- ○ *From Age-ing to Sage-ing* by Zalman Schacter-Shalomi and Ronald S. Miller[254]

- ○ *Another Country* by Mary Pipher[255]

- ○ *The Gift of Years: Growing Older Gracefully* by Joan Chittister[256]

- ○ *The Age of Dignity: Preparing for the Elder Boom in a Changing America* by Al-jen Poo[257]

As these book titles indicate, the authors have stepped far beyond the notion that older people should be put aside to languish in their later years without meaning or purpose—like old unused boats hauled out to rot away on land. As author Jack London reportedly said, "Better to wear out than rust out," and most Cruisers would smile and nod their heads in agreement. They want to remain active and involved; they want interesting people in their lives to socialize and discuss ideas with. They want to continue to be visible, a part of things, and they want to continue to do what they can to make a difference in the world. They seem intuitively aware that, as Sheehy stated, "The more we have worked our brain, the more it will continue to work for us."[258]

Being with Others

All of this may go fairly smoothly for Cruisers, if they are still able to get around and if they are surrounded by others whose interests, values, and goals are congruent with theirs. In many ways, this mirrors the challenges that Seekers have in their search for kindred spirits—other people who have a similar intellect and intensity. As Webb commented, "There is little doubt that other people are essential if we are to feel content and happy. This can be difficult for intense, sensitive, bright people who struggle to find others who will accept them as they are and with whom they can relate."[259] It is an important mission for a Cruiser's family members to help find places with activities and social groups that will be a stimulus and a "match" for their elder family member.

Staying "Put" or Moving Away

Some Cruisers plan ahead so they can do everything within their power to stay in their homes and in familiar surroundings, often near their children, grandchildren, and lifelong friends. If they can still drive their own cars, it is easier for them to stay put, to remain active, and to keep using their minds. Anita, in her mid-80s, found that she could do that through an organization for older adults dedicated to lifelong learning. She said it is "a Godsend" for her, especially since her immediate neighborhood is filling with younger families and the friends she used to socialize with there are all gone—either dead or moved. She no longer feels comfortable driving after dark; her night vision is not as good as it used to be, and, as she says, things look strange to her then. However, driving in the daytime is fine for her, and nearly every day she can be found participating in scheduled lectures and discussions at an LLI, speaking out and sharing precise and cogent thoughts and perspectives on the topics at hand. She enjoys meeting other people there for lively lunchtime discussions about wide-ranging subjects of interest and calls the LLI her "happy place."

In rural, isolated areas, Cruisers may have more difficulty finding ways to stay where they are while still attaining the mental stimulation they need and yearn for. Nonetheless, many are reluctant to leave and relocate somewhere else. They appreciate the close relationships and support that rural areas and small towns can provide.

Cruisers may need to hire someone or ask neighbors and family for more help than before—help with mowing grass, shoveling snow, home and auto maintenance, or housework (e.g., laundry and cooking). However, with this sort of assistance, they can stay in their homes where things are familiar and they already have a comfortable routine.

Even in their 80s and beyond, however, some Cruisers deliberately decide to move away, often heading to warmer climates to live in vibrant retirement communities with people and activities that appeal to them, even sometimes far away from friends and family and familiar places. They invite their friends and family to visit and hope they will. In the meantime, they travel back home when they can, phone frequently, and use technology to stay in touch while simultaneously creating a new life and establishing new friendships with like-minded people in their age group. One new option for bright older adults is a growing number of university-based retirement communities.[260] Each of these is affiliated with a university and offers an active, intellectually stimulating, and intergenerational retirement environment with a continuum of services to address the needs of residents as they age.

Adult Children and Their Concerns

Sometimes the Cruisers' adult children are partners in their decisions, but more often the Cruisers are strong-willed and determined to make their own decisions about where and how to live. They care a lot about being able to stay in charge of their own lives—feelings that are typical of their analytical minds, their intensity, and their need for autonomy. Like many older adults who plan to stay in their own homes, Cruisers may add safety features, such as handrails or grab bars, or widen the doorways to accommodate a walker or wheelchair. Alternatively, they may investigate retirement homes or communities in their area that offer amenities, such as a heated pool and exercise rooms, frequent lectures and films, clubs and activities, and occasional field trips to museums, botanical gardens, or other places of interest. Retirement communities with these amenities sometimes also offer various stages of care as needed, from independent living to assisted living, from rehab facilities to full-time nursing homes, and even hospice. Sadly, these graduated care communities are usually quite expensive, so they are not an option for everyone. But they bear looking into.

Some retirement communities provide a place where people buy a regular house but are located within a parklike setting with playground equipment, walking paths, and a community center they can use for family reunions or parties. Once the Cruisers who move there do not want to live in a separate house any more, they can relocate to a smaller apartment, with increasing care offered—all on the same campus. It's like a small town with plenty of sidewalks and close neighbors, but when you need more care, it's available just down the block.

Having a Plan B or Plan C in the event something goes wrong is just as important as planning ahead for the older years when mobility and other aspects of Cruisers' health may be problems. All family members should have advanced directives about what to do if they become unconscious or have a stroke. Cruisers should be sure to have conversations with loved ones about their final wishes—health care and resuscitation, burial versus cremation, the type of memorial service they would like, and so on.[261] With so many options today, it is helpful for family members to have this information—especially for the families of Cruisers, since most of these internally motivated

bright individuals are intensely determined to make their own decisions about everything.[262]

Cruisers who did not move to a place that will meet their mental,
physical, and social needs when they were Actualizers now may find
their grown children object to their desire to move someplace else
when they are 80 or more years old. The protectiveness that Cruisers
encounter often feels like they are being treated like children. Their
adult children want to get them to settle down someplace safe where
all of their needs will be met, not only for now but for any and all
eventualities in the future. This often implies permanent placement
in a retirement home or assisted living facility, something that many
Cruisers strongly resist and which can exacerbate problems they experience at this stage of life. They want to be in control of their own lives
and not have their children boss them around. For the Cruisers' adult
children, the tables are turned. Now they are parenting their parents
for the first time, with all of the tensions that go along with that.

Generativity!

Cruisers typically care a lot about communicating in depth to
their families about their most cherished beliefs and values, the lessons
they have learned in life, and their perspectives on their own experiences. An excellent way for them to do this is to create an "Ethical
Will," a concept that dates back to medieval times and even before,
according to *The Grandparents' Guide to Gifted Children.*[263] An ethical will is "a way to record and pass on your values, beliefs, faith, life
lessons, love and forgiveness."[264]

Along with Cruisers' need to exercise their minds is their desire
to be of service—to continue the course of generativity that they began
as Actualizers. For instance, Alberto worked at a music store during
his late 50s and taught guitar lessons in his spare time. He had seen
many young people living in poverty come into the store yearning to
get a guitar and learn to play. He knew that they dreamed of becoming
rock stars, but he was also well aware that music is uniquely good for
the mind and soul. He worked at the store part-time until he was 80,
and when he decided to retire at last, he approached his boss at the
music store about converting an unused storage space above the store
into a music studio. He contacted a local social service agency in his

city about collaborating on a grant to acquire used instruments and to provide lessons for young would-be guitarists who otherwise could not afford them. He began marketing the program through churches in poor areas of his city; he and the social workers and several ministers started giving lessons to just a handful of students with a few used guitars. News of their endeavor spread by word of mouth, and he found great satisfaction in this thriving program where he could teach and get other older musicians involved as well. The result was a growing number of satisfying success stories about how the program was keeping kids more motivated in school and removed from the gang activity that permeated their neighborhoods.

At this stage of life, as Jacobsen suggested, "The personality and soul become integrated, and complementary motivation emerges—the urge to apply abilities in ways that make a difference for others."[265] Cruisers may continue involvement in volunteer work, help in nearby classrooms, phone and write letters and emails to elected representatives, or submit letters to their local media.

Cruisers also look ahead to get their financial affairs in order and make legacy gifts to organizations they care about. Some paid close attention to financial and estate planning during the years when they were working and have everything in good order. Others did not and start to realize that they should do something about this now. They seek out information from trusted friends and get recommendations from them for professional sources for whatever help they need.[266]

Change is an inevitable part of the lives of Cruisers. The changes that they see in the world around them often spur them on to serve as a catalyst for positive change in any ways they can.

As they age, the ability to be out in the world enough to engage in generativity may become limited for some Cruisers. Those with vision problems will have to rely on others to help them get around. Even with good vision, some will need to give up driving. Annemarie observed:

As we age, we age unevenly. Our ability to walk may deteriorate, while our brains might function as well as ever. The asynchronicity between our dreams and desires and our ability to fulfill them also grows greater as we grow older. The most difficult change we have to accept is losing some of our independence and the need to rely on others.[267]

Getting Around and Out and About

One of the most difficult days in the lives of older adults is when they have to give up their driver's license—a disenfranchisement that is a blow to their identity as fully functioning adults. If you think about the euphoria that young people feel when they first get their driver's license, the sense of coming of age and being more independent, you can begin to understand how traumatic it is for older adults to lose theirs and the freedom that goes with it. They have to acknowledge that they will now be permanently dependent on others to get places they want or need to go. Having been independent and resourceful for many years, giving up a driver's license really concerns them. If they live in a city with good public transportation, the loss is not quite so devastating, but they still can be uncertain how they will be able to participate in their world as fully as they would like.

When one Cruiser's 80th birthday was approaching and the notice came in the mail that she would have to take the vision test in order to renew her driver's license, she was seriously worried because she'd had some trouble with her eyesight in the past. So she decided to go to the driver's license bureau right away before her license expired and see if she could pass the vision test. As it turned out, she was right to be concerned; she failed the eye test. However, they gave her two options: 1) She could take the test again any time before her birthday, which wasn't for a few more weeks; or 2) she could have her eyes examined by her own eye doctor and have him send in a form that verified her fitness to drive. After sharing her concerns with her friends in the small town where she lived and hearing from them that they would drive her anywhere she needed to go, she felt better. But she still made an appointment with her eye doctor. When he checked her vision, he said that her eyes were still good enough to drive, even at night. He filled out the necessary form and sent it to the driver's license bureau, and she was able to renew her license and was thrilled to find that it would be good for another five years.

Slowing Down...or Not?

Some Cruisers find that they tire quickly when they go on errands or other short trips. Some face various physical challenges that interfere with their mobility or prevent them from activities. A man who once jogged three times a week had to give it up because his arthritic knees became too painful. A woman who played tennis from her teen years into her 70s misses the sport terribly. A former golfer yearns for the good old days of being outdoors with friends and playing a few holes of golf. For some Cruisers, it is hard even to walk a block or two. It is difficult to be satisfied with slower and milder activities if you have been physically active your entire life. Cruisers find they need to make mental, emotional, and physical adjustments as they learn to accept their limitations and grieve about their losses.

The widest variation in physical capabilities for bright adults is within this age group. Many Cruisers have a vitality that goes on and on through their 80s and 90s—in some cases, past age 100. Some in their 90s show no sign of slowing down, physically or mentally. They still walk briskly and do their regular household chores. Others do well for a while and then suddenly seem to have difficulties—physical or mental or both. When she was 92, Marion Downs published a self-help book chock-full of practical suggestions for older adults who want to have vibrant, active lives into their 80s, 90s, and beyond.[268]

Cruisers who begin slowing down often mourn their inability to do everything they used to do. Some report memory issues, beginning with problems pulling out information they are trying to remember. Slower speed of memory retrieval is the first thing that Cruisers may notice. Some of them say, "It'll come to me, probably sometime later" and then find that whatever they wanted to remember does pop into their heads. They shrug and say that there's just too much data in their mental data bank; that's why it takes a little longer to find it. These Cruisers do remember what they were trying to think of because they do not give up. Others panic and throw up their hands in frustration, only making matters worse and finding themselves in a downward spiral of discouragement. However, regardless of issues with short-term memory, long-term memories may actually improve, especially the memories of events that happened in the far distant past.[269]

Role Model or "Elder"?

Despite limitations, many Cruisers make valuable contributions to their families and wider communities. They share historical knowledge of events that they experienced directly, and this helps others gain perspectives that they would not otherwise be able to obtain. Author, educator, speaker, and explorer Dan Buettner studied insights from centenarians about living life well. He wrote about how important it is to listen to the healthiest people who have lived long lives. He said, "If wisdom is the sum of knowledge plus experience, then these individuals possess more wisdom than anyone else."[270]

Although it seems as if it would be validating for Cruisers to hear this, many of them reject suggestions about sharing their vast wisdom with others. Many Cruisers just want to live their lives as best they can without anyone implying that they should be a font of knowledge and wisdom for anyone else. Some actually express discomfort with being seen as wiser than anyone else, because they feel that they themselves are still continuing to find their way. Annemarie eloquently expressed this feeling, saying, "…upon arrival in one's early 80s, the road one has been traveling, which, up until now had been relatively well lit, well described, and well worn, begins to peter out, until one is left standing in a field, no longer sure of the way."[271]

Often people in this age bracket are called *elders* with the intent of conveying great respect for their age and wisdom. In many countries other than the United States, elders are viewed and treated with great respect. For instance, elders have status and high regard in Hispanic cultures, in Native American cultures, within indigenous populations, and in many tribal cultures around the world. Author Mary Pipher shared information about the distinction that the Lakota people make between *elderly* and *elder*:

> The Lakota believe that if the old do not stay connected to the young, the culture will disintegrate. Older people tell stories that teach lessons and keep the culture alive. Because wisdom is highly valued among the Lakota, the older people are, the more they are loved. Older equals wiser equals more respected.[272]

This view contrasts sharply with the ways older adults are typically treated in the United States. Furthermore, many Cruisers in the United States object to being labeled *elders*, feeling it is a subtle allusion to their being *elderly* when they do not think of themselves that way at all.

In 2004, the travel adventure group for elders called Elderhostel selected a new name—Road Scholars—for their series of adventurous, experiential learning programs. This change seems to reflect a broader conceptualization of their focus on lifelong learning rather than focusing on the term *elders*. Their website affirms, "At the heart of today's organization are the participants, who are lifelong learners engaged in programs that foster camaraderie and a sense of community."[273] In addition, nothing on their website suggests specific ages for participants.

Pipher also suggested that this time of life "is really a search for a place in the universe, both figuratively and literally."[274] It is a time of asking existential questions, such as "How did my life matter?" "Was my time well spent?" "What did I mean to others?" "What can I look back on with pride?" "Did I love the right people?"[275]

Bright adults may agonize over the answers to questions such as these, seeing the ramifications of past decisions and events in multifaceted ways. They ruminate with their characteristic intensity and wisdom gained through their years of living. The more optimistic of them may tell themselves, "I did the best I could at the time, under the circumstances, given the knowledge and resources and the consciousness that I had." Others who have not developed as optimistic an explanatory style may find themselves filled with regret for the way things were and how they turned out, plagued with thoughts of "should've, could've, would've."

Spirituality may be a part of looking beyond the horizon at this stage of life and may also be related to Cruisers' broader perspectives. Whatever personally nurtures their spirit may or may not have anything to do with formal religion—i.e., something directly connected with organizationally prescribed beliefs and practices. Cruisers are often quite likely to make individual decisions about spiritual pursuits.

A thought-provoking distinction can be made between the "young-old and the old-old."[276] Pipher suggests that what changes someone from being young-old to being old-old is loss of health. However, several other factors also may come into play for Cruisers–– like whether their health issues are something fairly temporary (an accident, an illness, or surgery with the possibility of full recovery) or if the prognosis is for long-term increasing debilitation. Optimism affects how people respond to their health concerns and can help weather against becoming "old-old." Bright adults often use their intellectual abilities to respond and find ways to make their way through. However, they may still need to navigate a storm of intense emotions before this is possible.

Ageless

In many ways, Cruisers are really ageless. They are still youthful in manifestations of their intensity, their enthusiasm for learning, their creativity, and their childlike delight in new ideas and beautiful sights and sounds and other experiences. The phrase "young at heart" often describes these ageless adults. They keep their youthful zest for life. At the same time, they have mature concerns and a depth of wisdom commensurate with the years they have lived.

At times, other people expect Cruisers to act in more conventional ways and have trouble accepting their asynchrony. For instance, Herb's nieces and nephews wanted him to pay more attention to them and their children. They continually muttered to each other about his refusal to attend any weddings, baptisms, and other family events if they were held during the sailing season. Herb had a 35-foot sailboat that he maintained and raced on Lake Michigan from May through October, including participating in the race from Chicago to Mackinac Island every year. In his family's opinion, he should have given all of that up "at his age" since he was in his early 80s. However, he would smile and say, "If you want me to be there, plan things for when it isn't the sailing season." He told them that racing his sailboat was the only thing keeping him young, quoting an old Phoenician proverb: "God does not subtract from man's allotted time the hours spent in sailing."

Waypoints and Strategies for Cruisers

I have identified eight waypoints that are typical issues for Cruisers during ages 80 and beyond:

1. Being selective about how to spend their time and energy
2. Continuing to have vibrant, interesting lives
3. Dealing with physical changes
4. Intense drive to exercise their minds
5. Having meaningful relationships with others

6. Remaining independent as long as possible
7. Generativity
8. Being "ageless."

Being selective about how to spend their time and energy

Cruisers focus on designating what is and isn't important, and act accordingly. Their clarity about their personal identity helps them choose what they want their remaining years to be like insofar as possible. Bright adults at this stage continue to seek self-determination and want control over their own lives, just as in earlier stages of life, but they generally find that their energy is not quite the same as it once was. So they become increasing selective about how to spend their time. Here are some suggestions to help Cruisers allocate their time and energy:

○ Write options available to you on index cards, divide them into four piles, and color code each with stickers, highlighters, or markers: 1) top priority—to do as soon as possible or as often as possible (green); 2) second priority—to do whenever time and energy permits (yellow); 3) third priority—to put aside for later, if and when you are inclined (blue); and 4) last priority—things you do not want to do at all, ever (red).

○ Be quietly but firmly assertive about what you do and don't want to be involved in (especially when others badger you, attempt to make you feel guilty, or try to persuade you to do things you really don't want to do).

○ Say *no* to commitments that are only mildly interesting to you; decide on responses or phrases that you are comfortable using to say *no* and practice them.

○ Avoid spending time with people who drain your energy (e.g., with constant complaining).

○ Pay attention to what regularly works best for you for using your time, e.g., decide what part of the day is good for participating in activities versus more restful pursuits, such as reading or writing, playing music, or solving puzzles; determine what your own ideal sleep schedule is and stick to it as much as you can.

Barbara started to realize that she did not have as much energy as she used to and noticed that her mind seemed to work better early in the morning, right after breakfast. So she experimented with scheduling things that took more "brain power" for the morning hours—balancing her checkbook; dealing with other paperwork, such as filling out insurance forms; sorting through old mail that had piled up on her dining room table; and ruthlessly deciding to throw out things that she really did not need to keep. She carved out a specific block of time to do this, starting with spending only one hour at it before she stopped and did something more enjoyable, like phoning or emailing a friend.

After a week, she found that it was so satisfying to get these things done—tasks that she had been putting off for a long time—she decided to extend the time to an hour and a half. Then the rest of the day was hers to do whatever she wanted. She used that time to read, listen to music, take a nap, or occasionally go out to lunch without feeling guilty about the "gottas" that had been haunting her before. When someone who was always complaining about everything called her to set a date to get together, she gracefully declined, saying simply, "I'm sorry; I just can't."

Continuing to have vibrant, interesting lives

Cruisers need ongoing opportunities to pursue their interests and be involved in all kinds of activities. They enjoy discussing a variety of topics and ideas, and their values and goals give them direction for their lives. They continue to fine-tune these, making whatever course corrections are most appropriate for them. More and more, they realize how important to them it is to stay busy with things that interest them. They also find they need to be able to respond appropriately to ageism and to overcome stereotypic attitudes of others who attempt to classify them as "old folks." Here are some suggestions:

○ Reflect on what really has meaning for you in your life—i.e., why you get up in the morning; use this to refine your life purpose and craft a personal mission statement, communicating it to a trusted friend, along with your plans for implementation.[277]

○ Host book clubs or discussion groups of interest to you or create ones that you would like to have in your life; post a notice at your local library or coffee shop or any place other interested people might check.

○ Learn more about how to use technology and find out how best to put it to work for you.

○ Go on relevant bus tours organized by local centers for older adults.

○ Create your own personal field trips to places in your area that you always meant to visit (museums, botanical gardens, historical sites, etc.); invite along others with whom you want to share the experience.

○ Take a cruise; enjoy activities of interest to you and conversations with people you meet on board. [278]

Two very bright sisters went on their annual weeklong cruise together—a tradition they started years ago when their kids were teenagers and they both needed to get away. Initially, they left their husbands or their mom in charge at home; now they are both retired and their kids are grown and living their own lives. So, with more freedom than ever, they still go away together for a week each year without being particularly concerned about responsibilities either at home or at work, and their family members just say, "I guess it's that time again."

Their favorite cruise line catered to many fascinating people in their age group who thought the sisters' lives were interesting, too. They chose "anytime dining" for their meals, went to "tea time," and started conversations with people they met. They exchanged contact information and kept in touch with a number of them long after the cruise was over, even planning to book future cruises together, especially cruises that featured educational lectures and excursions.

Dealing with physical changes

At some point, Cruisers are likely to face physical challenges to their bodies. They have to pay attention to their health and wellness more than ever and give extra thought to living as healthy a life as possible. They characteristically use their excellent minds and intellectual intensity to figure out the best ways to do this. Some may have to cope with vision or hearing losses. Others may have issues with walking or personal mobility or other potentially limiting difficulties. Here are some recommendations that may be helpful:

○ Incorporate movement into your day-to-day activities without having to think about it, including walking (e.g., parking your car a little farther away from entrances or making a date to walk regularly with a friend), working in the garden, walking up or down stairs, joining a gym and taking classes there, participating in yoga or tai chi, etc.[279]

○ Pay attention to your diet and follow guidelines for healthy eating.

○ Get adequate quality sleep; if necessary, darken your room, reduce sound (or wear earplugs), or set a timer to play nature sounds or soft meditative background music. Take naps when you need to but avoid sleeping so much in the daytime that you have trouble sleeping at night.

○ Try not to obsess about minor aches or pains; however, pay attention to significant symptoms and confer with a trusted medical professional.[280]

○ Read up on any diagnosis you receive from medical professionals and write down questions to bring to your next appointment; bring an "extra pair of ears" with you (someone who can listen and take notes so that you can be sure you receive all important information).

○ Acquire the help you need to deal with vision or hearing loss and continue to work with whomever is prescribing glasses or hearing aids until you are satisfied; seek a second opinion, if what the experts are telling you doesn't ring true for you or isn't working well.

○ Continue to maintain physical mobility; appropriately use whatever tools you need when and if you need them, such as a cane for balance. [281]

Sam realized that he was spending too much time sitting and that he was starting to feel lethargic both mentally and physically. He wondered if getting more exercise would help, and he had heard that it might help him to sleep better at night, too. So he made a plan for the next month; he would park his car farther away from where he was going, and he would take the stairs up and down at least one flight rather than riding the elevator.

He also figured out ways to darken his room at night, even covering up the light on the charger for his phone and dimming the display on his clock radio. Because he lived someplace where noise was occasionally a problem and woke him up, making it difficult to get back to sleep, he tried different types of earplugs and found some that worked well for him.

After a month of doing both—exercising more and getting better sleep—he noticed that his energy level and thinking had improved. He was often heard telling his older friends that they should try doing what he had, and in return, they would recommend that he change his eating habits, too.

Intense drive to exercise their minds

Cruisers' minds are kind of like a GPS; they take into account wide-ranging data and put it together in meaningful ways to help them find where they are, where they want to go, and how they want to get there. But, just like a GPS, Cruisers' mental software needs to be used and updated with new ideas and information in order to function well. Cruisers' minds generally remain intensely active, but they need to overcome obstacles they encounter in finding mental stimulation. They need ample opportunities to continue to use their brains, even just having interesting people in their lives to exchange ideas with. Here are some suggestions:

○ Read—your favorite authors as well as ones that are new to you, classics that you have always promised yourself you would read, and books from different genres than those you typically enjoy; reread favorites to see what you notice now that you never saw before.

○ Bookmark interesting websites and go there regularly (e.g., the op-ed page of *The New York Times* or a blogger you find thought-provoking); read, absorb, think, and, if possible, discuss what you find there with other people.

○ Learn to play a musical instrument that always interested you or one that you used to play but have not touched in years; take lessons, establish a daily schedule for practice, and stay with it.

○ Join a choir or other singing group or take singing lessons; learn different genres of music (e.g., sea chanties, barbershop, musical comedy, folk music, 50s rock-and-roll, or jazz).

○ Master a new language or brush up on one you studied years ago—use audio recordings or podcasts, find a class or a tutor, and see if you can converse with someone who grew up speaking that language; research countries where that language is spoken and plan a trip there.

○ Become more computer literate, including experimenting with software that is new to you (e.g., Photoshop, Garage Band, iMovie, or Excel).

○ Play brain-challenging games on your computer, smartphone, or tablet.

○ Work your favorite kinds of puzzles—crossword, Sudoku, jigsaw, word jumble, etc.

○ Pursue a passion—anything you are interested in or think you might like to try or get back to doing (painting, writing poetry, bird-watching, etc.); find a mentor (perhaps even a younger person) to teach you more about it.[282]

○ Take advantage of local opportunities to keep your active mind engaged—e.g., adult learning courses, lectures at nearby colleges or universities, programs at your local library, book clubs, writers' workshops, or art classes.

Jenny had taken Spanish classes in high school and college, but she had never become fluent. She did fairly well reading Spanish and could even understand much of what she heard when other people spoke it. Even in her 80s, she found that she could remember a lot of the vocabulary. When she was younger, she had been uncomfortable when she tried to communicate in Spanish, being overly concerned about making mistakes and not saying things correctly. Now she regretted that and said to herself, "Well, that was then, and this is now. There's no time like the present to get over that!"

Jenny found that her library had audio CDs for learning Spanish, so she checked out several different sets to listen to so that she could find the right level for her, based on what she still remembered from years before. She knew she was not quite a beginning Spanish learner. After a few false starts, she discovered a set of audio CDs that she really liked. When she found that they were available online and reasonably priced, she bought her own copies and spent about 20 to 30 minutes each day listening to them, either at home, in her car, or on the bus, using a portable CD player that one of her grandchildren had given her.

In the building for older adults where Jenny lived, there were quite a few native Spanish speakers, including Violeta whose apartment was on Jenny's floor. They had often said *hola* to each other and a few other basic words. One day Violeta haltingly confided to Jenny in the hallway that she really wanted to improve her English, and Jenny said, "Yo, tambien—Español" ("Me, too—Spanish"). She and Violeta made a date to meet for coffee the following Monday afternoon. They set up a regular schedule of times when Jenny would speak only Spanish to Violeta (who would help her when she got stuck) and Violeta would speak only English to Jenny (who, in turn, would help her if she drew a blank on something). They laughed together over their struggles with each other's language and decided to go out to lunch from time to time—sometimes to a Columbian or Cuban restaurant where Jenny could practice ordering in Spanish and sometimes to an American restaurant so that Violeta could practice ordering in English.

Having meaningful relationships with others

All gifted adults need people in their lives who are similar to them—sharing their intensity and sensitivity and having interests, values, and goals that are congruent with theirs. However, this can be especially challenging for Cruisers when many of their lifelong friends and companions are no longer around. By this stage of life, they may have lost spouses, friends, and others. Unless these bright adults can find people on their wavelength, they are likely to be starved for companionship with like-minded friends. Here are some recommendations:

○ Reflect on what has always been especially meaningful for you in your most treasured relationships of the past. Write thumbnail sketches about some of your dearest friends, past and present; then go back and highlight or circle the words that describe what you had in common with them or why you enjoyed them so much.

○ Reconnect with valued friends and family via any means you can—phoning, writing letters, or connecting electronically (by email, video chat, texting, or social networking sites). Make an effort to contact those you have been out of touch with for a while. If possible, get together with friends and family face-to-face.

○ Find people who might be interested in things you are passionate about; make arrangements to connect with them regularly for conversation or to take part in meaningful events.

○ Attend lifelong learning classes or adult education courses that especially interest you; look for new friends there, exchange contact information, and follow up with them after the class or course is over.

○ Join local organizations that reflect your concerns about significant issues; get to know people there by working together on a common cause.

○ Get involved in community service by choosing or creating options that relate to what you love to do—work with gifted students at a local school, use your passion for gardening to plan or participate in a neighborhood beautification project, create an art project for your community, or find meaningful ways to work in a hospital, food pantry, soup kitchen, etc.; call the people in charge, explain your interest, offer your services, and see what relevant connections you might make with other volunteers.

○ Attend discussion groups that sound intriguing and get to know people there.

○ Invite interesting people to visit you or go to visit them.

○ Plan short-term excursions and whatever other travel is feasible with compatible friends or family; discuss details with each other ahead of time to prevent misunderstandings and hurt feelings.

○ Think about the people in your life who really understand and support you, who share your values, and who challenge you mentally; create a tangible "circle of stones" to represent your relationships by finding a stone to represent each of these people, along with one stone for yourself. Then place all of the stones in a circle on a flat surface someplace in your home. If possible, keep this circle of stones where you can look at it from time to time to remind yourself to stay connected with these people regularly, either through direct contact or just by keeping them in mind.

○ Listen thoughtfully to others whenever you connect with them, avoiding the temptation to do all the talking or interrupt them, even if you have all kinds of things you want to say.

Fred had always been an avid gardener, and after he had permanently moved South, he became intrigued by the kinds of plants he saw in his new location as compared to those in his old hometown up North. He read in the local newspaper about a community beautification project that was just about to get started near where he lived. He called the phone number in the article and offered to help. This led him to make friends with other garden enthusiasts who were also volunteering for the project, including another really bright man named Marco who had been a landscape architect before he mostly retired 10 years earlier.

Fred and Marco became good friends and spent many hours together talking about different kinds of plants and the environmental conditions they required. They discovered that they both cared a lot about the importance of green spaces for improving the quality of life in a community, and so they explored additional ways they could influence local government policies, including attending meetings of the City Council and the Planning Commission, speaking up and offering their ideas.

Fred and Marco, like other Cruisers, find that meeting interesting people is much like the instant bonding between boaters when they get together and raft off (i.e., tie their boats side by side, either at anchor or in a harbor). Cruisers enjoy the companionship of others who share their interests and enthusiasm about ideas and like to share stories about their lives with each other—much like boaters who enjoy swapping sea stories and the camaraderie of friends who share their love of being on the water.

Remaining independent as long as possible

Solo sailors usually celebrate their independence and ability to rely only on themselves. Bright Cruisers need that same kind of independence as long as possible. Their minds remain sharp, and they are often enthusiastic about a wide range of topics and involvements. Those in good health can still do nearly everything they want to do, including driving. Their reflexes, skills, and visual acuity let them keep their driver's licenses for a long time so that they can continue to get out and about easily without having to ask someone to take them.

Some Cruisers will have limitations and need to rely on others, becoming more dependent than they find comfortable. When the time comes to stop driving, even in the daytime or away from heavy traffic, these bright adults still need to be able to get around—a significant issue. Convenient ways of handling everyday tasks need to be addressed so that these Cruisers can continue being as independent as possible. Cruisers also must confront the protectiveness of their grown children who worry about them and want to be sure that they are safe and can handle any eventualities. Some Cruisers prefer to stay in their homes and in familiar surroundings and simply require ways to manage routine needs. Here are some suggestions:

○ Reflect on the ways you successfully maintain your independence; use journaling, writing poetry, or art to celebrate what works well for you. For instance, draw a cartoon about your "independent self," create an abstract painting, or play with writing a humorous poem about being independent.

○ Continue to stay active and involved in the things you enjoy and care about; resist anyone's implications that you are "too old" to do something.

○ Use your creative problem solving abilities to find solutions to challenges related to living your life as independently as possible.[283]

○ Regardless of whether you think driving might be an issue, either now or later, take a driver safety course for older adults, such as those offered by AAA, AARP, or other trusted sources in your local area.[284]

○ Make lists of the places and times you need to go; brainstorm your options for getting there and highlight the ones that are most interesting and feasible for you. Ask friends or family members for rides. Create a schedule with a neighbor and go grocery shopping together every week. If your community has good public transportation, use that. See if access is available to on-demand transportation for seniors, the disabled, and wheelchair users—such as Handi Car, services that work like a taxi. Or use various car services, such as Uber, or call a cab when you need one.[285]

○ If night driving becomes an issue, use family connections or post a notice on college bulletin boards or internet sites, such as Craigslist,[286] to find a dependable college student or young career person who would be available to drive you (including maybe even going with you to events of mutual interest). Be sure to ask for references and check them out, as well as considering your own intuition about whether this is someone you want in your life.

○ Delegate mundane tasks, such as housework, grocery shopping, and cooking, to others so that you can use your time and energy for more meaningful things. You can hire someone to do housework for you or ask someone if they are willing to do it in exchange for something else, perhaps teaching his or her children about things you are especially interested in or knowledgeable about.[287] For grocery shopping, use online ordering and delivery services.[288] Some communities have Meals on Wheels, which will deliver a hot meal once a day to seniors who request it.

○ Get someone (e.g., a professional organizer) to help you get through and organize your backlog of paperwork and other accumulated things in your life.

○ Find a bright graduate student to be your roommate by going through the graduate school at your local college, perhaps asking for suggestions from professors who teach in the field that you had worked in before retirement.

○ Share some time with anyone who interests you (e.g., at one or more mealtimes) before deciding to room together so that you can check out how compatible you are likely to be; before committing, set guidelines for how your arrangement will work.[289]

○ Avoid argumentativeness and defensiveness by preparing rational, well-thought-out responses to the concerns your grown children raise about where and how you live, about how you handle your money and affairs, and about how well you get around on your own.

○ Sort out when it is time to entrust others with some aspects of your life and when you can continue to rely on your past strengths and skills to manage on your own; do what you can to be logical and dispassionate about the distinction, as well as being honest with yourself about how you feel about this.

Some Cruisers have successfully maintained their independence by using several of these strategies simultaneously. One bright woman in her 80s posted a notice at a nearby coffee shop and found someone to help her organize her "stuff." She looked into alternative ways that she could get around, and she found that her county provided transportation services for the elderly that could take her where she needed to go (even though she did not think of herself as "elderly"). She made a trade with a neighbor to do her grocery shopping for her, and in return, she took care of her neighbor's young children for an hour or two each week. She called a nearby community college and talked to their student employment office and found a young woman who would do light housework. This worked out so well that the student moved in with her at the end of the school year and did cooking and laundry, too, in exchange for her room and board.

Generativity

The passion of gifted adults for making a difference in the world often becomes paramount at this time in their lives. Cruisers typically contemplate what their legacy might be, especially in terms of their core values. They want to be able to apply their abilities in ways that are significant for future generations, to live their lives in ways that are a logical outgrowth of their own spiritual beliefs, and to be a catalyst for better changes in the world. Here are some recommendations:

- ○ Consider the suggestions for generativity put forth for Actualizers in the previous chapter and implement those that seem relevant for you, including becoming a mentor for younger people who share your passion for causes that you have been committed to for years.

- ○ Write your own "legacy letter" or "ethical will" for the people who matter the most to you, talking about your feelings, your philosophy of life, and what means the most to you.[290]

- ○ Identify your most significant values—social justice, inter-dependence of all people, altruism, compassion, or philan-thropy—and do what you can to take action.

- ○ Search the Internet or go to the library to find practical ave-nues for collaborating with others who share your desire to make a difference in the world.

- ○ Return to old passions and share them with others—e.g., writing poetry or that novel you started years ago; start a writers' group for other "closet writers" to meet regularly to share your efforts and encourage each other, as well as helping each other find avenues for publication.

- ○ Mentor young entrepreneurs; regularly spend time with them face-to-face or via telephone or email.

○ Pool your knowledge and skills with other older adults on topics such as political activism; share your prior experience and get involved with them in causes you care about—voters' rights, social justice, environmental protection, etc.

○ Work with others on meaningful local projects—creating stimulating after-school programs for gifted children, establishing local arts programs, developing community vegetable gardens, setting up a food pantry, etc.

○ Continue to feed your spirit in ways that have served you well in the past—spending time in nature, attending religious services that still have meaning for you, or returning to those that formerly were important to you.

○ Visit other places of worship or attend study groups or other spiritually focused gatherings with friends who are on a spiritual path that is meaningful to them and that promotes peace in the world.

○ Check out spiritual practices that may be new to you—drumming, chanting, meditation, listening to audio presentations by spiritual leaders (e.g., those featured on "The Shift Network"), etc. [291]

George and Ellie were Cruisers who had always cared a lot about voters' rights and political activism, and they lived in a city where too many people seemed to be regularly disenfranchised. After talking with friends who shared their concerns, George and Ellie decided to do something. By collaborating with community leaders in the lowest-income areas of their city, they developed an effective plan of action to educate people about voting, to register them to vote, and even to help them get to the polls on Election Day.

Being "ageless"

The quality of agelessness that is so often readily apparent in gifted adults at this stage of life is like the beauty and functionality of classic wooden ships, restored, maintained, and sailed by people who choose to enjoy them rather than letting them rot away. Agelessness is a way to stay youthful throughout a lifetime—a satisfying way for Cruisers to live. Here are some ideas:

○ Reflect about times when you took the risk to feel as "young at heart" as you want to be; journal your thoughts about how risk-taking spices up your life.[292]

○ Tune out people who expect you to "act your age" or laugh at them and go ahead and enjoy whatever you like regardless of expectations.

○ Contemplate your response to the question, "How old would you be if you didn't know how old you are?"[293] See if your answer changes for you when you are with different people, in different circumstances, or at different times of your day or week.

○ Implement meaningful practices, e.g., mindfulness, meditation, focused thought, time in nature, writing, contemplative arts, and contemplative movement, or physical practices such as yoga (even "chair yoga") or tai chi.[294]

○ Bring your youthful spirit into play to energize discussions with other people who share your concerns about serious issues; find creative ways to join with them in taking action.

Vitality of Mind and Spirit

I have seen so many Cruisers who have struck me as "ageless," including Annemarie, Herb, and others in this chapter. Their intensity and lifelong asynchronous development defy their categorization into any particular age group. I have often said about Cruisers that their vitality of mind and spirit transcends chronological boundaries, and issues of age vaporize in the times I have shared with them.[295]

Cruisers should be accepted and recognized for all that they are and have always been—bright, talented, and gifted adults who still have much to offer the world. Whether through their active involvement or merely by their presence, their giftedness needs to be valued, not only by others but by these gifted adults themselves, most of whom are unaware of how their giftedness has been an important part of them throughout their lifespan.

CHAPTER 10

Under the Radar: The Invisible Ones and Those Who Run Aground

~ ~ ~

"The human heart is like a ship on a stormy sea driven about by winds blowing from all four corners of heaven."
—Martin Luther

"The waves rose high, but I had a good ship. Still, in the dismal fog I felt myself drifting into loneliness, an insect on a straw in the midst of the elements."
—Joshua Slocum

Once upon a time, an insightful, energetic, and talented youngster, full of promise, filled with enthusiasm, headed off into sunshine days filled with possibilities for the future. Little by little, clouds of confusion and damp despair rolled in like a fog bank, and after a while, all the potential that had shone so brightly seemed to disappear; none of it could be seen clearly any more, even though it was all still there, hidden from view.

Stealth Giftedness

This brief allegory describes various bright individuals whose gifts and talents seem to disappear. For some of them, their true nature—their giftedness—was never recognized, encouraged, or nurtured, and their potential talent was not developed to begin with. For others, despite being launched into a future filled with promise, their abilities somehow disappeared from sight. Regardless of when or why this happened, Invisible Ones need help to come out of the fog that shrouds them so that they can sail into new days filled with sunshine and satisfaction.

In his 40s, one highly gifted man was living a subsistence kind of life. He and his dad had not seen each other for a long time, and when they got together again, they talked about why that was. He said he was concerned that his dad was disappointed in him—"because of the whole gifted child thing." He knew that his dad had expected him to be a success in life, had high hopes, and had always referred to him as "gifted." His dad pointed out the evidence of his son's abilities and potential that had been so apparent to others throughout the latter's youth but that the younger man had dismissed out of hand. When it came to good grades in school or high test scores, he would say, "Oh, I was just lucky" or "They only asked questions that I knew the answers to—not any of the stuff that I didn't know." Sometimes he would just say, "I guess my teachers (or later on, my boss) just liked me; that's why I seemed smart to them." He commented to his dad, "I'm really not gifted; I don't think I ever really was. I was just good at taking tests; that's why they labeled me as gifted."

Whether or not he realizes it, this 40-year-old man is still as gifted as he ever was, although only a few people who know him now might label him as such. The abilities that he and others like him possess have simply disappeared from most people's sight. This is why I call them the Invisible Ones; they are under the radar—possessing a sort of "stealth giftedness." Their abilities are no longer easily seen—not even by these bright individuals themselves.

A few who are very close to them may recognize the depth of their thinking, feeling, and understanding and may still see them as truly bright, talented, or creative, regardless of what they are doing (or not doing) in the way of worldly achievements. However, the hearts of some of their closest friends and family members often ache for the ongoing struggles that these Invisible Ones face.

Periods of being invisible are not rare. Most bright adults hit a snag, run aground, or get lost in the fog at times in their lives and need the tools and desire to get themselves off of the sandbar or the courage to trust their compass during the fog and stay the course.

Many gifted individuals, too, may be achieving externally, but experiencing a fog inside. Though they are doing well in their accomplishments, they are battling internal storms and having substantial personal difficulties that are invisible to others. The intensity and sensitivity that goes along with being bright can be a challenge to manage, particularly if the person feels alone and misunderstood.

For yet other bright persons, it is quite obvious that life has ground them down or that they have been damaged and scarred by previous traumas. Still other adults who are clearly of high ability have lives that are a mess, and it is puzzling to understand why.

Rough Going

Some Invisible Ones, like this 40-year-old man, spend their lives working one menial job after another, periodically struggling with unemployment and financial challenges. Their journeys take them far afield from what others thought they would do—others who knew about the potential they showed earlier in life.

Some of the Invisible Ones are really only partly invisible—sort of a "now you see me, now you don't" way of being. At times they function well and openly, are recognized by others, and accept their own abilities. But then they slip back into the fog, often to try to hide from others because of their excessive self-criticism, where they believe their own negative self-talk. Sometimes they even sabotage themselves as a way of showing themselves—and others—that they really aren't gifted after all.

Some of these talented people find their way into addictive behaviors, including substance abuse, knowingly or unknowingly numbing themselves to the pain they otherwise experience. As Tolan commented, "Not understanding the source of their frustration or ways to alleviate it, they may opt to relieve the pain through the use of alcohol, drugs, food, or other addictive substances or behaviors. Or they may simply hunker down and live their lives in survival mode."[296]

In the introduction to his book *Why Smart People Hurt,* author Eric Maisel wrote about how so many intelligent people have had to deal with addictions. He described how clever people in our contemporary world are plagued by sadness—a reflection of "anxiety that is connected to their very ability to think."[297] Discovering meaning in their existence, achieving their goals, and finding life worthwhile are crucial concerns for bright adults.

In writing about ways that bright people avoid confronting existential issues, Webb identified three general coping styles and the underlying reasons associated with them. Although these mechanisms are not healthy, they usually feed the bright individual's illusions about how the world works. Bright adults may gravitate toward using these, and other "not so healthy coping styles" singly or in combination:

1. *Moving away from*—avoiding and rejecting traditional society by withdrawing; being nontraditional and arcane. These bright adults often have been hurt in childhood, and their sensitivity prompts them to withdraw and hide themselves from others and from society.

2. *Moving toward*—accepting society's traditions; conforming; working the system to become successful. Because these gifted adults participate in the system, their abilities are usually recognized by others. However, they are prone to feeling as if they are imposters and, later in life, to feeling that their efforts have been shallow and without meaning.

3. *Moving against*—rebelliously rejecting society; being angry and openly nonconforming.[298] The intensity of gifted children and adults can be a major asset, or it can be a liability. If they have been hurt, particularly repeatedly, gifted adults may strike out at "the system" or at others close to them, often in ways that are creative, such as computer hacking or fraud.

In *Searching for Meaning: Idealism, Bright Minds, Disillusionment, and Hope*, Webb also offered alternative coping strategies that are healthier than those above for dealing with existential issues. Some of these strategies include creating your own life script, affiliating with other idealists, becoming involved in causes, developing authentic relationships, compartmentalizing, and learning optimism and resiliency.[299]

Complex Causes

Bright adults become invisible for complex reasons as diverse as they themselves are. Many have families who did not understand and support the social and emotional aspects of giftedness. Some parents expected and even demanded high achievement in whatever talent areas they, themselves, particularly valued. The result in some cases was to lead the students into cheating, dishonesty, and manipulation.[300] Some gifted individuals were criticized repeatedly for behaviors that accompanied their giftedness, including their asynchrony, creativity, or inclination to challenge traditions and question the motives of others. Some continue to suffer from the residual effects of physical, sexual, or psychological abuse, made more acute by their sensitivity and intensity.

In discussing difficulties and obstacles faced by bright individuals in developing their gifts, Jacobsen commented on the negative effect of preconceived ideas that other people have about them. They often were typecast at an early age and repeatedly heard comments such as "You're so good at _____; you should be a _____ when you grow up."[301] Or "You're so smart; you can be anything you want to be." Gifted young adults often must face unwanted indoctrination by authority figures in their lives—authority figures who seem to act as if *they* have the only answers to life's big questions. This can result in these bright adults developing a sense of self that "falters under the weight of life's deeper truths and emerging self-knowledge"[302] and leaves them confused and in turmoil. In too many cases, bright adults lose interest in pursuing the possible futures that were predicted for them. They join the ranks of the Invisible Ones. Unanticipated course changes throughout their lives come from multiple sources that compound the effects of any single factor.

For some talented students who later became invisible as adults, the underlying factors were family dynamics or other relationships that did not nurture their inherent giftedness and talent. Difficult experiences in childhood or adolescence are often at the heart of the matter.[303] This may be painful to hear for many parents of Invisible Ones—parents who have done their best, given the understanding and ability to respond that they had at the time.

Veering Off Course

Some students "lose" their giftedness even in elementary school, particularly if they also have a learning disability, ADHD, or other condition that hinders their capacity to achieve in school. At parent-teacher conferences, parents hear, "He's so bright; he could do a lot more if only he'd apply himself." Before long, the teachers start to question whether these students are really capable at all. If they were identified for a gifted program, the teachers become convinced that they were misidentified, and the parents and the students themselves get progressively more alienated from the school.

For others, the disappearance happens later. In middle school, fewer gifted programs exist to challenge them and peer group approval may take precedence in their lives. In high school, the only services offered are typically high-pressure, heavily academic programs, such as Advanced Placement classes. Some bright students opt out in favor of an active social life, involvement in extracurricular activities, or risky behaviors that provide them with the stimulation they long for. Other bright students may leave high school or college with a promising future predicted for them, but little by little they veer off course for various reasons.

A course toward invisibility often starts with underachievement in school—usually because a child's educational, social, and emotional needs were not addressed, whether or not their abilities were recognized. They drift through unchallenging classrooms, fly under the radar, become the class clown, or engage in open rebellion and power struggles. They encounter one teacher after another who is either oblivious to their giftedness or who is threatened by their knowledge, awareness, and insights. Teachers like this have been heard to say, "I don't know what to do with her; she's smarter than I am."

Despite the disturbing lack of teacher education courses about how to provide for gifted students, many dedicated teachers do make concerted efforts to offer challenging, differentiated learning experiences for their bright students. However, these teachers continually struggle against the prevailing educational winds where there is more concern with group scores on high-stakes standardized tests than with matching bright students with optimal educational experiences. [304]

Some Invisible Ones had few opportunities in or out of school to find anyone else like them. Lacking a peer group with kindred spirits to share their advanced thoughts and intense feelings, they settle for whatever peers they can find—sometimes others their age or anyone who can provide excitement to fill their need for some sort of stimulation.[305] Others grew up in poverty and had few opportunities for putting their gifts and talents to use in socially acceptable and meaningful ways. So they may immerse themselves intensely in gangs, which provide them with what they are seeking and cannot find elsewhere.

Other Invisible Ones, particularly if they are handicapped by unhealthy perfectionism, become frozen in the face of too many options, being painfully aware that any path they might take could result in leaving other alternatives behind forever. They are unwilling or unable to choose. As British psychologist Joan Freeman said, "To be lost in a jungle of extreme potential, born with gifted abilities to do almost anything, your life choices can be overwhelming."[306] In the back of their minds, they hear nagging questions: "What if it's the wrong choice? What if I should've gone in a different direction?" Sadly, they may decide to hide their abilities rather than to be wrong.

Gender Issues

Talented women sometimes lose themselves in gender-prescribed roles, and the end result is that their gifts and talents become invisible. Kerr and McKay poignantly describe how this still plays out in the 21st century:

> Young women, particularly upon entering college, are at risk of becoming entangled in the culture of romance, which revolves around the pressure for young women to become heavily involved in the romantic world. Rather than focusing on academic goals and career development, women often find themselves being pressured to make themselves attractive, participate in parties and dances, and go to places like bars and clubs, all with the sole purpose of meeting eligible men. These female students are pressured, both subtly and overtly, to participate in romantic pursuits, which requires them to devote much of their time and energy into beautification and finding men to date who will boost their societal position.[307]

Some bright women disappear into roles that match what others expect when they get married or when they become mothers. Even if they never marry, or were formerly married and now are single, societal pressures may get to them. The expectations of conformity and subservience even for bright women are still widespread in our culture, including in the workplace—issues that exist even after decades of the women's movement working to change things.[308] A further complication is that gifted girls and women tend to be more androgynous (not in appearance, but in character traits), and those who do not fit into prevailing thoughts of what it means to be "feminine" run into trouble.[309]

Giftedness in adult men can become invisible for similar reasons—attempts to conform to socially prescribed behavior, preconceived ideas about bright people, and unwanted indoctrination. They have no doubt about the culture's expectations for them as husbands, fathers, and employees, and many of them obscure their true inner nature in an effort to get by and "do the right thing." Additionally, gifted boys and men tend to be more androgynous than most other boys and men, and their androgyny and sensitivity make them painfully aware of being out of sync with the "macho" image portrayed in media and popular culture.[310] So they hide those aspects of themselves that do not fit with that image until even they, themselves, lose sight of them. As Barbara Kerr and Sanford Cohn note in their book, *Smart Boys: Talent, Manhood, & the Search for Meaning*, "Most gifted boys try to fit in with the traditional expectations of their families and society, and in fact continue to do so throughout their lives… Their life paths were linear and generally conservative, or at least traditional, with few detours for self-discovery."[311]

There is an old saying about being careful of the masks you wear; you may become what you pretend to be. This can happen to the Invisible Ones—women and men alike. However, the underlying causes and manifestations may differ for each gender.[312] As Lovecky indicated, the dilemma for a perceptive gifted adult is "whether to hide the insights and respond superficially to the social facade or to use the gift and risk rejection. Either course may produce constraint and difficulty with spontaneity. Finding interpersonal support is a major priority for these gifted adults; the risk is fear of closeness and intimacy."[313]

Many gifted individuals experience their own variation of what is known as imposter syndrome.[314] They think it is a fluke that they were identified as gifted—that the tools that were used to identify them were wrong or that someone made a mistake in scoring the tests or in using the rating scales. Those caught in the imposter phenomenon feel like charlatans who do not deserve the success they have achieved. They believe that they got ahead for reasons other than their own capabilities. Because they do not think they are gifted, they experience an ongoing undercurrent of anxiety, fearful that someday they will be found out. These bright adults who feel like imposters often don a cloak of invisibility—at least to themselves—because they, themselves, do not see their own gifts and talents. They deny their own abilities even though their giftedness is readily acknowledged by others. As Tolan suggested, gifted adults frequently take their gifts and talents for granted and think that the really bright ones are people with different capabilities than theirs.[315]

In Jacobsen's terms, gifted adults "are constantly faced with the dilemma of making a splash with their expanded perspectives, or swimming silent laps in the norm pool."[316] Some resolve this dilemma by consciously deciding not to conform to what the world expects of them because of their abilities. They may silently drop out or deliberately choose to hide how capable they are; others become openly rebellious. In either case, these particular Invisible Ones do not feel like imposters. Though under the radar to others, they are clear about who they are and their perspectives on what they do and do not want in their lives. They systematically remove themselves from view, choosing deliberately to have a low profile. Sometimes they have done this as early as their elementary, middle, and high school years—sometimes later on, in their 20s, 30s, 40s, or beyond. Those who rebel choose not to "play the game" on anyone else's terms regarding success.

Playing the Game?

"You need to learn to 'play the game,'"
That's what they always say,
To get along in what they call
The "real world!"
"It's a jungle out there,
Don't you know?"
"You've got to learn some day
Just to get along."
"You don't see eye to eye with them?

Then, close your eyes.
Give in; pretend.
What's wrong with that?"

Don't they know that if I do
I run a major risk
Of losing all I am?
If I were to close my eyes,
Pretend I didn't see,
Deny the vision that's my gift,
Buy in and go along,
Then, where would I be?
Where's the person that I am
Who sees a better way,
A better world, another choice,
A new reality?

Sometimes I hear the "experts" speak.
They talk of "self-abuse,"
And then they turn around and say
That I should "play the game"
As if their game
Is worth it.
Buying in, for me, is selling out.
Conforming to some norm,
Becoming what they want
Just isn't how I see it.
That isn't what I see
I'm here to be.

The worst form of self-abuse
Is not to be myself:
The truest, finest Self
That I can be.
Denying that means dying
Day by day, inch by inch,
Giving in and giving up
Until there's nothing left
Of Me--

Just a robot, programmed
By those who want to
"Protect" me or change me.

For those of you who think
That teaching me
To play the game
Is doing me a favor,
Are you sure it isn't just
That you would rather not
Have me disrupt your world
With changing it,
With questioning,
With taking a stand,
Standing up for
My Self.

As Jacobsen said, "Fitting in is a high price to pay when it means selling out."[317] Even those who choose to challenge tradition need to analyze the costs of doing so versus the benefits.[318]

Special Needs

Bright adults also may become invisible because of their differing abilities and disabilities. Under the large umbrella of special needs are a wide range of issues or problems with the ways some individuals learn and process information. This group of Invisible Ones are gifted in all kinds of different ways, too, but they may have difficulties or disabilities that cause them to function differently from other people. Difficulties include learning disabilities, emotional and behavioral disorders, problems with speech and language, vision and hearing impairments, physical challenges, and various other exceptional educational needs such as ADHD and Asperger's Syndrome.[319]

In educational terms, students who are gifted and who also have other special needs are classified as twice exceptional—abbreviated as 2e—whether or not their learning challenges or their giftedness were ever recognized.[320] Gifted education experts today recommend that teachers of 2e children pay attention to their strengths as well as their weaknesses and use the strong areas to help the weaker ones.

Bright adults can be 2e, too, though many years ago, when current adults were in grade school, it was even more unlikely that they were ever appropriately identified as 2e. Whether or not anyone ever explained it to them, gifted individuals at any age can have various special needs that come under the big umbrella of 2e. They may not have a clue as to how capable they are and how their learning differences resulted in their invisibility and prevented them from receiving the appropriate responses at home or in school.[321]

In school, many of them unknowingly managed to use their abilities to compensate for their learning difficulties so that no one noticed how they were struggling, while their learning difficulties concealed just how capable they really were. The schools were satisfied with average performance, and that was that. This continued for many gifted students into adulthood, with the result that the abilities of many of these bright adults remain invisible. Their abilities continue to be underestimated, because they, as well as others, focus on what they cannot do rather than what they can do and have done. Because schools have always been slow to recognize the possibility of 2e students, the older these Invisible Ones are, the less likely it is that either their abilities or their disabilities were ever recognized—a tragic loss of understanding that might have brought innumerable ways for better and happier lives.

Regardless of the obstacles that being 2e brings, many gifted adults have overcome their difficulties and gone on to have full and satisfying lives. Some found their niche in professions where the coping skills that they developed for dealing with their disabilities served them well. Others used dedication, perseverance, and dogged determination to make their mark on the world, achieving eminence and accomplishing much.[322]

Running Aground

Mental illness claims some bright adults, and some are institutionalized. Some get appropriate treatment; others do not. Though biological factors may have contributed to their vulnerability to mental illness, some bright adults found their mental health threatened by living in a world where an overwhelming number of people around them seemed focused only on materialistic goals and superficial ideas promulgated by mass media and popular culture. As Webb observed, "Bright, intense, sensitive, caring, idealistic people are more likely to be disillusioned than many others."[323] Disillusionment about the society they see around them is enough to tip some of the Invisible Ones over the edge and into a state in which they feel that they are the only sane ones in a world that is simply crazy.

A small minority of gifted adults recognize how much better they are at some things than others and become arrogant, narcissistic, and full of themselves, thinking that somehow they are a better species of human, rather than just better at certain skills. They frequently have significant interpersonal problems with co-workers or family and may end up running aground by getting fired, yet blaming their employers for being too stupid to recognize their skills, knowledge, and abilities. A few bright people can be extremely manipulative, antisocial, and even psychopathic.[324]

Some of the Invisible Ones who have run aground by turning to crime end up in prison. Others have used their abilities so adeptly that they escape detection or incarceration. Streznewski indicated that gifted people may represent as much as 20 percent of the prison population but further noted, "If we combine lack of sufficient stimulation from the environment with maturity and self-image problems, we have a potential criminal, one who often has more than enough equipment to get away with crimes for a long time."[325]

The absolute worst-case scenario for Invisible Ones is suicide. As Streznewski said, this is "a tragic waste of precious lives."[326] Some researchers have found that those who complete an attempt at suicide "tend to be brighter than average."[327] Statistics that correlate high ability with suicide are difficult to find, largely because the capabilities of those who attempt or complete suicide have, in general, already become invisible. Bright individuals who attempt suicide may well be responding to specific issues they face during each stage of their lives—issues that are magnified by their intensity, sensitivity, and depth of thinking.[328]

Invisibility as a Choice

All of this notwithstanding, some bright adults merely make the choice to be invisible, at least some of the time. Even though they know how intelligent and knowledgeable they are, they have come to the conclusion that they do not always have to correct everyone else or demonstrate their abilities. They have chosen the premise that silence does not mean agreement and that there is a place for tact in social situations. The key for them is deciding which things are worth fighting for and which they can let go—at least for now.

Pursuing Passions

One group of the Invisible Ones, usually those who choose invisibility, quietly pursue their individual passions, even though the fruits of their labors may never be seen. This may be because they do not need external validation from others for what they do, or it may be because their creative inventions are not yet recognized by society as relevant or valuable. Some may simultaneously be struggling financially or even dealing with addictions or other problems, including difficulties in relationships. According to Goertzel, et al., "A great many highly creative people have unresolved emotional problems, and some of them suffer economic, health, or safety problems."[329] However, in spite of difficulties in their lives, these particular Invisible Ones still feel compelled to pursue their heartfelt desire to paint, compose music, write, or follow whatever their inner calling is. Many of these are creative people whose ingenious work may go unrecognized, and some of them hesitate for various reasons to share what they are working on. Their emotional intensity makes them reluctant to face evaluation, criticism, or rejection.

The journey through life as a gifted adult is not always simple and straightforward. An intriguing website called "The College Dropouts Hall of Fame" lists an impressive number of successful and prominent individuals who never completed college degrees and whose giftedness was not necessarily apparent when they dropped out.[330] Some did not even complete high school. The listing includes notables from such widely varying fields as technology, business, politics, the restaurant industry, entertainment, sports, and more. These former Invisible Ones are no longer invisible. They have fulfilled some or perhaps most of their potential and are now visible again. The list of formerly Invisible Ones includes familiar names, such as Steve Jobs, Ray Bradbury, Tony Bennett, Rosa Parks, Albert Einstein, Coco Chanel, B. B. King, J. Paul

Getty, Diane Keaton, Hiroshi Yamauchi, Doris Lessing, Ray Kroc, Pablo Picasso, Mark Twain, Florence Nightingale, Walt Disney, Quincy Jones, Abraham Lincoln, Stan Musial, and Jane Austen.

Waypoints and Strategies for the Invisible Ones

None of us likes to dwell on thoughts of bright adults lost in a fog, running aground, disappearing from view, plodding through meaningless lives, sinking into depression, getting caught up in addictive behavior, turning to lives of crime, succumbing to mental illness, or committing suicide. Some of what happens to the Invisible Ones, with all of their potential, is difficult to think about. Although giftedness is a large factor, the underlying causes for invisibility in bright adults are far more complex than only the impact of giftedness on their lives. Instead, it is an interaction of giftedness with other issues.

Six waypoints are key for the Invisible Ones. Some of these factors are only true for some of them; some are generally true for all of them. Significant issues for the Invisible Ones include:

1. Accepting giftedness
2. Dealing with overwhelming options
3. Numbing themselves to pain
4. Dealing with gender-prescribed roles
5. Coping with how they learn and process information
6. Finding a satisfying, meaningful life.

Accepting giftedness

Bright Invisible Ones are typically deep in denial. Even if identified for gifted programs during their younger years, they think either that they were never really gifted or that they outgrew any abilities they previously had. Part of what is at the heart of their denial often is their own misunderstanding of giftedness as something someone does (or doesn't do) to be "successful" in life.[331] In order to sail beyond this, the Invisible Ones need to find ways to accept that giftedness is really about who a person is—their inner qualities—rather than about performance or achievement. If the Invisible Ones give any consideration at all to the possibility that they might be bright, talented, creative, or gifted, they worry about what others might expect of them, and they may wonder if they will be seen as arrogant or elitist if they ever acknowledge their abilities. A significant number of bright adults who have accomplished noteworthy things feel like imposters and attribute their successes to external factors, such as luck or favoritism, rather than their own abilities. Furthermore, many Invisible Ones may have trouble accepting any recognition for their giftedness. Many of those in denial have quirks and may even have been diagnosed as disordered because of those idiosyncrasies. Here are some suggestions to help Invisible Ones accept their giftedness:

○ Listen to people in your life who see you as bright, talented, or gifted; ask them to explain why they see you that way and thoughtfully consider what they say even when you have trouble believing it.

○ Use descriptions and lists of characteristics of gifted adults, such as those provided in Chapter 2, to honestly appraise yourself.

○ If your behavior can be described as "quirky," do some research to find out if such quirks are common in gifted children and adults.

○ Explore whether your interpersonal difficulties might be explained by giftedness and lack of understanding by others, rather than as pathology.

○ Reflect on what you were like as a child by using questions such as those listed in Appendix 9; jot down specific examples that you can recall that go along with your answers to those questions.

○ Read books, articles, websites, and blogs and participate in webinars about gifted adults; see what information matches what you know about yourself.[332]

○ Investigate more about asynchronous development; think about how it plays out in others like you.[333]

○ Keep a journal with your responses to the question, "What would happen if it turned out that I'm actually gifted?" Add your thoughts and feelings about this over a period of a month or more, and label your responses *plus*, *minus*, or *interesting*.[334]

○ Work with a counselor who has expertise in understanding gifted adults.[335]

One of Joan's friends whose children were in a gifted program had started reading more about giftedness and told Joan what she was learning, saying that she kept seeing Joan on the pages of what she read. Joan, though baffled, eventually asked her friend to explain what she meant.

When her friend started telling her why she thought the descriptions of a gifted person fit her, Joan was still unconvinced. So she went online and started doing her own research, finding information about gifted adults on websites like Hoagies' Gifted Education Page, SENG, and the Gifted Development Center.[336] After reading that information, she started to think that maybe, just maybe, there was something there that could explain many of the issues and challenges that she had faced during her life's journey—times when she had run aground or felt like she was lost in the fog.

Dealing with overwhelming options

Because of their multipotentiality, bright adults commonly find themselves facing an abundance of possibilities and feeling overwhelmed when confronted with making decisions. Some lose interest in pursuing futures that were predicted for them and struggle with the negative effect of preconceived ideas that others have about them, not wanting to conform to what the world expects of them because of their abilities. They may feel disillusioned about what they see around them and grapple with whether to hide their insights and respond superficially or to speak up and risk rejection. Here are some strategies for coping with overwhelming options:[337]

○ Search the Internet for values clarification tools that look interesting; try out one or more of them to help you identify what you care most about. [338]

○ Establish goals that focus on your values; decide to search for meaning rather than a job and rule out possibilities that do not reflect what is most important to you.[339]

○ Use systematic approaches for making decisions to prioritize your many options and select one or two from the top of your list to do "for now," reserving the next ones to do after these if you are still interested in them.[340]

○ Determine which of your greatest interests might be good for finding employment and which might be better suited to pursue as a hobby or avocation; figure out how to delegate your time so that you can do both.

○ Identify the expectations you believe other people have of you; reflect on how you feel about those and whether they differ from the expectations you have of yourself. [341]

○ Reconnect with your unlived life by giving form and expression to suppressed yearnings that you have never allowed yourself to pursue—e.g., doing creative work, getting involved in humanitarian causes, or breaking free of outmoded lifestyles.[342]

So many choices, so little time! That is how Rob felt about the options he wanted to pursue in his life. His friends would say to him, "You're never going to live long enough to do everything you want to do. Just *decide* on something and get started!" Meanwhile he took whatever jobs he could find just to get by, but that was not very satisfying and he was starting to get depressed.

Rob remembered that back in school they used to do something called "values clarification," which he always found pretty interesting. So he went online and searched under that term and saw many helpful suggestions. He randomly picked one that sounded good, tried it, and began to see that what he really cared the most about was having a purpose in life and making a contribution in the world—specifically, work related to social justice employment and labor rights. The next question for him became, "Okay, so what do I want to do about it?" That led him toward examining what kind of work he might pursue that would relate to this and how to obtain the necessary training. He realized that using his creativity to write and perform music was really important to him. So he decided that he would continue with that as a hobby for now and eventually see if he might use it in his work.

Numbing themselves to pain

Some Invisible Ones find that everything they see around them makes day-to-day living extremely difficult. Their intensity and sensitivity give them a heightened awareness of so much that's wrong, not only in their own lives, but also in the world—hunger, poverty, senseless wars, people's inhumanity to one another, lack of concern for the environment, abuse of power, etc. They may numb themselves through substance abuse and other addictive behaviors, including overeating, gambling, compulsive shopping, and more—seeking refuge, often unknowingly, from the pain they would otherwise experience. Webb suggested that a primary underlying cause for bright people to numb themselves to pain through alcohol or other substance addiction is disillusionment with what is going on for them—in their relationships, in their jobs, and in the direction of their lives. Indicating that "dulling their ability to feel disappointment and dissatisfaction seems like the only answer," Webb further noted that the relief only lasts until whatever substance they are using wears off and that the aftereffects may lead to spiraling downward into deeper and deeper addictive behavior until, in some cases, they have to hit bottom before they will do anything differently.[343] Overcoming a need to numb oneself to pain can be quite challenging, but here are some suggestions for beginning:

○ Learn about your intensity and sensitivity and how that plays out in your life; make notes about ways that others have managed that might work well for you and try some of them.[344]

○ Seek one or two people who accept you as you are and who can provide a meaningful and supportive relationship for you; spend time with them so that you feel connected and less isolated.[345]

○ Try changing your life script by looking at what you tell yourself about your life and then choosing to change it in ways that are important to you.[346]

○ Monitor how you respond to world events, local news, natural disasters, etc.; turn off the television and reduce the attention you pay to news sources, including those on your computer and other electronic devices.

○ Find physical outlets to burn off your feelings of frustration about personal situations rather than resorting to substance abuse or other addictive behaviors—walking, swimming, bicycle riding, cross-country skiing, rowing, etc.; go out in nature as often as possible.

○ Get help to deal with addictions and their underlying causes by finding an addictions counselor who relates well to bright adults.[347] Be aware that few counselors know much about giftedness, and be prepared to help foster your counselor's knowledge and understanding.

○ Join a 12-step program or other recovery group that addresses the specific issues you are dealing with, including the related emotional components; keep up with the effort even if you backslide or get discouraged.

Roberta, a bright and cynical high school biology teacher who had been mired in "gloom and doom" for most of her life, was known by her friends for her pessimistic outlook. Unknown to them, she had grown up in an alcoholic family, always feeling on edge and uncertain about what might happen next, expecting the worst, and holding others at a distance. Despite the "bad example" of the family she had grown up in, she had slipped into numbing herself with more and more glasses of wine at night.

After her second marriage fell apart and she had a few close calls with negative evaluations at school, Roberta took a long, hard look at her life and realized that it was up to her if things were ever going to change. She met with a counselor and decided to write a new script for her life—one in which she was the hero, not the victim. She asked everyone to call her by her middle name, Dawn, as a reminder of her determination to have this be the dawning of a new day in her life—a life that would be different from here on. She entered a doctoral pro- gram, found interesting new friends, completed her Ph.D. in chemistry, and became a valued member of the faculty at a small college for girls. On the rare occasions when she got together with people from her past, they were amazed by how optimistic and enthusiastic she had become—a total contrast to the "Roberta" they remembered.

Dealing with gender-prescribed roles

Bright men and women often must confront gender-prescribed roles—roles that limit them. They often feel like they are sailing against the tide of popular opinion that says they should think and act the way the rest of the population does and the way in which women and men are depicted in the media. They need to find ways to transcend social stereotypes rather than just live conventional lives. Here are some suggestions:

○ Consider "What do the words 'masculine' and 'feminine' mean?" "What are the rights and responsibilities of each partner in a marriage or other committed relationship?" "How should they divide domestic responsibilities, including child care?" "How should women and men decide how much time and energy to invest in careers?"[348] Journal your responses to such questions to see which established customs and practices differ for women and men. Then write about those you want to change in your own life.

○ Using creative visualization, take a mind trip into your future to see what your vision or quest might be and how you might accomplish your goals and dreams, regardless of typical gender-prescribed roles.

○ Find a mentor who seems to have broken free of traditional expectations for women and men and is living the kind of life you would like to live; ask questions about how that person did it and see which answers might work for you.

○ On a large sheet of paper, draw your own representation of internal and external barriers to your living your life the way you want; color code the barriers to indicate those you could break through immediately (green), those you could change soon (yellow), those that will require more long-term effort (purple), and others that you do not intend to do anything about right now (red).

○ Listen carefully to people who encourage you and take risks to develop your gifts and talents regardless of any societal expectations based on gender.

○ Thoughtfully consider valuable advice for bright women, such as that offered in Kerr's "Rules for Real Women." See which rules make you squirm because they reveal flaws in the ways in which you have generally behaved and start to implement a plan to change.[349]

○ Write your own set of "Rules for Bright Men" to provide advice to men who want to leave gender-based stereotypical behavior behind; implement as much of your advice as possible in your own life.

After a late night of sitting around talking about the dumb movies, programs, and commercials on television that focused on macho men, Gary and a couple of his bright buddies began making up a tongue-in-cheek list of "Rules for Men" loaded with all of the stereotypes they could think of. This prompted Gary to reflect, and later he decided to start his own list of "Rules for Bright Men" for breaking away from the old rules of being a "regular guy" that had been part of their lifelong indoctrination, and he shared these with his bright friends. They decided to make a pact to change as many of their stereotypical behaviors as possible and to text each other about their progress as they did so, with the idea of potentially starting a blog about their experiences.

Coping with how they learn and process information

Some Invisible Ones learn and process information in ways that prevent them and others from seeing how capable they are. Perhaps they are visual thinkers and can hardly express themselves in words. Perhaps they are 2e because of a learning disability, Asperger's Syndrome, etc. Here are some helpful ideas for managing how you learn and process information:

○ Learn more about being 2e by reading relevant books and websites.[350]

○ From books and websites, learn about how thinking and learning styles influence people's lives.

○ Get accurate assessments of your abilities and your learning profile from a professional, such as a neuropsychologist—someone who is knowledgeable about individuals who are 2e; can clearly explain your gifts, talents, and learning differences to you; and can give you valuable guidance.[351]

○ Be honest with yourself about any anger you may have surrounding how your gifts and talents or your learning differences were neglected by others when you were younger. Write down your feelings about this and create your own ceremony to allow you to put resentment behind you—e.g., have a symbolic "funeral" and bury or burn what you have written.

○ Identify the tools you have used over the years to compensate so that you could function successfully; decide which to build on now and which to eliminate if they are no longer useful.

○ Use your favorite forms of creative expression (drawing, painting, photography, film, drama, music, poetry, dance, etc.) to represent your unique strengths and celebrate them; share the results however you would like (or not).

○ Mentor 2e students or other adults who are just discovering information about their learning differences.

○ Become an activist on behalf of 2e children and adults.

Judy's long childhood history of periodic bouts with school phobia and struggling in classes never gave her any clue that learning disabilities were at the heart of her troubles. Because of ideas that Judy shared in class discussions, however, a few of her teachers occasionally noticed that she was really bright, but they mostly assumed that she was just lazy or just plain didn't care about doing well in school. By the time she finished high school, she decided that was it; she was never going to go back to school.

After a series of mundane jobs, Judy was so frustrated that she decided to see if the local tech school had something to offer her. She had heard that it was pretty different from typical college classes. When she went to the tech school to check it out, they gave her a battery of tests that revealed the extent of her learning disabilities but also showed that she had a strong propensity for visual-spatial thinking. So she enrolled in an auto mechanics program and found it intriguing.

The tech school offered accommodations for her learning disabilities, and she was able to graduate and get a good job doing foreign car repair, which eventually led her to a position as a designer in the auto industry overseas.

Finding a satisfying, meaningful life

The route that Invisible Ones travel in their lives may feel a lot like sailing upwind—tacking back and forth in order to move forward. They may be moving, even at a fairly good rate of speed, but their progress is slow because they are not traveling in a straight line. Here are some suggestions that may help:

○ Create a "chart" of your life, depicting islands, coastal features, areas of deep and shallow water, harbors, anchorages, navigational aids (e.g., lighthouses and buoys), etc. Use these as metaphors for your interests, your goals and values, your abilities, and the people who are supportive of you; label your chart in any way you see fit and determine what it reflects about what is important to you.

○ Think about the causes you care most deeply about—promoting literacy, supporting soldiers returning from war, reducing poverty, cleaning up the environment, immigration reform, improving health care, animal rights, disaster relief, seeking peaceful solutions to world conflicts, etc. Find a local organization that has a good track record of progress toward goals that you value; volunteer for that organization.

○ Pursue your passions regardless of whether the fruits of your labors will ever be seen; make room in your life for your desire and follow whatever you yearn to do—inventing, sculpting, playing music, writing poetry, or designing software.

○ Decide if you are willing to share your creative work and, if so, take some small steps for getting it recognized—develop a Kickstarter project to obtain funding, show your sculptures at an art fair, perform your music at an "open mic" at a coffeehouse, participate in a poetry reading, self-publish an e-book, submit a software application to either Apple's App Store or Google's Android App Store, etc.

○ Identify sources of interpersonal support—people who are good listeners and accept you and appreciate you for who you are without laying burdensome expectations on you; spend quality time with one or another of these people regularly. Learn to appreciate those good friends who tell you what you need to hear, even if it is not necessarily what you want to hear.

○ Write a letter to yourself as if the person writing it is your dearest friend—someone who sees everything about you and wants to encourage you to be totally authentic, to use your gifts and talents in meaningful ways, and to follow your heart's desire.

○ Experiment with the ideas shared by Tolan for changing your life into how you want it to be by changing the stories you tell yourself.[352]

○ Think of what you really want to do that you do not think you can by following the four steps in Appendix 10 to transform "Yes, but…" into "Yes, and…"[353]

○ Find ways to be at peace with who you are as a bright adult; consider yourself as a "work in progress," rather than becoming immobilized by self-criticism.

Every time Lucas thought about getting involved in projects related to his concerns about human rights, he would shrug and say to himself, "What good would it do? I'm just one person." After reading an article about Amnesty International, he wondered if it would be possible to get involved in some of their efforts. He found that he could become an online volunteer for the organization to join with others who shared his concerns and that they had all kinds of concrete suggestions, tools, and tips for effective activism that he could use without ever leaving home.[354] He found that taking action on a cause that was important to him helped him feel as if his life had more meaning and that he could make a difference in the world in some small way. This led him to find a local human rights organization where he could get even more directly involved with others close at hand who shared his values and ideals.

Coming Out of the Fog

Invisible Ones often lose sight of who they are and where it is they want to go, feeling as if they are drifting in the midst of a dense haze. Seeing their own abilities and how they might use them to find their way can be as hard as peering through heavy fog. If they are willing to try some strategies with an open mind and to suspend judgment about themselves, they have a good chance of sailing into greater clarity and coping with those discouraging times when the fog closes in on them again. It is important to hold onto hope even when setbacks occur and you find yourself feeling disoriented again, thinking "I thought I was done with this!"

It is helpful to identify tools that worked as you navigated your way through the fog before; then you can determine if the same strategies will be effective again or if you should try a different approach. Resilience and courage are keys to avoiding becoming totally immobilized when you feel as if you have run aground or are drifting aimlessly. Take some small action—even if it seems unrelated to making forward progress—e.g., journaling, going outdoors for a strenuous walk or run, taking a long drive to someplace new, visiting an elderly friend or relative, or doing any kind of artwork (even finger painting). Overcoming inactivity can help you see what direction to take next.

It is not necessary for Invisible Ones to achieve lofty levels of fame and fortune in order to have satisfying and meaningful lives. Whether the Invisible Ones can ever emerge from under the radar and find their way to smooth sailing and safe harbors where they can be at peace with who they are remains an open question—but one that is worth seeking answers to.

CHAPTER 11

Tying the Knot—Conclusion

~ ~ ~

"Indeed, the cruising of a boat here and there is very much of what happens to the soul of man in a larger way. We set out for places which we do not reach, or reach too late; and, on the way, there befall us all manner of things which we could never have awaited."

—Hilaire Belloc

When sailors circumnavigate the world, they talk about the end of their voyage as "tying the knot."[355] For sailors, it is as if they have trailed a very long rope behind them, winding it around the globe throughout their journey, and are now securing the final end to the beginning—the end that they left back in the harbor at the start of their expedition. In much the same way, we are tying the knot on the journey we have been traveling together across the lifespan of bright adults.

Bob Bilhorn, a man I know well, set off at age 70 to sail around the world. He tied the knot on his voyage six years later. Much like the journey gifted adults take throughout their lives, he experienced starts and stops, taking time out to explore various ports along the way and even occasionally flying back home for a while before returning to wherever he had left his boat to continue his circumnavigation.

Bob had assorted crew members join him for different legs of his journey for varying periods of time.[356] In the same way, various people are part of our lives for different chunks of time—some for a little while, some for longer, and some who come back into our lives after a prolonged absence. When I shared the quotation from the beginning of this chapter with Bob, he thought that the following phrase should be added: "And all worked toward a higher sense of good and fulfillment." That is how Bob described the outcome of his circumnavigation, and he hoped that others felt that way, too.[357]

Similarly, my hope for you and the bright adults in your life is that your journey will lead you to a higher sense of good and fulfillment. Most people encounter storms along the way. You may feel cast adrift at times or blown off course, wondering if you are alone in what you are going through. Because of the sensitivity and intensity typical of bright adults, the ever-changing storms of life may feel much more severe to you and those around you. When you discover that other people like you have traveled the same routes, you find that you are not really alone and that there are resources, markers, and buoys along the way that can help.

Looking Astern and Looking Ahead

Seasoned sailors rely on navigational aids to guide them through rough conditions that they encounter on their voyages. In much the same way, bright adults benefit from knowing about common issues for people like them at each of life's stages. Strategies for responding to these issues on each leg of life's journey are like those navigational aids—they provide guidance for moving forward throughout the lifespan toward smoother sailing.

Some of the experiences of bright adults are like home ports for sailors—places that they return to throughout the lifespan. For instance, all bright adults want acceptance and kindred spirits in their lives. They grapple with discovering how to live with their intensity while facing important challenges. They need to have consistent access to appropriate resources. And they yearn to find meaning in life.

Each stage of development for bright and gifted adults has its own specific issues and unique experiences, although many similar concerns may crop up during several stages. The kinds of challenges that these bright adults typically face play out differently at various times in their lives. Thus, recommendations for each of the age groups vary, too, and the suggestions provide practical approaches for navigating narrow channels, bad weather, and stormy seas.

Sailors embarking on long voyages need to know what factors may affect their course. They need to know how to calibrate their compasses and recalibrate them when necessary to correct for deviation. Likewise, bright adults need to be aware of issues for people like them that might send them off track. By implementing strategies that were useful for others, they can better steer in whatever directions work best for them.

Let's go back to the metaphor of the lifespan of bright adults as a voyage around the world—your own world, with its own unique ports of call and experiences along the way. The crewmates who have shared your journey and the conditions you encounter along the way are yours and yours alone, to respond to in your own way—learning as you go. Your "sailing vessel" (your mind and your body) changes along the way. After all, no one else is exactly like you. In essence, paraphrasing poet William Ernest Henley from his poem "Invictus," "You are the master of your fate and the captain of your soul."[358]

It does not matter whether you chose this book to learn more about someone else or to learn about yourself and aspects of your own life. You may have started out thinking about someone else and then made discoveries about yourself and others you have known. This often happens for people who do not see themselves as bright, talented, or gifted until they start learning more about what it means.

Many bright, intense adults find it intimidating to consider the whole idea of being at the helm and steering, especially when contemplating the kinds of challenges they are likely to face at various stages of life. When you first got your hands on this book, you may have decided to skim through it, but it is not a book designed to be put on the shelf and forgotten. Just like sailors cannot see everything about an interesting port of call when they first dock their boat or anchor in a new harbor, this book is one to read, reflect on, and revisit, not only as you sail onward through different stages in your own life, but also as different issues come up, regardless of your age. Some of the ideas suggested here may interest you now—others will be useful later on. And some you may find worth implementing more than once.

This may be a good time for you to glance back astern and look at where you have been in your life, to contemplate your journey so far, and to think about how your past relates to what is important to you now—whether those were your school years or the years since then. Who had an impact on your life, either positive or negative? What were some of the most memorable moments for you? If you could start your journey over again knowing what you know now, what would you change? What did you learn from the things that you would change if you could? What can you change now about your thoughts and feelings about "way back when" (including school years)? What does this tell you about how you want to live your life now? If you were "captain of the educational world," what would you have educators do differently for bright children that would help them when they set off on their own journeys through adulthood?

Now or Later?

When describing the 25 years after age 50, which she dubbed "The Third Chapter," Lawrence-Lightfoot had some specific suggestions about how education needs to change:

> *I believe that the designers of childhood education need to consider the developmental tasks of adulthood and old age as well as those of childhood when they construct curricula, develop effective pedagogies, and build school cultures. So much of childhood socialization in school is aimed at intellectual competence and achievement motivation, at helping children learn to compete successfully against their peers, gain public recognition for solo work, and demonstrate mastery by rapid response rates, quick articulation of ideas, and high scores on standardized tests. But these often turn out to be the very competencies that may interfere with successful aging and learning in the Third Chapter, where collaboration, relationship building, slowness and deliberateness, risk-taking, and irreverence are the coin of the realm; where work and play, restraint and expressivity, discipline and improvisation are joined.*[359]

Regardless of your current age, how do these comments about the importance of collaboration, relationship building, deliberateness, risk-taking, and irreverence relate to your own life? In what ways do you see yourself merging work and play, restraint and expressivity, discipline and improvisation in your life now?

Hopes and Dreams or Expectations?

As you reflect on the ideas in this book, what are your own hopes and dreams for yourself and others like you? Hopes and dreams are different from expectations. Expectations are like commands—orders to do or be something that you may not want to do or be. They seem heavy, like a burden that may be too much to carry—one you would rather put down and walk away from so that you can head off in your own chosen direction. Hopes and dreams are light and filled with joyful possibilities—similar to how sailors feel as they head out at the start of a well-planned voyage. It is the difference between the "gottas" and the "wannas"—obligations and preferences, requirements and electives, "shoulds" and "desires." Which of these do you want more in your own life, and how can they translate into your day-to-day choices? How can you be your most authentic self and share whatever gifts and talents you have?

A blogger, recently writing about "The Crossroads of Should and Must," describes "must" as being "who we are, what we believe, and what we do when we are alone with our truest, most authentic self. It's our instincts, our cravings and longings, the things and places and ideas we burn for, the intuition that swells up from somewhere deep inside of us."[360] Basically, she is talking about your "calling"—what you sense you are really meant to do rather than what others think you *should* do.

Questions for Reflection

In her book *The Gifted Adult: A Revolutionary Guide for Liberating Everyday Genius*, Jacobsen lists what she calls "signs of advanced development." As you read these, think about the following questions: "How many of these concepts would you like to be a part of your own life?" "Which fit with your own hopes and dreams right now?" "Are there some that might be more relevant to your life in the future than they are today?" "Which do you want to pack into your seabag to take along with you?"

1. A conscious awareness of life as process

2. Increased respect for self and others, and a strong preference for diversity

3. Greater vitality and satisfaction in your endeavors

4. Acceptance of setbacks and pressure as catalysts that crystallize talents

5. Becoming comfortable with necessary risks

6. Willingness to be more authentic across situations

7. Growing intolerance for being out of balance

8. Powerful compulsion to use special abilities to contribute to society

9. Heightened trust in intuitive powers and transcendent experience

10. Growing sense of cooperating with a universal plan for the greater good.[361]

After thinking about life as a journey, we end our travels through this book with a lot of questions. By contemplating your responses to these queries, you can focus on your own goals and values to help chart a course through your lifespan. Your answers to some questions will remain the same, year after year. Others will change as you travel through life, encounter new people, learn more, and have novel experiences.

One strategy that I use in my work with teachers is "Stop for now." At the end of a thought-provoking discussion, I put up a stop sign and say, "Stop for now." Then I come back later to the same question or issue. The pause may be for five minutes, five hours, five days, or five weeks, but everyone is bound to have new thoughts about the topic whenever the discussion continues. So the end of this book is simply a "Stop for now"—a pause to contemplate what you have read and to consider the ideas that were offered. You can go back to reread it whenever it might be most useful to you and put into action whichever suggestions best fit whatever is going on in your life. You can also use the ideas in this book as a springboard to talk with others who share your journey.

Solo sailors often report that they feel as if they "find themselves" when sailing alone. This book is my invitation to you to take time out to know yourself and others better. It can be a time for you to come back to an ever-clearer sense of who you are and where you want to go and to consider the people and experiences that enrich your journey through life.

"There are many points on the compass rose. I had to locate the few that were meant for me and head for those that summoned me with a passion, for they were the ones that gave meaning to my life."

—Richard Bode

Background for My Model

Here are some authors whose theories are particularly relevant to my thinking about bright, intense adults at various times in their lives.

Erik Erikson

Erik Erikson's work, based on his book *Childhood and Society*, published in 1951, has often been a key part of courses in psychology and child development. He examined issues at each stage of life and divided the adult years into three stages of development: Young Adulthood—approximately ages 18 to 35, characterized by concerns with intimacy versus isolation; Middle Adulthood—approximately ages 35 to 55 or 65, characterized by dilemmas of generativity versus stagnation, and Late Adulthood—approximately ages 55 or 65 to death, characterized by challenges of integrity versus despair.[362]

Erikson's first stage of adult development—Young Adulthood—still seems relevant in the 21st century, though his theory is less consistent with the lives of adults during their middle years and into late adulthood. I have expanded significantly on his ideas in those later decades. Erikson's time frame was more appropriate in the mid-20th century when he formulated his theory than it is now.[363] People live much longer and remain far more active now than they did in the 1950s when Erikson's theory was published. But even then, bright adults often had significantly different issues and concerns to deal with than people in the general population. The inner experiences and awareness of bright and talented people, including their intensity, their insights, and their perceptions, set them apart from others.

David Shaffer and Daniel Levinson

In addition to Erikson, other authors designated different stages and age ranges of adult development. Psychologist David Shaffer specified ages 20 to 40 as young adulthood, ages 40 to 65 as middle adulthood, and the rest of life as old age.[364] Daniel Levinson also divided adult life into three "eras" or developmental periods: early adulthood, ages 17 to 45; middle adulthood, ages 40 to 65; and late adulthood, ages 60 and beyond. With the metaphor of "seasons" to describe human development, Levinson's *The Seasons of a Man's Life* focused on stages in the lives of men; another, *The Seasons of a Woman's Life*, written nearly 10 years later, centered on women throughout their lifespans.[365]

Thomas Armstrong

Thomas Armstrong saw the human lifespan as an odyssey that reflects our physical, psychological, and spiritual journey through life, and he described 12 stages of life, 5 of which encompass the adult years: Early Adulthood, Midlife, Mature Adulthood, Late Adulthood, and Death and Dying. Though each stage has challenges, he also proposed that "each stage of life has its own unique gift."[366] His book *The Human Odyssey: Navigating the Twelve Stages of Life* explores his ideas about the gifts that each stage of life brings.

Mary-Elaine Jacobsen

Rather than looking specifically at life stages, Mary-Elaine Jacobsen focused on adults who have potential for advanced development. In her 1999 book, *Liberating Everyday Genius*, she emphasized the importance of developing self-understanding in order to become freed from the constraints that prevent them from being themselves. She called these adults "everyday geniuses," a term that she coined to indicate that these people are those who can and will see beyond the obvious. Delving into their personality and psychology, she pointedly said that these adults are "the most under-identified group of potential achievers in our society."[367]

Marylou Streznewski

Marylou Streznewski, in her 1999 book, *Gifted Grownups*, zeroed in on three categories of bright adults whom she designated as "strivers, superstars, and independents." From interviewing 100 gifted adults and gathering stories of their experiences, she described what she called the "mixed blessings of extraordinary potential" at various ages and stages throughout the lifespan. She devoted one entire chapter to specific issues for gifted women and another to what she called "The Dark Side," dealing with those situations where some gifted individuals defy society's apparent lack of understanding or acceptance.[368]

Willem Kuipers

Willem Kuipers created the acronym "XIP" to describe gifted adults, his abbreviation for "Extra Intelligent People." In his book *Enjoying the Gift of Being Uncommon,* he stated that these are people who "are a colourful [sic] lot; they can be brilliant, exasperating, full of ideas, dramatic, galvanizing or depressing, hilarious, persistently destructive, aloof or overwhelmingly helpful, and show many of these aspects even simultaneously." Further, he indicated, "The list can be much longer, but the shared aspects are 'intense,' 'uncommon,' and 'diverse.'"[369] Kuipers described in detail the characteristics of these bright adults, the complexity of their lives, and the challenges associated with acknowledging and applying their abilities so that they can have happy and effective lives.

Gail Sheehy

Although not specifically written about gifted adults, Gail Sheehy's popular 1974 book, *Passages: Predictable Crises of Adult Life,* spoke so well to the experiences of many bright people at various ages and stages of life that many of her ideas are relevant and worth including.

Her book, updated in 2004 with a new introduction, continues to offer timely information about each decade of people's lives from their 20s through their 30s, into their 40s, and to some extent into their 50s and beyond.

Resources

Books and Book Chapters

Armstrong, T. (2007). *The human odyssey: Navigating the twelve stages of life.* New York: Sterling Publishing.

Arnett, J. J., Kloep, M., Hendry, L. B., & Tanner J. L. (2011). *Debating emerging adulthood: Stage or process.* New York: Oxford University Press.

Aron, E. N. (1998). *The highly sensitive person.* New York: Broadway Books.

Bateson, M. C. (1989). *Composing a life.* New York: The Atlantic Monthly Press.

Bateson, M. C. (2010). *Composing a further life: The age of active wisdom.* New York: Alfred A. Knopf.

Battaglia, M. M. K., Mendaglio, S., & Piechowski, M. M. (2014). A life of positive maladjustment (1902–1980). In A. Robinson & J. Jolly (Eds.), *A century of contributions to gifted education: Illuminating lives,* pp. 181–199. New York: Routledge.

Berger, S. L. (2014). *College planning for gifted students.* Waco, TX: Prufrock Press.

Bode, R. (1993). *First you have to row a little boat.* New York: Warner Books.

Bolen, J. S. (2001). *Goddesses in older women: Archetypes in women over fifty.* New York: HarperCollins.

Bowlby J. (1969). *Attachment. Attachment and loss: Vol. 1. Loss.* New York: Basic Books.

Brown, B. (2010). *The gifts of imperfection: Let go of who you think you're supposed to be and embrace who you are.* Center City, MN: Hazelden.

Buettner, D. (2012). *The blue zones: 9 lessons for living longer from the people who've lived the longest.* Washington, D.C.: National Geographic.

Butler, R. N. (2010). *The longevity prescription: The 8 proven keys to a long, healthy life.* New York: Avery.

Cain, S. (2013). *Quiet: The power of introverts in a world that can't stop talking.* New York: Random House.

Chittister, J. (2008). *The gift of years: Growing older gracefully.* Katonah, NY: BlueBridge.

Cohen, G. D. (2005). *The mature mind: The positive power of the aging brain.* New York: Basic Books.

Columbus Group (1991) cited in Silverman, L. K. (1993). The gifted individual. In L. K. Silverman (Ed.), *Counseling the gifted and talented.* Denver, CO: Love.

Daniels, S. & Piechowski, M. M. (2009). *Living with intensity.* Scottsdale, AZ: Great Potential Press.

Downs, M. P. (2005). *Shut up and live! (you know how).* Nashville, TN: Cold Tree Press.

Ellis, N. (2004). *If I live to be 100: Lessons from the Centenarians.* New York: Three Rivers Press.

Erikson, E. (1951). *Childhood and society.* New York: W. W. Norton.

Erikson, E. (1959). *Identity and the life cycle.* New York: International Universities.

Erikson, E. (1963). *Childhood and society.* 2nd ed. New York: W. W. Norton.

Erikson, J. M. (1997). *The lifecycle completed: A review/Erik H. Erikson–Extended version.* New York: W. W. Norton & Company, Inc.

Farrell, C. (2014). *How baby boomers are changing the way we think about work, community, and the good life.* New York: Bloomsbury Press.

Fiedler, E. D. (1999). Gifted children: The promise of potential/the problems of potential. In V. Schwean & D. Saklofske (Eds.), *Handbook of psychosocial characteristics of exceptional children,* pp. 401–441. New York: Kluwer/Plenum.

Fiedler, E. D. (2009). Advantages and challenges of lifespan intensity. In S. Daniels & M. M. Piechowski (Eds.), *Living with intensity* (pp. 167–184). Scottsdale, AZ: Great Potential Press.

Fiedler, E. D. (2013). You don't outgrow giftedness: Giftedness across the lifespan. In C. S. Neville, M. M. Piechowski, & S. S. Tolan (Eds.). *Off the charts: Asynchrony and the gifted child* (pp. 183–210). Unionville, NY: Royal Fireworks Press.

Findsen, B. & Formosa, M. (2011). *Lifelong learning in later life.* Rotterdam, the Netherlands: Sense.

Fonda, J. (2011). *Prime time.* New York: Random House.

Freeman, J. (2010). *Gifted lives: What happens when gifted children grow up.* London: Routledge.

Gatto-Walden, P. (2009). Living one's spirit song: Transcendent experiences in counseling gifted adults. In S. Daniels & M. M. Piechowski (Eds.), *Living with intensity* (pp. 203–223). Scottsdale, AZ: Great Potential Press.

Goertzel, V. & Goertzel, M. G. (2004). *Cradles of eminence: Childhoods of more than 700 famous men and women.* (2nd ed. with updates by T. G. Goertzel & Ariel M. W. Hansen). Scottsdale, AZ: Great Potential Press.

Goldberg, E. (2006). *The wisdom paradox: How your mind can grow stronger as your brain grows older.* New York: Gotham Books.

Gould, R. L. (1978). *Transformations: Growth and change in adult life.* New York: Simon and Schuster.

Gross, M. U. M. (2000, Winter). Exceptionally and profoundly gifted: An underserved population. *Understanding Our Gifted.* Retrieved from: www.hoagiesgifted.org/underserved.htm

Hollis, J. (1993). *The middle passage: From misery to meaning in midlife.* Toronto, Canada: Inner City Books.

Hollis, J. (2005). *Finding meaning in the second half of life: How to finally, really grow up.* New York: Gotham Books.

Holt, J. (1978). *Never too late.* Boston, MA: Da Capo Press.

Jacobsen, M-E. (1999). *Liberating everyday genius.* New York: Ballentine

Kane, M. (2009). Annemarie Roeper: Nearly a century with giftedness. In S. Daniels & M. M. Piechowski (Eds.), *Living with intensity* (pp. 185–202). Scottsdale, AZ: Great Potential Press.

Kane, M. & Fiedler, E. D. (2011). Into the stratosphere: Providing curriculum for highly, exceptionally, and profoundly gifted students. In N. Hafenstein, E. Honeck, & A. Tung (Eds.), *Greatest potential, greatest need: Soaring beyond expectations—Conference proceedings and selected articles focusing on the highly gifted.* Denver, CO: Institute for the Development of Gifted Education, Ricks Center, University of Denver.

Keating, D. P. (2009). Developmental transitions in giftedness and talent: Adolescence into adulthood. In F. D. Horowitz, R. F. Subotnik, & D. J. Matthews (Eds.), *The development of giftedness and talent across the lifespan* (pp. 189–208). Washington, D.C.: American Psychological Association.

Kennedy, C. (2011). *She walks in beauty: A woman's journey through poems.* New York: Hyperion.

Kerr, B. A. (1985). *Smart girls, gifted women.* Columbus, OH: Ohio Psychology Publishing.

Kerr, B. A. (1994). *Smart girls: A new psychology of girls, women and giftedness.* (Revised ed.). Scottsdale, AZ: Great Potential Press.

Kerr, B. A. & Cohn, S. J. (2001). *Smart boys: Talent, manhood, & the search for meaning.* Scottsdale, AZ: Great Potential Press, Inc.

Kerr, B. A. & McKay, R. (2014). *Smart girls in the 21st century: Understanding talented girls and women.* Tucson, AZ: Great Potential Press.

Kiersey, D. (1998). *Please understand me II.* Del Mar, CA: Prometheus Nemesis Book Co.

Kuipers, W. (2010). *Enjoying the gift of being uncommon: Extra intelligent, intense, and effective.* Zoetermeer, the Netherlands: CreateSpace.

Lawrence-Lightfoot, S. (2009). *The third chapter: Passion, risk, and adventure in the 25 years after 50.* New York: Sarah Crichton Books.

Levinson, D. J. (1978). *The seasons of a man's life.* New York: Ballantine Books.

Levinson, D. J. (1996). *The seasons of a woman's life.* New York: Ballantine Books.

Maisel, E. (2013). *Why smart people hurt: A guide for the bright, the sensitive, and the creative.* San Francisco, CA: Conari Press.

Maslow, A. (1970). Religion, values, and peak experiences. New York: Viking.

Maslow, A. H. (1970). *Motivation and personality.* 2nd ed. New York: Harper & Row.

Miller, A. (2008). *The drama of the gifted child: The search for the true self.* New York: Basic Books.

Nauta, N. & Ronner, S. (2013). *Gifted workers.* St. Maartenslaan, the Netherlands: Shaker Media.

Neville, C. S., Piechowski, M. M., & Tolan, S. S. (Eds.). (2013). *Off the charts: Asynchrony and the gifted child* (pp. 158–210). Unionville, NY: Royal Fireworks Press.

Palmer, P. J. (2000). *Let your life speak.* San Francisco, CA: Jossey-Bass.

Pauley, J. (2014). *Your life calling: Reimagining the rest of your life.* New York: Simon & Schuster.

Pestalozzi, T. (2009). *Life skills 101: A practical guide to leaving home and living on your own.* Cortland, OH: Stonewood Publications.

Piechowski, M. M. (1997). Emotional giftedness: The measure of intrapersonal intelligence. In N. Colangelo & G. A. Davis (Eds.), *Handbook of gifted education (2nd ed.)* (pp. 366–381). Needham Heights, MA: Allyn and Bacon.

Piechowski, M. M. (2006). *"Mellow out," they say. If only I could: Intensities and sensitivities of the young and bright.* Madison, WI: Yunasa.

Pipher, M. (1999). *Another country: Navigating the emotional terrain of our elders.* New York: Riverhead Books.

Raines, R. (1997). *A time to live: Seven steps of creative aging.* New York: Penguin Putnam.

Rivero, L. (2010). *A parent's guide to gifted teens: Living with intense and creative adolescents.* Scottsdale, AZ: Great Potential Press.

Rivero, L. (2010). *The smart teens' guide to living with intensity: How to get more out of life and learning.* Scottsdale, AZ: Great Potential Press.

Roberts, C. (2009). *We are our mothers' daughters.* New York: Harper Perennial.

Roeper, A. (1995). *Selected writings and speeches.* Minneapolis, MN: Free Spirit.

Roeper, A. (2011). *Beyond old age: Essays on living and dying.* Berkeley, CA: Azalea Art Press.

Sauder, A. E. (2010). *Gifted adults' perception of giftedness: How giftedness influenced their graduate education.* Saarbrücken, Germany: VDM Verlag Dr. Müeller

Schachter-Shalomi, Z. & Miller, R. S. (1995). *From age-ing to sage-ing: A profound new vision of growing older.* New York: Grand Central.

Seligman, M. E. P. (2006). *Learned optimism: How to change your mind and your life.* New York: Vintage.

Seligman, M. E. P. (2007). *The optimistic child: A proven program to safeguard children against depression and build lifelong resilience.* New York: Houghton Mifflin.

Sheehy, G. (1995). *New passages: Mapping your life across time.* New York: Random House.

Sheehy, G. (1998). *Understanding men's passages: Discovering the new map of men's lives.* New York: Ballantine Books.

Sheehy, G. (2006). *Passages: Predictable crises of adult life.* New York: Ballantine Books.

Silverman, L. K. (1993). The gifted individual. In L. K. Silverman (Ed.), *Counseling the gifted and talented* (pp. 3–28). Denver, CO: Love.

Silverman, L. K. (1995). The universal experience of being out-of-sync. In L. K. Silverman (Ed.), *Advanced development: A collection of works on giftedness in adults* (pp. 1–12). Denver: Institute for the Study of Advanced Development.

Silverman, L. K. (2013). *Giftedness 101.* New York: Springer.

Sinetar, M. (1987). *Do what you love, the money will follow: Discovering your right livelihood.* New York: Dell.

Smith, C. G. (2013). *Creative problem solving techniques to change your life.* CreateSpace.

Streznewski, M. L. (1999). *Gifted grownups: The mixed blessings of extraordinary potential.* New York: John Wiley & Sons.

Subotnik, R. F. (2009). Developmental transitions in giftedness and talent: Adolescence into adulthood. In F. D. Horowitz, R. F. Subotnik, & D. J. Matthews (Eds.), *The development of giftedness and talent across the lifespan* (pp. 155–170). Washington, D.C.: American Psychological Association.

Sykes, B. (2001). *The seven daughters of Eve: The science that reveals our genetic ancestry.* New York, W.W. Norton & Company.

Tan, C-M. (2012). *Search inside yourself: The unexpected path to achieving success, happiness (and world peace).* New York: HarperOne.

Taylor, J. B. (2006). *My stroke of insight.* New York: Penguin.

Terman, L. M. & Oden, M. H. (1947). *The gifted child grows up. Genetic studies of genius Vol. 4.* Stanford, CA: Stanford University Press.

Terman, L. M. & Oden, M. H. (1959). *The gifted group at mid-life. The gifted child grows up. Genetic studies of genius Vol. 5.* Stanford, CA: Stanford University Press.

Tolan, S. S. (2009). What we may be: What Dabrowski's work can do for gifted adults. In S. Daniels & M. M. Piechowski (Eds.), *Living with intensity* (pp. 225–235). Scottsdale, AZ: Great Potential Press.

Tolan, S. S. (2011). *Change your story, change your life.* CreateSpace.

Viorst, J. (1976). *How did I ever get to be forty and other atrocities.* New York: Simon & Schuster.

Viorst, J. (1989). *Forever fifty and other negotiations.* New York: Simon & Schuster.

Viorst, J. (2000). *Suddenly sixty.* New York: Simon & Schuster.

Viorst, J. (2005). *I'm too young to be seventy and other delusions.* New York: Free Press.

Webb, J. T. (2013). *Searching for meaning: Idealism, bright minds, disillusionment, and hope.* Tucson, AZ: Great Potential Press.

Webb, J. T., Amend, E. R., Webb, N., Goerss, J., Beljan, P., & Olenchak, F. R. (2005). *Misdiagnosis and dual diagnoses of gifted children and adults: ADHD, Bipolar, OCD, Asperger's, Depression, and other disorders.* Scottsdale, AZ: Great Potential Press.

Webb, J. T., Gore, J. L., Karnes, F. A., & McDaniel, A. S. (2004). *Grandparents' guide to gifted children.* Scottsdale, AZ: Great Potential Press.

Webb, J. T., Meckstroth, E. A., & Tolan, S. S. (1982). *Guiding the gifted child: A practical source for parents and teachers.* Columbus, OH: Ohio Psychology Press.

Welker, D. H. (1996). *Hen Medic: Woman doctor indeed!* Lake Nebagamon, WI: Paper Moon.

Welker, D. H. (1998). *Hen medic II: Woman doctor indeed!* Lake Nebagamon, WI: Paper Moon.

Willings, D. (1980). *The creatively gifted.* Cambridge, Great Britain: Woodhead-Faulkner.

Articles

Alvarado, N. (1989). Adjustment of gifted adults. *Advanced Development, (1)*, 77–86.

Cross, T., Gust-Brey, K., & Ball, P. (2002). A psychological autopsy of the suicide of an academically gifted student: Researchers' and parents perspectives. *Gifted Child Quarterly, 46*(4). Retrieved from www.davidsongifted.org/db/Articles_id_10337.aspx.

Feldman, D. H. (1984). A follow-up of subjects scoring above 180 IQ in Terman's genetic studies of genius. *Exceptional Children, 50*(6), 518–523. Retrieved from www.davidsongifted.org/db/Articles_print_id_10192.aspx.

Fiedler, E. D. (2005, Summer). Two sides of the same coin: Teachers developing creativity. *CAG Communicator, 36*(2), 29–32.

Fiedler, E. D. (2012). You don't outgrow it! Giftedness across the lifespan. *Advanced Development Journal, 13*, 19–37.

Freedman, M. (January 1, 2014). The dangerous myth of reinvention. *Harvard Business Review.* Retrieved from http://blogs.hbr.org/2014/01/the-dangerous-myth-of-reinvention/

Guetzloe, E. (1994). Risk, resilience, and protection. *Journal of Emotional and Behavioral Problems, 3*(2), 2–5.

Jacobsen, M. (1999). Arousing the sleeping giant: Giftedness in adult psychotherapy. *Roeper Review, 22*(1), 36–40.

Kaufmann, F. (1981). The 1964-1968 Presidential Scholars: A follow-up study. *Exceptional Children, 48*(2), 164–169.

Kaufmann, F. (1992). What educators can learn from gifted adults. *Talent for the Future, Van Gorcum.* Retrieved from www.davidsongifted.org/db/Articles_print_id_10023.aspx.

Kerr, B. & Claiborn, C. D. (1991). Counseling talented adults. *Advanced Development Journal, 3.* (Reprinted in the 1995 Special Edition of *Advanced Development Journal*, pp. 163–171.)

Kottmeyer, C. (2007). Optimum intelligence: My experience as a too-gifted adult. *Advanced Development, 11,* 125–129.

Kuipers, W. (2007). How to charm gifted adults into admitting giftedness: Their own and somebody else's. *Advanced Development, 11,* 9–25.

Lewis, R. B., Kitano, M. K., & Lynch, E. W. (1992). Psychological intensities in gifted adults. *Roeper Review, 15*(1), 25–31.

Lovecky, D. (1986). Can you hear the flowers singing? Issues for gifted adults. *Journal of Counseling and Development, (64),* 590–592.

Lovecky, D. V. (1993). Creative connections: Perspectives on female giftedness. *Advanced Development, 5,* 117–129.

Munsey, C. (2006). Frisky, but more risky. *American Psychological Association Monitor, 37* (7). Retrieved from www.apa.org/monitor/julaug06/frisky.aspx

Nauta, N. (2013). What can parents, teachers, and counselors learn from the knowledge on gifted adults? *NAGC Counseling and Guidance Newsletter, 9,* 19–21.

Noble, K. D., Robinson, N. M., & Gunderson, S. A. (1993). All rivers lead to the sea: A follow-up study of gifted young adults. *Roeper Review, 15*(3), 124–130.

Perrone, K. M., Perrone, P. A., Ksiazak, T. M., Wright, S. L., & Jackson, Z. V. (2007). Self-perception of gifts and talents among adults in a longitudinal study of academically talented high-school graduates. *Roeper Review, 29*(4), 259–264.

Peterson, J. S. (2001). Successful adults who were once adolescent underachievers. *Gifted Child Quarterly, 45*(4), 236–250.

Piechowski, M. M. (2002). Experiencing in a higher key: Dabrowski's theory of and for the gifted. *Gifted Education Communicator, 33*(1), 28–31, 35–36.

Raines, A., Reynolds, C., Venables, P. H., & Mednick, S. A. (2002). Stimulation seeking and intelligence: A prospective longitudinal study. *Journal of Personality and Social Psychology, 82*(4), 663–674.

Rocamora, M. (1992). Counseling issues with recognized and unrecognized creatively gifted adults: With six case studies. *Advanced Development Journal, 4.* (Reprinted in the 1995 Special Edition of *Advanced Development Journal,* p. 153.)

Roeper, A. (1982). How the gifted cope with their emotions. *Roeper Review, 5*(2), 21–24.

Roeper, A. (1991). Gifted adults: Their characteristics and emotions. *Advanced Development, 3,* 85–98

Seligman, M. P. & Csikszentmihalyi, M. (2000). Positive psychology: An introduction. *American Psychologist, 55*(1), 5–14.

Subotnik, R. F., Karp. D. E., & Morgan, E. R. (1989). High IQ children at midlife: An investigation into the generalizability of Terman's genetic studies. *Roeper Review, 11*(3), 139–144. Retrieved from www. davidsongifted.org/db/Articles_print_id_10176.aspx.

Surry, J. (1993). Self-in-relation: A theory of women's development. *Advanced Development, 5,* 1–11.

Tolan, S. (1994). Discovering the gifted ex-child. *Roeper Review, 17*(2), 134–138.

Tolan, S. S. (1999). Self-knowledge, self-esteem and the gifted adult. *Advanced Development Journal, 8,* 147–150.

Willings, D. (1985, Sept.). The specific needs of adults who are gifted. *Roeper Review, 8*(1), 35–38.

Internet Sources

Advanced Development Journal, the first journal on adult giftedness: All volumes, including the 1995 Special Edition, are available. Retrieved from www.gifteddevelopment.com/product-category/ advanced-development-journal.

Angell, R. (February 17, 2014). This old man: Life in the nineties. *Onward and outward: The New Yorker.* Retrieved from www.newyorker.com/ magazine/2014/02/17/old-man-3.

Azpeitia, L. (n.d.) Gifted, Talented, and Creative Adults. Retrieved from http:// gifted-adults.com/characteristics-of-gifted-talented-creative-adults.

Bailey, D. (November 1, 2014). David Bailey: This is what 100 looks like. *The Guardian.* Retrieved from www.theguardian.com/ artanddesign/2014/nov/01/david-bailey-this-is-what-100-looks-like.

The Davidson Gifted Database includes a lengthy list of articles on gifted adults. Retrieved from www.davidsongifted.org/Search.aspx?output= xml_no_dtd&client=davidsongifted_frontend&site=dgdb_ all&q=gifted%20adults.

Eby, D. Both of Douglas Eby's websites include many different resources that relate to gifted adults: http://highability.org and http://talentdevelop. com. Just do a search using the keywords "gifted adults."

Fiedler, E. (2003, April). *Diversity in the classroom: Assimilating differences among adult learners and gifted students.* Article based on interview retrieved from www.glencoe.com/ps/teachingtoday/ educationupclose.phtml/print/10.

Fonda, J. (2011). Life's third act. From TEDxWomen2011. Retrieved from www.ted.com/talks/jane_fonda_life_s_third_act.html.

The Gifted Adults Foundation in the Netherlands (IHBV)—an organization for knowledge, projects and networking meant to improve life for gifted and talented adults. Retrieved from http:// ihbv.nl/international/english/ihbv/.

The Gifted Development Center website includes several articles on gifted adults. Retrieved from www.gifteddevelopment.com/search/node/ gifted%20adults.

Gross, T. & Sendak, M. (September 20, 2011). *This pig wants to party.* Interview by Terry Gross with Maurice Sendak on NPR's "Fresh Air." Retrieved from NPR: www.npr.org/2011/09/20/140435330/ this-pig-wants-to-party-maurice-sendaks-latest.

Gustke, C. (April 4, 2014). Going back to school, without the pressure. Retrieved from *New York Times:* www.nytimes.com/2014/04/05/your-money/college-retirement-communities-expected-to-grow.html.

Hoagies' website has an extensive list of sources of information on gifted adults. Retrieved from www.hoagiesgifted.org/gifted_adults.htm.

Jaffe, I. (March 6, 2013). For midwife, 71, delivering babies never gets old. Retrieved from NPR: www.npr.org/2013/03/06/ 173156161/for-midwife-delivering-babies-never-gets-old?ft= 3&f=111787346&sc=nl&cc=es-20130310.

Jampolsky, J. & Cirincioni, D. (2011). How to heal your attitudes: Interview. *SC Super Consciousness Website.* Retrieved from www.superconsciousness.com/topics/health/letting-go-blocks-healthy-attitudes.

Keillor, G. (2014). *The view from Mrs. Sundberg's window.* Retrieved from www.publicradio.org/columns/prairiehome/sundberg/2014/02/ 08.shtml?elq=bf404a48b4a546ca956be80f1b919511&elq CampaignId=5517.

National Association for Gifted Children. (2009). *White paper: Twice Exceptionality.* Retrieved from www.nagc.org/sites/default/files/Position%20Statement/twice%20exceptional.pdf.

Navan, J. (2014, November). Gifted Comes of Age: A SENG initiative. *Supporting Emotional Needs of the Gifted: Changing lives, changing futures!* Retrieved from www.sengifted.org/archives/articles/gifted-comes-of-age-a-seng-initiative?utm_source=November+2014+SENGvine&utm_campaign=Nov+2014-Sengvine&utm_medium=email.

Nickish, C. (May 20, 2013). *Seeing the (northern) light: A temporary arctic retirement.* Retrieved from NPR: www.npr.org/2013/05/20/183910777/seeing-the-northern-light-a-temporary-arctic-retirement?

Prober, P. (2008). Counseling gifted adults. Retrieved from www.sengifted.org/archives/articles/counseling-gifted-adults-a-case-study.

Roeper, Annemarie: Celebrating an extraordinary life: Special Commemorative Edition of *Keeping in Touch* from The Roeper School honoring the life and work of Annemarie Roeper. Retrieved from http://issuu.com/theroeperschool/docs/kit.amr.commem.1212.

SENG (Supporting Emotional Needs of the Gifted). Their website has many sources of information on gifted adults. Retrieved from www.sengifted.org/search-results?cx=003473141502989371879%3Ae7t044sohde&cof=FORID%3A11&q=gifted%20adults&sa.

Silverman, L. K. (1997–2013). *Giftedness in adults.* Retrieved from www.gifteddevelopment.com/sites/default/files/Characteristics%20of%20Giftedness%20in%20Adults.pdf.

Weeks, L. (March 28, 2013). *Maybe we should retire the word 'retire'.* Retrieved from NPR: www.npr.org/2013/03/28/175461789/maybe-we-should-retire-the-word-retire

Zernike, K. (July 10, 2010). *Turn 70. Act your grandchild's age.* Retrieved from the New York Times: www.nytimes.com/2010/07/11/weekinreview/11zernike.html?_r=0.

APPENDIX 3

Journal Writing: Exploring Inner Space

Self-discovery ➠ Self-awareness ➠ Self-understanding ➠ Self-actualization

Bright adults need opportunities to find out who they are *(self-discovery)*, to tune in to their feelings and their perceptions of the world around them *(self-awareness)*, and to make meaning out of their responses to life *(self-understanding)* in order to use their potential fully and lead satisfying, productive lives *(self-actualization)*. Journal writing can be a highly effective strategy for facilitating this process.

What Journals Are

○ Journals are tools for reflection and introspection.

○ Journals are personal and private (even though the writer may allow someone else to read them).

○ Journals are a way to slow down the galloping thought processes to allow for self-examination and contemplation of a universe of intriguing ideas.

○ Journals provide opportunities to get in touch with and express feelings.

○ Journals are an avenue for exploring the inner world, for making sense out of what otherwise might appear to be chaos and confusion.

○ Journals are beneficial for reducing stress, fostering good health, facilitating problem solving and decision-making, enhancing personal growth, and promoting creativity.

What Journals Are Not

○ Journals are not diaries or daily chronologies of events.

○ Journals are not designed for winning the approval/acceptance of others.

○ Journals are not a means for simply parroting back others' ideas without personal reaction and interpretation.

○ Journals are not solely affective, nor are they solely cognitive.

○ Journals are not a guarantee that the outer world can always be perceived as reflecting order, logic, and sanity.

○ Journals are not a panacea.

Ellen D. Fiedler, Ph.D., Wings for Education, Inc., New Buffalo, Michigan •
ellenfiedler@comcast.net •

Suggestions for Keeping a Journal

Find the kind of journal you *want* to write in; pick something *you* like to write with. If you don't know, ask yourself these questions:

○ Are you going to write by hand? On a typewriter? On a computer?

○ Do you want loose-leaf paper or a bound notebook?

○ Do you like a book that is highly tactile (corduroy, silk, or velvet) or the kind of black-and-white speckled notebook you used in your early years in grade school?

○ What colors speak to you and invite you to write?

○ When and where do you feel safe to express yourself?

○ What kind of setting works best for you?

○ How important is being in a quiet space, and, if that is important, where are you likely to find one?

Take appropriate security measures to make sure that what you write will be private.

- Discuss issues of confidentiality with anyone you allow to read your journal.
- Have an understanding that they will *not* read anything you cover over and mark *private*.
- Don't just list events.
- Share feelings, concerns, opinions, and reflections on the meaning of your actions and those of others.
- Just write down events that elicited strong feelings, either negative or positive.
- Leave out anything that *didn't* have an impact.

If you need a bit of a jump-start, use open-ended idea-jolters (such as the ones listed below) to spark your thinking and get you moving forward in the process of keeping a journal.

- Write a one-page autobiography.
- Make a "collage of today"—headlines, a photo or drawing of yourself, weather notes (both internal and external).
- Write a letter to yourself; write letters to other people (even letters that you might not really want to send).
- Write down a dream and your interpretation of it.
- Draw the path you are currently walking. What does your life look like, symbolically? What are some of the landmarks you notice along the way?
- Write to yourself about your life path. What do you know about where you are coming from and where you are going?
- Make up "What if?" questions and answer them (e.g., What if you won the lottery? What if you had three wishes? What if you were captain of the world?)

○ Make a list of things that you wonder about, that you find wonderful, and that you find to be sources of wonder. How are these alike? How are they different?

○ What were you wondering about the day after you were born? At age 5? Age 10? What will you be wondering about at age 50? Age 75? What are you wondering today?

○ What are the little choices that influence your day? What choices do you want to make differently? What gets in the way of making satisfying choices? What choices do you celebrate?

○ What would your "ultimate learning experience" be?

Journal writing is a journey—a journey of discovery into your own inner world. Enjoy the trip!

Ellen D. Fiedler, Ph.D., Wings for Education, Inc., New Buffalo, Michigan •
ellenfiedler@comcast.net •

Dealing with Expectations

1. Identify significant people in your life—those who have expectations of you. List them down the left-hand column of the chart on the next page.

2. Identify areas of your life where people have expectations of you. List them across the top of the chart. Examples might include:

   ○ Performance on the job or in school
   ○ Socialization
   ○ Relationships
   ○ Clubs/organizations
   ○ Family involvement
   ○ Family responsibilities
   ○ Community activities
   ○ Competitions/awards
   ○ Involvement in religious activities

3. Moving vertically, indicate the level of expectations each person has for you in each area of your life. Conclude with your expectations of yourself in each area.

4. Do different people in your life have different expectations of you in each of these areas? How do these compare with the expectations you have of yourself?

Note: It may be interesting to have some of the people you have listed on your chart fill out a chart for you, too, based on their perceptions of expectations that have an impact on your life.

Adapted by Dr. Ellen D. Fiedler, Professor Emerita, Northeastern Illinois University, Chicago, Illinois, from a process developed at the Guidance Institute for Talented Students (G.I.F.T.S.), University of Wisconsin–Madison.

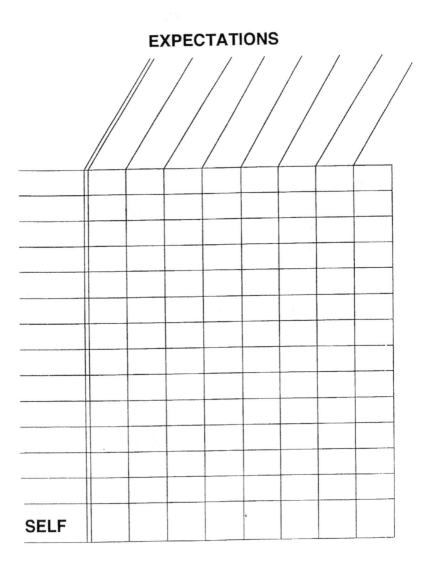

How to Listen So Others Will Talk with You

The Language of Acceptance

1. Acceptance must be demonstrated, not just felt.

2. Communicate acceptance nonverbally by:
   a. Nonintervention (letting others "do their thing")
   b. Passive listening (silence).

3. Communicate acceptance verbally by:
   a. Avoiding the "Typical 12 Roadblocks to Communication"
   b. Using "Door Openers" (*"I see,"* *"Oh,"* *"Mm hmm,"* *"Is that so,"* etc.)
   c. Active listening ("You" messages that reflect their feelings back to them, such as any of the phrases listed below for helping you focus on feelings and emotions).

The Typical 12 Roadblocks to Communication

1. Ordering, directing, commanding: Telling someone to do something, giving an order or command, e.g., *"Don't talk to me like that!"*

2. Warning, admonishing, threatening: Telling someone what consequences will occur if they do something, e.g., *"If you do that, you'll be sorry!"*

3. Exhorting, moralizing, preaching: Telling someone what they "should" or "ought" to do, e.g., *"You shouldn't act like that."*

4. Advising, giving solutions or suggestions: Telling someone how to solve a problem, giving advice or suggestions, providing answers or solutions, e.g., *"Why don't you...?"*

5. Lecturing, teaching, giving logical arguments: Trying to influence someone with facts, counterarguments (e.g., *"Yes, but..."*), logic, information, or your own opinions (e.g., *"It just doesn't make sense to think that way."*).

6. Judging, criticizing, disagreeing, blaming: Making a negative judgment or evaluation of someone, e.g., *"That's a silly point of view."*

7. Blindly praising, agreeing: Offering a positive evaluation or judgment, agreeing, without deeply considering the matter, e.g., *"Well, I think you're really capable."*

8. Name-calling, ridiculing, shaming: Making someone feel foolish, putting someone into a category, shaming, e.g., *"You're a hothead."*

9. Interpreting, analyzing, diagnosing: Telling someone what their motives are or analyzing why they are doing or saying something, communicating that you have them figured out or diagnosed, e.g., *"You're saying that to bug me."*

10. Reassuring, sympathizing, consoling, supporting: Trying to make someone feel better, talking them out of their feelings, trying to make their feelings go away, denying the strength of their feelings, e.g., *"Everyone goes through this sometime."*

11. Probing, questioning, interrogating: Trying to find reasons, motives, causes, searching for more information to help you solve the problem, e.g., *"Why do you suppose that happened?"*

12. Withdrawing, distracting, humoring, diverting: Trying to get someone away from the problem, withdrawing from the problem yourself, distracting them, kidding them out of it, pushing the problem aside, e.g., *"Come on; let's talk about something more pleasant."*

The "Language of Acceptance"—Why Use It?

○ Helps people free themselves of troublesome feelings by expressing them openly

○ Helps people become less afraid of negative feelings

○ Promotes a positive relationship between people

○ Helps people move ahead with solving their problems.

○ Influences others to be more willing to listen to your thoughts and ideas

○ Keeps the problem with the person who owns it (i.e., helps them think for themselves)

Attitudes Required for "Active Listening"

1. You must *want* to hear what others have to say. This means you are willing to take the time to listen. If you don't have the time, you need only say so.

2. You must genuinely *want* to be helpful with this particular problem at that time. If you don't want to, wait until you do.

3. You must genuinely be able to *accept others' feelings*, whatever they may be or however different they may be from your own feelings or from the feelings you think someone "should" feel. (This attitude takes time to develop.)

4. You must have a deep feeling of *trust* in others' capacity to handle their feelings, to work through them, and to find solutions to their problems. (You'll acquire this trust by watching others solve their own problems.)

5. You must appreciate that feelings are *transitory*, not permanent. Feelings change—hate can turn into love, discouragement may quickly be replaced by hope. Consequently, you need not be afraid of expressing feelings; they will not become forever fixed. (Active listening will demonstrate this to you.)

6. You must be able to see the others as *separate* from you—unique persons, separate individuals with their *own* lives and their *own* identity. This "separateness" will enable you to "permit" others to have their *own* feelings, their *own* way of perceiving things. Only by feeling "separateness" will you be able to be a helping agent for others. You must be "with" them as they experience their problems, but not joined to them.

Adapted by Dr. Ellen Fiedler, Professor Emerita, Northeastern Illinois University, Chicago, Illinois, from: *P.E.T., Parent Effectiveness Training*, by Dr. Thomas Gordon.

Responding to Their Feelings

Phrases to help you focus on *feelings* and *emotions:*

You feel…
Tell me more…
As you see it…
Sounds like…
As I hear it, you…
You believe…
What I hear you saying is…
It seems to you…
From your standpoint…
You think…
I'm picking up that you…
You figure…
Could it be that…
From your point of view…
Something tells me that maybe you…
I get the impression that…
What I think I hear you saying is…
I really hear you saying…
I wonder if…
You're really…
From what you've said, I wonder…
You find it difficult to talk about…
I guess you feel…
You sound as though…

You must have been…
Your primary concern is…
When I listen between the lines…

Based on materials developed by Dr. Maureen Neihart and shared by Dr. Ellen Fiedler, Professor Emerita, Northeastern Illinois University, Chicago, IL Wings for Education, Inc., New Buffalo, MI ~ ellenfiedler@comcast.net

Strategies for "Organizationally Challenged" Bright Adults

Note: These suggestions for bright adults have been adapted from the following article: Fiedler, E. D. (2013). "Organizationally challenged?" Helping gifted students develop executive functions. IAGC Journal, 79–81.

Bright adults often are "organizationally challenged." In fact, the brighter they are, the more likely it is that they will have issues with organization (or the more likely others in their lives will have concerns about their disorganization). The more complicated their lives become, the more these bright adults find that the ability to remain organized eludes them.

Some typical behaviors found in bright individuals who are organizationally challenged include managing time poorly and losing important papers or possessions. Many have difficulty with transitions. They get totally absorbed in what they are doing and don't want to move on, whether it is dinner time, time to change activities, time to go home, or time to go to bed. These bright adults often skip steps in multistep processes and have problems with identifying important information when working on a project.

Does any of this sound familiar? If you or someone in your life fits this description, it might be useful to know a little something about "executive functions." Executive functions are defined as "cognitive processes that allow people to plan, organize, make decisions, pay attention, and regulate behavior."[370] These processes are brain functions pertaining to having and setting goals and not getting sidetracked or distracted along the way. They also relate to the ability to shift gears and change plans when faced with obstacles, making mistakes, or even when discovering new information.[371]

The good news is that executive functions can be developed. We just need to consider strategies particularly tailored for gifted individuals.

Let's start with looking at some specific issues for bright adults. Problems with executive functions can lead to difficulties with self-concept. No matter how high their abilities really are, some bright adults simply don't feel good about themselves, and others who misguidedly try to reassure them or praise them find their efforts to be in vain. They are frequently frustrated and have little tolerance for their own errors. They have trouble dealing with their self-expectations and their expectations of others. Also, other people in their lives often have trouble understanding their inability either to get things done or express their thoughts and feelings accurately. They frequently make decisions that are impulsive or lack depth. Long-term goals elude them; in fact, they often really don't know how to establish goals. Those who have problems with executive functions may have a pessimistic, gloomy view of the future.[372]

So why are bright people so often "organizationally challenged"? Among the reasons for this are: a) they have good memories and can rely on remembering where they saw something last, and b) they have so many interests and so many things going on at once that their lives simply spin out of control. Also, bright individuals are typically internally motivated and resist all external efforts to get them to conform to anyone else's ideas of how they should live their lives. Furthermore, they often are unaware of the knowledge or lack the skills that would help them be more organized. Besides, organization requires mundane work, and their brains aren't wired that way.[373]

Strategies for Bright Adults

Let's look at some strategies that may be effective for helping bright adults get more organized. These approaches are especially designed with bright individuals in mind and honor their need to have control over as many aspects of their lives as possible. You may have already implemented a number of these, perhaps not realizing their effect on developing your executive functions.

Color-coding. Use different colored notebooks, folders, index cards, markers, or sticky notes for different categories of things you need to keep track of in your life. You need to figure out what those categories might be and decide which colors should be used for which. Some kind of chart or "key" can be posted on the wall of your room or in some other convenient location (e.g., in the kitchen or bathroom, or on your computer). You should decide whether/where the chart should be posted.

Timers. Use a wind-up or electronic timer to keep track of when it is time to change activities, quit doing whatever you are doing, or for whatever purpose you think might be most useful. Some people like to play "beat the clock" by setting a timer for doing some of their least favorite chores or tasks and seeing if they can finish before the timer goes off. When using timers, set a trial run for a week; then see how it works or what modifications you might want to implement to make it work out better.

Alarms. Whether your alarm comes on a clock, watch, or phone, brainstorm situations in which it might be useful to have an alarm remind you of what you need to do at a particular time. Then make a list of the ideas you want to use. You also can decide how much "advance warning" you need. Just as with using a timer, it is a good idea to set a trial run for a week and then see how it goes or what you might like to change.

Appointment books/"agendas"/calendars. Some people like to have a hands-on calendar for all of their activities and appointments. You can also use it for notes about things to do, addresses, and other things you want to remember. An appointment book can either be one you carry with you (although there is always the danger of losing it), one that hangs on the wall, or one on your computer that can sync up with your other electronic devices, such as your phone or tablet. Bright adults typically have jam-packed schedules, and having a system to keep track of *what*, *when*, and *where* is essential for helping you manage your life. This is especially good for appointments, due dates, and other calendar events, with reminders as far ahead of time as you would like to be reminded of each. Having a "master calendar" for the family is always useful, too, posted in a prominent place, such as the refrigerator.

Technology. Most bright adults love using technology and are good at doing so, and it can be hugely useful in innumerable ways. Smartphones, tablets, and computers can be synced with each other or used independently as stand-alone devices.

We have already discussed timers, alarms, and calendars, so here are some other ideas that can help you with organizing your life using technology:

- ○ *Contacts.* Phone numbers and addresses (email and snail mail) can all be kept electronically, and the devices all have search functions that make the information easy to find.

- ○ *Notes and reminders.* Notes, "to do's," reminders, and all kinds of miscellaneous information that would get lost if it were on scraps of paper can be kept electronically. These items can be color-coded, as well, using whatever system you find most useful for your purposes.

- ○ *Podcasts/video tutorials/other Internet sources.* An unbelievable assortment of useful information is available free for downloading as podcasts. These podcasts can be accessed directly or downloaded to a computer, a smartphone, an iPod, or a tablet for mobile listening whenever and wherever it might be most convenient.

Mind mapping. Mind mapping is "a diagram used to visually outline information."[374] A mind map is often created around a single word or text, placed in the center, to which associated ideas, words, and concepts are added. Major categories radiate from a central node, and lesser categories are sub-branches of larger branches. Categories can represent words, ideas, tasks, or other items related to a central key word or idea. Try Googling "mind mapping." Among the sources listed are websites with free mind-mapping software, including the following one: http://freemind.sourceforge.net/wiki/index.php/Main_Page.

Role models/mentors. Find out how successful adults organize their lives; check out their wide range of methods and then choose those that you think would be useful for you to use yourself. Also look at the lives of remarkable individuals from history (e.g., Leonardo da Vinci) and find out how they kept their lives organized. Then imagine what those people might do today if they had the resources available to them that are available now, including modern technology.

Creative problem solving. The Creative Problem Solving Model is a tried and true method for breaking complex problems into manageable stages. You start with the "Mess" (actually now called "Objective Finding") and proceed through "Fact Finding," "Problem Finding," "Idea Finding," "Solution Finding," and "Acceptance Finding." This website provides a quick overview: http://members.optusnet.com. au/charles57/Creative/Brain/cps.htm.

The Creative Problem Solving Model is especially helpful for getting beyond the simple pleasures of brainstorming ideas and on to actually selecting and implementing solutions.

Conclusion

Remember that some of us really do work better under pressure and can cope better than others with what appears to be chaos and confusion. As one gifted girl who is now a successful obstetrician said, "I thrive under stress."[375] However, some who typically cope well with apparently chaotic conditions can get themselves into a real bind when too many things build up at once. They need to get more organized before things run out of control and they go ballistic. Also, some "deadline workers" do run out of time as they push the deadline. One idea that may help them is to start the planning process with "Day Zero" (the due date) and plan backwards—i.e., begin with what needs to be done the day before it is due, the day before that, etc.

One final suggestion: Start small and avoid trying to implement too many ideas at once. Chose two or three that you think are especially appealing and try those approaches first, choosing one to take on a "test drive." Then after a suitable time interval, think about how it is going, make modifications as needed, and go from there. If several members of your family are organizationally challenged, different strategies might be applicable for each of them. So you might think about making this a joint project in which you each try one or two of these suggestions and then share your results with each other. In general, developing executive functions results in less anxiety—for you and certainly for others in your life.

APPENDIX 7

Self-Assessment Wheel

○ Take a marker and draw a circle on a sheet of paper.

○ Divide your circle into eight pie-shaped sections labeled, respectively: Intellectual, Creative, Physical, Social, Emotional, Family, Spiritual, and Other. *(Note: You can choose other categories that are more relevant to you as well as deciding what area of your life you would like to focus on for the category of "Other.")*

○ Color in each section of the pie chart to the extent that you are currently satisfied with that area of your life.

○ Share your observations with someone you trust or keep them private. Look especially for those areas in which there is complete satisfaction or complete dissatisfaction.

○ File your sheet away in a safe place and then redo this activity in a month or more before looking at what you did the first time. Then take out your original sheet and make comparisons with the one just completed, noting any areas of change.

Purpose: To help you assess your level of satisfaction in all areas of your life and to assist you in developing goals and strategies for meeting your needs.

Adapted by Dr. Ellen Fiedler from "Eight Effective Activities to Enhance the Emotional and Social Development of the Gifted and Talented" by G. T. Betts and M. F. Neihart, (1985), *Roeper Review, 8* (1), 18–23.

S.P.I.C.E.S. Activity for Risk-Taking

Social
Physical
Intellectual
Creative
Emotional
Spiritual

Rank each of these areas of your life in terms of how difficult you find risk-taking to be for you (1 = the most difficult, and 6 = the easiest).

If you were given an "assignment" to take a risk in one of these areas, would you choose your easiest? Your most difficult? Or one in between? What would represent a risk for you in that area of your life? Consider that, select one or more to do, and use journaling to reflect on your choice and how it goes for you.

Adapted by Dr. Ellen Fiedler from an activity shared by Dr. Maureen Neihart.

Questions for Gifted Adults about Childhood

Are you an undetected gifted adult who needs more information on adult giftedness?

When you were a child, how many of the following questions applied to you?

- Were you advanced in your development of speaking, reading, or other skills in early childhood?
- Were you fascinated with words or ideas?
- Did you ask a lot of questions?
- Did you have an unusual perspective of things and events?
- Were you a good problem solver?
- Did you have a good memory?
- Were you exceptionally sensitive?
- Did you have a great sense of humor?
- Were you insightful?
- Were you perfectionistic?
- Were you intense?
- Did you collect things and organize your collections?
- Were you a rapid learner?

○ Did you show compassion for others?

○ Did you enjoy older playmates and the company of adults?

○ Were you argumentative?

○ Did you have a large vocabulary?

○ Did you have a creative imagination?

○ Were you an avid reader?

○ Did you have a wide range of interests?

○ Did you like puzzles, mazes, or numbers?

○ Did you have a great deal of energy?

○ Did you have a long attention span?

If many of these characteristics fit you, you are probably a gifted adult. Giftedness was not commonly identified in children until recently, so many adults are unaware that they were gifted as children. But even those who were identified tend to believe their giftedness disappeared before adulthood.

Excerpted from: www.gifteddevelopment.com/ADJ/adj.htm.[376]

Transforming "Yes, but…" into "Yes, and…"

1. Write down your responses to the phrase "I really want to…"

2. Follow each response with "but…" and fill in whatever you think is stopping you.

3. Cross out the word *but* and replace it with the word *and*. Look at your sentence as it is written now and see what it shows you about what you need to do to remove the obstacles.

4. Determine what you need to do to accomplish what you want.

For example:

Step 1: I really want to work with people like me…

Step 2: …*but* I don't know what qualifications I'd need.

Step 3: Cross out the word *but*; your sentence would look like this:

I really want to work with people like me, ~~but~~ *and* I don't know what qualifications I'd need.

Step 4: Do the research to find out what qualifications you would need by looking up information online or talking to people who are doing the kind of work you are interested in.

Developed by Dr. Ellen Fiedler based on an idea shared by Dr. Felice Kaufmann.

References

Alvarado, N. (1989). Adjustment of gifted adults. *Advanced Development, 1*, 77–86.

Armstrong, T. (2007). *The human odyssey: Navigating the twelve stages of life.* New York: Sterling.

Aron, E. N. (1996). *The highly sensitive person: How to thrive when the world overwhelms you.* New York: Broadway Books.

Baines, B. K. (2006). *Ethical wills: Putting your values on paper.* 2nd ed. Kansas City, MO: Center for Practical Bioethics.

Bateson, M. C. (2010). *Composing a further life: The age of active wisdom.* New York: Alfred A. Knopf.

Battaglia, M. M. K., Mendaglio, S., & Piechowski, M. M. (2014). A life of positive maladjustment (1902–1980). In A. Robinson & J. Jolly (Eds.), *A century of contributions to gifted education: Illuminating lives,* pp. 181–199. New York: Routledge.

Berger, S. L. (2014). *College planning for gifted students.* Waco, TX: Prufrock Press.

Berne, E. (1992). *Games people play: The basic handbook of transactional analysis.* New York: Ballantine Books.

Betts, G. T. & Neihart, M. F. (1985). Eight effective activities to enhance the emotional and social development of the gifted and talented. *Roeper Review, 8*(1), 18–23.

Bode, R. (1993). *First you have to row a little boat: Reflections on life and living.* New York: Warner Books.

Bowlby J. (1969). *Attachment. Attachment and loss: Vol. 1. Loss.* New York: Basic Books.

Boyes, R. (2007). Forget burnout, boreout is the new office disease. *The Times,* Sept 15, 2007. Retrieved from www.thetimes.co.uk/tto/career/article1792702.ece.

Buettner, D. (2012). *The blue zones: 9 lessons for living longer from the people who've lived the longest.* Washington, D.C.: National Geographic.

Butler, R. N. (2010). *The longevity prescription: The 8 proven keys to a long, healthy life.* New York: Avery.

Cain, S. (2013). *Quiet: The power of introverts in a world that can't stop talking.* New York: Random House.

Caswell, C. (2004). *The quotable sailor.* Guilford, CT: The Lyons Press.

Chessman, A. (n.d.). Distinguishing levels of giftedness: What does it mean for our practice? Retrieved from www.curriculumsupport.education.nsw.gov.au/policies/gats/assets/pdf/plk12gtlvls.pdf.

Chittister, J. (2008). *The gift of years: Growing older gracefully.* Katonah, NY: BlueBridge.

Clance, P. R. (1986). *The imposter phenomenon: When success feels like a fake.* New York: Bantam Books.

Cohen, G. D. (2005). *The mature mind: The positive power of the aging brain.* New York: Basic Books.

Columbus Group. (1991). Cited in Silverman, L. K. (1993). The gifted individual. In L. K. Silverman (Ed.), *Counseling the gifted and talented,* p. 3. Denver, CO: Love.

Cross, T., Gust-Brey, K., & Ball, P. (2002). A psychological autopsy of the suicide of an academically gifted student: Researchers' and parents' perspectives. *Gifted Child Quarterly,* 46(4). Retrieved from www.davidsongifted.org/db/Articles_id_10337.aspx.

Daniels, S. & Piechowski, M. M. (2009). *Living with intensity.* Scottsdale, AZ: Great Potential Press.

Downs, M. P. (2005). *Shut up and live! (You know how).* Nashville, TN: Cold Tree Press.

Ellis, N. (2004). *If I live to be 100: Lessons from the Centenarians.* New York: Three Rivers Press.

Erikson, E. (1951). *Childhood and society.* New York: W. W. Norton.

Erikson, E. (1959). *Identity and the life cycle.* New York: International Universities.

Erikson, E. (1963). *Childhood and society.* 2nd ed. New York: W. W. Norton.

Erikson, E. H. & Erikson, J. M. (1997). *The life cycle completed: Extended version with new chapters on the ninth stage of development by Joan M. Erikson.* New York: W. W. Norton.

Faludi, S. (1991). *Backlash: The undeclared war against American women.* New York: Three Rivers Press.

Farrell, C. (2014). *Unretirement: How baby boomers are changing the way we think about work, community, and the good life.* New York: Bloomsbury Press.

Fiedler, E. (1998, Spring). The bird and the fish (Editorial). *Heritage Hailer, 17*(1), 11.

Fiedler, E. D. (1995). Some people. *Gifted & Talented Children's Association —South Australia—Newsletter, 99,* 14.

Fiedler, E. D. (1998, March). Some people. *ABC Newsmagazine: A Quarterly Publication of the Association for Bright Children of Ontario.*

Fiedler, E. D. (2005, Summer). Two sides of the same coin: Teachers developing creativity. *CAG Communicator, 36*(2), 29-32.

Fiedler, E. D. (2007, April). *Intensity at home: What's a parent to do?* Presentation at the 2007 Bay City Spring Conference, Bay City, MI.

Fiedler, E. D. (2009). Advantages and challenges of lifespan intensity. In S. Daniels & M. M. Piechowski (Eds.), *Living with intensity,* pp. 167–184. Scottsdale, AZ: Great Potential Press.

Fiedler, E. D. (2012). You don't outgrow it! Giftedness across the lifespan. *Advanced Development Journal, 13,* 19–37.

Fiedler, E. D. (2013). "Organizationally challenged?" Helping gifted students develop executive functions. *IAGC Journal,* 79-81.

Fiedler, E. D. (2013). You don't outgrow giftedness: Giftedness across the lifespan. In C. S. Neville, M. M. Piechowski, & S. S. Tolan (Eds.). *Off the charts: Asynchrony and the gifted child,* pp. 183–210. Unionville, NY: Royal Fireworks Press.

Fiedler, E. D. & Webb, J. (2011, November). *Adult gifted: You don't just outgrow it! Advantages and challenges of lifespan intensity.* Presentation at the 58th Annual Convention of the National Association for Gifted Children, New Orleans, LA.

Fonda, J. (2011). *Prime time.* New York: Random House.

Freedman, M. (January 1, 2014). The dangerous myth of reinvention. *Harvard Business Review.* Retrieved from http://blogs.hbr.org/2014/01/the-dangerous-myth-of-reinvention/.

Freeman, J. (2010). *Gifted lives.* London: Routledge.

Gatto-Walden, P. (2013). The heart of the matter: Complexities of the highly gifted self. In C. S. Neville, M. M. Piechowski, & S. S. Tolan (Eds.). *Off the charts: Asynchrony and the gifted child,* pp. 158–182. Unionville, NY: Royal Fireworks Press.

Goertzel, V., Goertzel, M. G., Goertzel, T. G, & Hansen, A. M. W. (2004). *Cradles of eminence: Childhoods of more than 700 famous men and women.* Scottsdale, AZ: Great Potential Press.

Guetzloe, E. (1994). Risk, resilience, and protection. *Journal of Emotional and Behavioral Problems, 3*(2), 2–5.

Hollis, J. (2005). *Finding meaning in the second half of life.* New York: Gotham Books.

Jacobsen, M. E. (1999). *Liberating everyday genius.* New York: Ballantine.

Kane, M. (2009, October). *Executive functions: Another look at disorganization, meltdowns, lack of initiative and focus.* Presentation at the Annual Conference of the Wisconsin Association for Talented and Gifted, Sheboygan, WI.

Kane, M. & Fiedler, E. D. (2013, August). *Changing family structures: Helping gifted families find their way.* Presentation at the 20th Biennial World Conference of the World Council for Gifted and Talented Children, Louisville, KY, USA.

Kaufman, F. (1981). The 1964–1968 Presidential Scholars: A follow-up study. *Exceptional Children, 48*(2), pp. 164–169.

Kaufman, F. (1992). What educators can learn from gifted adults. Retrieved from www.davidsongifted.org/db/Articles_print_id_10023.aspx

Keating, D. P. (2009). Developmental transitions in giftedness and talent: Adolescence into adulthood. In F. D. Horowitz, R. F. Subotnik, & D. J. Matthews (Eds.), *The development of giftedness and talent across the lifespan*, pp. 189–208. Washington, D.C.: American Psychological Association.

Keillor, G. (2014). *The view from Mrs. Sundberg's window.* Retrieved from www.publicradio.org/columns/prairiehome/sundberg/2014/02/08. shtml?elq=bf404a48b4a546ca956be80f1b919511&elqCampaignId=5517

Kerr, B. (1985). *Smart girls, gifted women.* Columbus, OH: Ohio Psychology Publishing.

Kerr, B. A. (1994). *Smart girls: A new psychology of girls, women, and giftedness.* (Revised ed.). Scottsdale, AZ: Great Potential Press.

Kerr, B. & Claiborn, C. D. (1991). Counseling talented adults. *Advanced Development Journal, 3.* (Reprinted in the 1995 Special Edition of *Advanced Development Journal,* pp. 163–171.)

Kerr, B. A. & Cohn, S. J. (2001). *Smart boys: Talent, manhood, & the search for meaning.* Scottsdale, AZ: Great Potential Press.

Kerr, B. & McKay, R. (2015). *Smart girls in the 21st century: Understanding talented girls and women.* Tucson, AZ: Great Potential Press.

Kottmeyer, C. (2007). Optimum intelligence: My experience as a too-gifted adult. *Advanced Development, 11,* 125–129.

Kuipers, W. (2010). *Enjoying the gift of being uncommon: Extra intelligent, intense, and effective.* Zoetermeer, the Netherlands: CreateSpace.

Lawrence-Lightfoot, S. (2009). *The third chapter: Passion, risk, and adventure in the 25 years after 50.* New York: Sarah Crichton Books.

Levinson, D. J. (1978). *The seasons of a man's life.* New York: Ballantine Books.

Levinson, D. J. (1996). *The seasons of a woman's life.* New York: Ballantine Books.

Lovecky, D. (1986). Can you hear the flowers sing? Issues for gifted adults. *Journal of Counseling and Development, 64,* 590–592.

Mach, A., Vatcha, D., & Harris, Z. (2008, February). *Focus on function: Executive function skills for adolescents with LD.* Presentation at 45th Annual International Conference of the Learning Disabilities Association of America, Chicago, IL.

Maisel, E. (2013). *Why smart people hurt: A guide for the bright, the sensitive, and the creative.* San Francisco, CA: Conari Press.

Maslow, A. H. (1970). *Motivation and personality*. 2nd ed. New York: Harper & Row.

Maupin, K. (2014). *Cheating, dishonesty, and manipulation: Why bright kids do it.* Tucson, AZ: Great Potential Press.

Miller, A. (2008). *The drama of the gifted child: The search for the true self.* New York: Basic Books.

Morhaim, D. K. & Pollack, K. M. (2013). End-of-life care issues: A personal, economic, public policy, and public health crisis. *American Journal of Public Health, 103*(6).

Munsey, C. (2006). Frisky, but more risky. *American Psychological Association Monitor, 37*(7). Retrieved from www.apa.org/monitor/julaug06/frisky.aspx

National Association for Gifted Children. (2009). *White paper: Twice Exceptionality.* Retrieved from www.nagc.org/sites/default/files/Position%20Statement/twice%20exceptional.pdf.

Nauta, N. (2013). What can parents, teachers, and counselors learn from the knowledge on gifted adults? *NAGC Counseling and Guidance Newsletter, 9,* 19–21.

Nauta, N. & Ronner, S. (2013). *Gifted workers.* St. Maartenslaan, the Netherlands: Shaker Media.

Neville, C. S., Piechowski, M. M., & Tolan, S. S. (Eds.). (2013). *Off the charts: Asynchrony and the gifted child.* Unionville, NY: Royal Fireworks Press.

Newman, M. (December 5, 2013). *American Music & Dance: Baby Boomer Era and Rock'n Roll—1946 to 1964.* Presented at the Lifelong Learning Institute, Nova Southeastern University, Davie, FL.

Noble, K. D., Robinson, N. M., & Gunderson, S. A. (1993). All rivers lead to the sea: A follow-up study of gifted young adults. *Roeper Review, 15*(3), 124–130.

Palmer, P. J. (2000). *Let your life speak: Listening for the voice of vocation.* San Francisco: Jossey-Bass.

Pauley, J. (2014). *Your life calling: Reimagining the rest of your life.* New York: Simon & Schuster.

Pestalozzi, T. (2009). *Life skills 101: A practical guide to leaving home and living on your own.* Cortland, OH: Stonewood Publications.

Piechowski, M. M. (1997). Emotional giftedness: The measure of intrapersonal intelligence. In N. Colangelo and G. A. Davis (Eds.), *Handbook of gifted education,* 2nd ed., pp. 366–381. Needham Heights, MA: Allyn and Bacon.

Piechowski, M. M. (2006). *"Mellow out," they say. If only I could: Intensities and sensitivities of the young and bright.* Madison, WI: Yunasa.

Pipher, M. (1999). *Another country: Navigating the emotional terrain of our elders.* New York: Riverhead Books.

Raines, R. (1997). *A time to live: Seven tasks of creative aging.* New York: Plume.

Raines, A., Reynolds, C., Venables, P. H., & Mednick, S. A. (2002). Stimulation seeking and intelligence: A prospective longitudinal study. *Journal of Personality and Social Psychology, 82*(4), 663–674.

Rivero, L. (2010). *A parents' guide to gifted teens: Living with intense and creative adolescents.* Scottsdale, AZ: Great Potential Press.

Rocamora, M. (1992). Counseling issues with recognized and unrecognized creatively gifted adults: With six case studies. *Advanced Development Journal, 4.* (Reprinted in the 1995 Special Edition of *Advanced Development Journal,* p. 153.)

Roeper, A. (1982). How the gifted cope with their emotions. *Roeper Review, 5*(2), 21–24.

Roeper, A. (1990). *Educating children for life: The modern learning community.* Monroe, NY: Trillium Press.

Roeper, A. (2011). *Beyond old age: Essays on living and dying.* Berkeley, CA: Azalea Art Press.

Rothlin, P. & Werder, P.R. (2008) In *Boreout!: Overcoming workplace demotivation.* London: Kogan Page.

Rush Neurobehavioral Center. (n.d.) *Executive Function.* Retrieved October 13, 2012, from http://rnbc.org/education/a-focus-on-executive-function/

Schacter-Shalomi, Z. & Miller, R. S. (1995). *From age-ing to sage-ing: A profound new vision of growing older.* New York: Grand Central.

Seligman, M. E. P. (2006). *Learned optimism: How to change your mind and your life.* New York: Vintage.

Seligman, M. E. P. (2007). *The optimistic child: A proven program to safe-guard children against depression and build lifelong resilience.* New York: Houghton Mifflin.

Seligman, M. P. & Csikszentmihalyi, M. (2000). Positive psychology: An introduction. *American Psychologist, 55*(1), 5–14.

Shaffer, D. R. (1988). *Social and personality development,* 2nd ed. Pacific Grove, CA: Brooks/Cole.

Sheehy, G. (1995). *New passages: Mapping your life across time.* New York: Random House.

Sheehy, G. (1998). Understanding men's passages: Discovering the new map of men's lives. New York: Ballantine Books.

Sheehy, G. (2006). *Passages: Predictable crises of adult life.* New York: Ballantine Books.

Shideler, M. (2014, January). *The Villages Magazine,* p. 38.

Silverman, L. K. (1993). The gifted individual. In L. K. Silverman (Ed.), *Counseling the gifted and talented,* pp. 3-28. Denver, CO: Love.

Silverman, L. K. (1997–2013). *Giftedness in adults.* Downloaded 3/4/14 from www.gifteddevelopment.com/sites/default/files/Characteristics%20of%20Giftedness%20in%20Adults.pdf.

Silverman, L.K. (1999). How to Care for Introverts. https://www.facebook.com/notes/the-introvert-entrepreneur/the-original-source-for-how-to-care-for-introverts/331076146950389.

Silverman, L. K. (2010). Foreword. In Kuipers, W. *Enjoying the gift of being uncommon: Extra intelligent, intense, and effective.* Zoetermeer, the Netherlands: CreateSpace.

Silverman, L. K. (2013). Asynchronous development: Theoretical bases and current applications. In C. S. Neville, M. M. Piechowski, & S. S. Tolan (Eds.). *Off the charts: Asynchrony and the gifted child,* pp. 18–47. Unionville, NY: Royal Fireworks Press.

Sinetar, M. (1987). *Do what you love, the money will follow: Discovering your right livelihood.* New York: Dell.

Smith, C. G. (2013). *Creative problem solving techniques to change your life.* CreateSpace.

Sternberg, R.J (2002). *Why smart people can be so stupid.* New Haven, CT: Yale University Press.

Streznewski, M. L. (1999). *Gifted grownups: The mixed blessings of extraordinary potential.* New York: John Wiley & Sons.

Subotnik, R. F. (2009). Developmental transitions in giftedness and talent: Adolescence into adulthood. In F. D. Horowitz, R. F. Subotnik, & D. J. Matthews (Eds.), *The development of giftedness and talent across the lifespan,* pp. 155–170.

Thoreau, H. D. (1854/2004). *Walden: A fully annotated edition.* (Edited by Jeffrey S. Cramer.) New Haven & London: Yale University Press.

Tolan, S. (1994). Discovering the gifted ex-child. *Roeper Review, 17*(2), 134–138.

Tolan, S. S. (1999). Self-knowledge, self-esteem, and the gifted adult. *Advanced Development Journal, 8,* 147–150.

Tolan, S. S. (2009). What we may be: What Dabrowski's work can do for gifted adults. In S. Daniels & M. M. Piechowski (Eds.), *Living with intensity,* pp. 225–235. Scottsdale, AZ: Great Potential Press.

Tolan, S. S. (2011). *Change your story, change your life.* CreateSpace.

Tolan, S. S. (2013). Hollingworth, Dabrowski, Gandhi, Columbus, and Some Others: The History of the Columbus Group. In C. S. Neville, M. M. Piechowski, & S. S. Tolan (Eds.). *Off the charts: Asynchrony and the gifted child,* pp. 9–17. Unionville, NY: Royal Fireworks Press.

U.S. Department of Education. (2001). *No Child Left Behind.*

Webb, J. T. (2013). *Searching for meaning: Idealism, bright minds, disillusionment, and hope.* Tucson, AZ: Great Potential Press.

Webb, J. T., Amend, E. R., Webb, N., Goerss, J., Beljan, P., & Olenchak, F. R. (2005). *Misdiagnosis and dual diagnoses of gifted children and adults: ADHD, Bipolar, OCD, Asperger's, Depression, and other disorders.* Scottsdale, AZ: Great Potential Press.

Webb, J. T., Gore, J. L., Amend, E. R., & DeVries, A. L. (2007). *A parent's guide to gifted children.* Scottsdale, AZ: Great Potential Press.

Webb, J. T., Gore, J. L., Karnes, F. A., & McDaniel, A. S. (2004). *Grandparents' guide to gifted children.* Scottsdale, AZ: Great Potential Press.

Webb, J. T., Meckstroth, E. A., & Tolan, S. S. (1982). *Guiding the gifted child: A practical source for parents and teachers.* Dayton, OH: Ohio Psychology Publishing.

Welker, D. H. (1996). *Hen Medic: Woman doctor indeed!* Lake Nebagamon, WI: Paper Moon, Inc.

Willings, D. (1980). *The creatively gifted: Recognizing and developing the creative personality.* Cambridge, Great Britain: Woodhead-Faulkner.

Endnotes

1   Thoreau, 1854; Thoreau, 2004.

2   Bateson, 2010.

3   Subotnik, 2009.

4   Webb, 2013, p. 118.

5   Kuipers, 2010, p. 4.

6   "In the most basic terms, gifted adults are obviously different to the untrained eye in fundamental ways." Jacobsen, 1999, p. 26.

7   Gatto-Walden, 2013, p. 163. Patricia Gatto-Walden, a licensed counseling and clinical psychologist in private practice, has spent more than three decades working with gifted and talented children, adolescents, and adults.

8   Fiedler, 2009.

9   Alvarado, 1989, p. 77.

10   Tolan, 2009, p. 225.

11   Webb, 2013, p. 37.

12   "Even those who were tested as children and placed in gifted programs often believe that their giftedness disappeared by the time they reached adulthood." Silverman, 2010, p. ix.

13   Rocamora, 1992.

14   Luke, 12:48, *New International Testament*.

15   Kottmeyer, 2007, p. 129.

16   Fiedler, 2009, pp. 168–169.

17   Daniels & Piechowski, 2008.

18   Webb, 2013, pp. 49–50.

19   Jacobsen, 1999, Excerpted and adapted from list on pp. 27–28.

20   Another useful list of characteristics of gifted adults can be found at http://www.gifteddevelopment.com/ADJ/scale.htm.

21   Professor Miraca Gross from the University of New South Wales wrote about levels of giftedness in 2000 in her article originally published in *Understanding our Gifted*. Retrieved from: http://hoagiesgifted.org/underserved.htm. The levels of giftedness that she identified were also included in the 2000 publication of the *International Handbook of Research and Development*

of Giftedness and Talent (second edition) by K.A. Heller, F.J. Monks, R. J. Sternberg, & R.F. Subotnik (Eds.).

22   Subotnik, 2009, p. 158.
23   Tolan, 1999.
24   Welker, 1996.
25   Tolan, 1994, p. 134.
26   In 1991, several leading proponents of this view convened in Columbus, Ohio, to draft a new definition of giftedness that would help convey to parents, educators, and officials the reality of the gifted experience. It seemed to them that one of the most significant and often unrecognized consequences of giftedness was that it led to *asynchronous* development. In other words, while the child might be highly advanced in some areas of learning, the same child could be at a more average level in other aspects of development, or even delayed, particularly in social development through lack of contact with like others. When this uneven development is combined with the heightened intensity with which gifted children react to experience, it creates enormous stresses and tensions for the child and for parents and teachers, all of whom (including the child) may be bewildered by these apparent contradictions.

The members of the Columbus Group, all eminent researchers, practitioners, and writers, have continued to work individually and in collaboration to advance our understanding of giftedness. Their research and their experience continue to illuminate our thinking. Their definition has had a powerful influence on the development of gifted education. It has helped countless teachers and parents to gain a better comprehension of what it means to be a gifted child. But, frustratingly, there are still many who have not heard of it, including, it would seem, those who determine our education policies. http://www.giftedreach.org.nz/pdf/columbus_background_info.pdf. More details about the Columbus Group and the origins of the Columbus Group's definition of giftedness can also be found in Tolan, 2013, pp. 9–17.

The Columbus Group definition was a focus of the 11th World Congress on Gifted Education in 1995, with the opening keynote by Dr. Linda Silverman titled "The Universal Experience of Being Out-of-Sync." For a long time, it was the first definition listed on the NAGC website, and it is now included on the NAGC website under social-emotional issues: http://www.nagc.org/resources-publications/resources/social-emotional-issues/asynchronous-development. For nearly 20 years, it has been a significant part of presentations nationally and internationally by various members of the Columbus Group and others, and was the purpose of a major conference presented by members of the Columbus Group in Albuquerque in 2014. It is the entire reason the first International Symposium by the Columbus Group was created and scheduled for New Zealand in April of 2015: http://www.giftedreach.org.nz/news.htm.

27 The complete Columbus Group definition states: *Giftedness is asynchronous development in which advanced cognitive abilities and heightened intensity combine to create inner experiences and awareness that are qualitatively different from the norm. This asynchrony increases with higher intellectual capacity. The uniqueness of the gifted renders them particularly vulnerable and requires modifications in parenting, teaching, and counseling in order for them to develop optimally.*—The Columbus Group, 1991, cited in Silverman, 1993, p. 3.

28 Annemarie Roeper was a seminal leader in gifted education. A prolific writer, she was actively involved in the field throughout her lifetime. She and her husband, George, founded the Roeper School for the Gifted and the *Roeper Review*.

29 Roeper, 1982, p. 21.

30 The U.S. Federal Definition states: The term 'gifted and talented,' when used with respect to students, children, or youth, means students, children, or youth who give evidence of high achievement capability in areas such as intellectual, creative, artistic, or leadership capacity, or in specific academic fields, and who need services or activities not ordinarily provided by the school in order to fully develop those capabilities.—U.S. Department of Education, 2001, p. 544.

31 Silverman, 1997.

32 Most studies of gifted children have found Verbal IQ scores for gifted children to be higher than Performance IQ scores, sometimes dramatically so (Brown & Yakimowski, 1987; Malone, Brounstein, von Brock, & Shaywitz, 1991; Sattler, 2001; Wilkinson, 1993). For example, Webb and Dyer (1993) found that Verbal IQ and Performance IQ scores for gifted children often differ widely—as much as 45 points in one case—yet do not relate to a neurological or significant psychological problem. 27% of gifted children in that study whose Verbal IQ exceeded Performance IQ showed patterns in which Verbal IQ was at least 20 points greater than Performance IQ, and 8% of these children showed differences of 30 or more points. For children whose Performance IQ was greater than Verbal IQ, 11% showed a 20 or more point difference. Silver and Clampitt (1990) similarly found that 20% of gifted children had Verbal IQ scores 21 or more points higher than their Performance IQ scores.

33 Sternberg, 2002; Webb, Gore, Amend, & DeVries, 2007.

34 Webb, 2013, pp. 49–53; Fiedler, 2009, pp. 167–169.

35 Jacobsen, 1999, p. 126.

36 Webb, 2013, p. 11.

37 Willings, 1980, p. 27.

38 Webb, 2013.

39 Webb, et al., 2005.

40 For a more complete understanding of the problem of misdiagnosis, see http://sengifted.org/programs/seng-misdiagnosis-initiative.

41 Jacobsen, 1999, p. 182; Fiedler, 1991, p. 182.

42   Erikson, 1951.
43   Jacobsen, 1999; Streznewski, 1999; Kuipers, 2010; Sheehy, 1995; Sheehy, 2006.
44   See Appendix 1 of this book for an extensive list of relevant books and articles.
45   Erikson, 1951.
46   Fiedler, 2013, p. 192.
47   Cohen labeled this "Phase I: Reevaluation, exploration, and transition (midlife reevaluation)." He stated, "Most people experience this period not as a crisis but as a quest—a desire to break new ground, answer deep questions, and search for what is true and meaningful in their lives." Cohen, 2005, p. xviii.
48   Jacobsen, 1999, p. 8.
49   Streznewski, 1999, p. 6.
50   Kuipers, 2010, p. xiii.
51   Maslow, 1970.
52   Erikson, 1951.
53   Mary Lou Streznewski (1999), in her chapter on "The Dark Side," has good information about this group of invisible bright adults and their challenges
54   An Internet search for the phrase "Life is a journey, not a destination" (or another variation of it, "Happiness is a journey, not a destination") yields a wide range of sources to which it is attributed, including Ralph Waldo Emerson—e.g., see http://quoteinvestigator.com/2012/08/31/life-journey/.
55   Several generations ago, adults did not think about happiness very much. It was enough to have a good house and food on the table, to hold a steady job, and to live a conventionally acceptable life that was generally deemed the "right and proper" way to live.
56   Bode, 1993.
57   Maslow noted that *belonging* is one of the basic needs of human beings. Maslow, 1970.
58   Three chapters of the book *Living with Intensity,* edited by S. Daniels & M. M. Piechowski, are devoted to gifted adults, and the other chapters can be very helpful in understanding what intensity is like for bright people at any age.
59   Webb, 2013.
60   Fiedler, 2013, p. 202.
61   Fiedler, 2009, p. 167.
62   Streznewski, 1999, p. 134.
63   Nauta, 2013.
64   Tolan, 2009, p. 235. Some other sources that relate directly to finding meaning in life are: *Searching for Meaning: Idealism, Bright Minds, Disillusionment, and Hope* (Webb, 2013); *Finding Meaning in the Second Half of Life* (Hollis, 2005); *Smart Boys: Talent, Manhood, and the Search for Meaning* (Kerr & Cohn, 2001); *The Third Chapter: Passion, Risk, and Adventure in the 25 years after 50* (Lawrence-Lightfoot, 2009); and *From Age-ing to*

Sage-ing: A Profound New Vision of Growing Older (Schacter-Shalomi & Miller, 1995).

65   Tolan, 2011.

66   Webb, 2013, p. 88.

67   A great deal of information can be gleaned about Mike Matoin from *The Best of Mike* audiocassette tape set that was produced and distributed by Unity in Chicago, whose tagline is "A spiritual community of light, love, and laughter." http://www.unitychicago.org.

68   A tribute written about Mike Matoin in the *Chicago Tribune* reflects the impact that he had: "Rev. Mike Matoin, 63, the founder and senior minister of Unity Church, used a message of love and laughter rather than guilt and fear to build his congregation from 100 to more than 1,500 people in 15 years." Downloaded 3/13/14 from http://articles.chicagotribune.com/1995-03-24/news/9503240375_1_unity-church-message-korean-war.

69   For example, see http://www.lifehack.org/articles/lifestyle/wake-up-call-write-your-obituary.html, http://obituaryguide.com/writeyourown.php, and http://obitkit.com.

70   Tolan, 2011.

71   Webb, 2013, pp. 106–121.

72   Raines, 1997, p. 159.

73   Fiedler, 2005. Figures 2 and 3 in this article include detailed information about ways to use journaling as a valuable tool for self-discovery and for making meaning out of life.

74   Jacobsen, 1999.

75   Jacobsen, 1999, pp. 376–377.

76   This quote is often credited to Mark Twain, but it cannot absolutely be attributed to him: http://www.twainquotes.com/Discovery.html.

77   Webb, Meckstroth, & Tolan, 1982.

78   Webb, 2013, p. 21.

79   Berger, 2014, included the following questions:
Will I be satisfied with this choice?
Will I be happy with this choice?
Will others (parents) approve of this choice?
How will I feel about this choice in 6 months? In 1 year? In 5 years? (p. 81)

80   Kerr & Cohn (2001) describe multipotentiality as "a term used in reference to people who exhibit a broad range of abilities…a common situation in which a gifted child has the ability to select and develop any number of career options, all with an equal likelihood of success" (p. 130).

81   Their multipotentiality reflects a pattern of intense interests that can make it difficult for gifted adults to zero in on college majors or just one career path or to decide how to spend their leisure time.

82   Berger, 2014, p. 28.

83   Simpson & Kaufmann, 1981.

84   Kerr & Claiborn, 1991.

85   Fiedler, 2005.

86   Kerr & Claiborn, 1991, p. 165.
87   Nauta & Ronner, 2013.
88   Home Economics is now also called Family and Consumer Sciences.
89   Erikson, 1959.
90   Webb, et al., 2005.
91   Streznewski, 1999, p. 106.
92   Sheehy, 2006.
93   Noble, Robinson, & Gunderson, 1993.
94   Keating, 2009, p. 194.
95   Guetzloe, 1994.
96   Good sources for service learning and service learning projects can be found in Berger, 2010; Lewis, 1998; and Lewis, 2009.
97   Keating (2009) mentioned the importance of social opportunities and support throughout the lifespan. (See especially pp. 203–205.)
98   Kerr & Claiborn, 1991.
99   Cain, 2013. Also, a TED talk by Susan Cain on this topic is available at https://www.youtube.com/watch?v=c0KYU2j0TM4.
100 "Metacognition" means thinking about thinking—reflecting on your own thought processes and what that means about what you know. Metacognition is seen much earlier in bright individuals than in others and is one of the ways bright adults are different from other people.
101 See Appendix 3 for suggestions for keeping a journal.
102 See Appendix 4 for instructions and a blank sample "Expectations Chart."
103 See Appendix 5 for suggestions on "How to Listen So Others Will Talk to You."
104 See https://www.ted.com/talks/browse.
105 Kerr & Claiborn, 1991, p. 164.
106 An online copy of the Holland Self-Directed Search can be found at http://www.self-directed-search.com. Other interest inventories are also available online.

     Information about the Strong Interest Inventory can be found at http://careerplanning.about.com/od/selfassessment/a/strong-interest-inventory.htm.
107 The Creative Problem Solving (CPS) process is a tried and true method for decision-making. Information about CPS can be found at http://www.creativeeducationfoundation.org/creative-problem-solving/the-cps-process/.
108 Many resources are available on the internet for developing a functional resume, including the following: http://jobstar.org/tools/resume/tempfun.php and http://office.microsoft.com/en-us/templates/functional-resume-TC102919188.aspx.
109 University of Massachusetts is one good online source of information about decision-making: https://www.umassd.edu/fycm/decisionmaking/process/.
110 See Appendix 6 for an article with suggestions for getting organized.

111 Suze Orman has many books that are particularly relevant for Seekers: http://www.amazon.com/s/ref=nb_sb_ss_i_2_7?url=search-alias%3D-stripbooks&field-keywords=suzy+orman+books&sprefix=suzy+or%2C-stripbooks%2C203. Also see Pestalozzi, 2009.

112 Jacobsen, 1999, pp. 39–40.

113 Kaufman, 1992.

114 Roeper, 1990.

115 Rivero, 2010, p. 70.

116 Kerr, 2014, p. 210.

117 Streznewski, 1999, p. 134.

118 "Boreout" was described by Roger Boyes in his 2007 article titled "Forget burnout, boreout is the new office disease" published in *The Times*, Sept. 15, 2007. Retrieved from http://www.thetimes.co.uk/tto/career/article1792702.ece. The first ones to write about boreout were Rothlin, P. & Werder, P.R. (2008) in their book *Boreout!: Overcoming workplace demotivation*. London; Philadelphia: Kogan Page.

119 Noks Nauta, personal communication, Dec. 29, 2014.

120 We'll take a closer look at addictions in Chapter 10 when we consider the group I call the Invisible Ones.

121 Adrienne Sauder, personal communication via email, Sept. 10, 2013.

122 Armstrong, 2007, p. 159.

123 Levinson, 1978, pp. 98–99.

124 Levinson, 1996, p. 239.

125 Kerr & McKay, 2014.

126 Kaufman, 1992.

127 Brighter people are more likely to be introverts and need fewer friends than extroverts typically do: https://www.facebook.com/notes/the-introvert-entrepreneur/the-original-source-for-how-to-care-for-introverts/331076146950389.

128 Some interesting insights about these feelings of sadness can be found in Eric Maisel's book, *Why Smart People Hurt: A Guide for the Bright, the Sensitive, and the Creative.*

129 Women tend to have a broader zone of tolerance than do men. Fiedler & Webb, 2011.

130 GLBT is a common abbreviation for Gay, Lesbian, Bi-sexual, and Transgender.

131 Couples who do this have to caution themselves to stick to discussing ideas and not slip into personal attacks related to whose point of view is "right," something that sometimes happens when one is more educated or articulate than the other.

132 Kerr & McKay, 2014.

133 Supporting Emotional Needs of Gifted (www.sengifted.org) is an excellent place to start, as are various books written specifically for parents of gifted and talented children.

134 Webb, Meckstroth, & Tolan, 1982.

276 Bright Adults

135 DeVries & Webb, 2007.
136 Therapist Andrew S. Mahoney has focused a great deal of his practice on the topic of giftedness and identity. Detailed descriptions of his "Gifted Identity Formation Model" are included in articles provided on his website, http://www.counselingthegifted.com/articles.html, and can provide valuable information for Voyagers as well as for counselors who work with them.
137 See the previous chapter for more comments, suggestions, and ideas about keeping a journal or look at Appendix 3, which is all about journal writing.
138 O*Net is offered online by the Occupational Information Network and provides detailed descriptions of the world of work to help with career exploration and job analysis. See https://www.onetonline.org.
139 The OOH is offered by the Bureau of Labor Statistics from the U.S. Department of Labor. It provides detailed information about hundreds of occupations, including job summaries, entry-level education required, and median pay. See http://www.bls.gov/ooh/.
140 Use your favorite browser to search online for jobs and/or job training in your state or for any state you are interested in. Just put "job search" or "job training" and the state's name in the search line.
141 For example, CPS (http://www.creativeeducationfoundation.org/creative-problem-solving/the-cps-process/) or ideas about decision-making from the University of Massachusetts: https://www.umassd.edu/fycm/decisionmaking/process/.
142 LinkedIn is one online source that is especially aimed at helping people connect professionally: https://www.linkedin.com/about-us?trk=hp-about.
143 https://www.onetonline.org
144 http://www.lifecoach.com or http://www.lifecoaching.com/pages/life_coaching.html
145 http://www.mynextmove.org
146 One good source for learning about this is *Please Understand Me II* by David Kiersey.
147 The Internet has an abundance of resources on conflict resolution, including http://www.helpguide.org/articles/relationships/conflict-resolution-skills.htm and http://stress.about.com/od/relationships/a/conflict_res.htm. You can start with the ideas on these websites or do a search and look at others; then pick and choose the approaches that seem to fit you best.
148 Hoagies' website is a good place to start: http://www.hoagiesgifted.org.
149 Kaufman, 1992, p. 2. http://www.davidsongifted.org/db/Articles_prnt_id_10023.aspx.
150 Fiedler, 2009.
151 Streznewski, 1999, p. 131.
152 Erikson, 1951.
153 http://www.experts123.com/q/how-often-does-the-average-american-family-move.html
154 Fiedler, 2012.
155 Jacobsen, 1999, p. 356.

156 Fiedler, 2013, p. 195.

157 Hollis, 2005, p. 1.

158 Sheehy, 2006, p. 34.

159 Sheehy, 1998, p. 34.

160 This may actually reflect what is described in Dabrowski's Theory of Positive Disintegration (TPD) as Level III: spontaneous, multilevel disintegration. *Spontaneous* because it seems so surprising, almost as if it comes out of the blue; *multilevel* because of the tension between lower and higher values; and *disintegration* because it "shakes up the psyche." This disintegration is related to "the anguish of those who see and feel far beyond the mundane." Described as a journey from "what is" to "what ought to be," the driving force in these individuals' lives is their vision of an inner ideal, and this plays out both personally and professionally. Battaglia, Mendaglio, & Piechowski, 2014, p. 190. An especially good source of information about Dabrowski's levels and other aspects of his theory is the book *Living with Intensity*. For details about the levels of TPD, see especially Chapter 2 in Daniels & Piechowski, 2009, pp. 19–29.

161 Fiedler, 2009.

162 Aron, 1996, p. 119.

163 Retrieved from http://macdrifter.com/pages/about.html.

164 Retrieved from http://www.merriam-webster.com/medical/generativity.

165 Webb, 2013, p. 161.

166 See video presentation downloaded 12/14/13 from http://link.bright-cove.com/services/player/bcpid70868678001?bckey=AQ~~,AAAAE-EcdhlE~,gr325-mFBbzbMHq608vPXRPVjeranI_R&bclid=0&bc-tid=2924560389001.

167 Cohen, 2005, p. 57.

168 Webb, 2014, p. 97.

169 Fiedler, E., 1998, p. 11.

170 Kane & Fiedler, 2013.

171 One website cites pioneering psychologist Mihaly Csikszentmihalyi specifically with regard to his considering androgyny a "crucial aspect of the creative mindset." Retrieved from http://www.brainpickings.org/2014/11/07/psychological-androgyny-creativity-csikszentmihalyi/.

172 Kerr & McKay, 2014, p. 115.

173 Kerr & Cohn, 2001, pp. 52 and 158.

174 Palmer, 2000, p. 9.

175 Some examples include: breath awareness (closing your eyes and concentrating on your breath), focusing on a peaceful image or repeating a sound or word, or listening to an audio recording of ocean waves or gentle rain.

176 A new copy of the "Expectations Chart" suggested for Seekers can be completed again for this stage of life. (See Appendix 4.)

177 For example: Sinetar, 1987.

178 Retrieved from http://www.friendsofthestirlingroadbranchlibrary.com.

179   Information about events such as these was retrieved from http://www.naturenearby.org/upcoming-events.

180   Jacobsen, 1999, p. 353.

181   Newman, 2013.

182   Fiedler, 2012.

183   Streznewski, 1999, p. 139.

184   Fiedler, 2009, p. 173.

185   Seligman & Csikszentmihalyi, 2000.

186   Webb, 2013, p. 163.

187   Tolan, 1994, p. 137.

188   Bateson, 2010, p. 87.

189   Seligman, 2006.

190   Lawrence-Lightfoot, 2009, p. 6.

191   Fiedler, 2013, p. 193.

192   Tolan, 1994, p.135.

193   LGBT is a commonly used abbreviation for individuals who are Lesbian, Gay, Bi-sexual, or Transgendered. The Q refers to *queer* or *questioning*.

194   Personal communication, Rick Karlin, Dec. 24, 2013.

195   Cohen, 2005, p. 60.

196   Fiedler, 2009, p. 173.

197   Aron, 1996.

198   Fiedler, 2013.

199   Retrieved from http://www.peacecorps.gov/volunteer/response/.

200   Retrieved from http://www.peacecorps.gov/about/fastfacts/.

201   See especially Chapters 8 and 9 in Neville, Piechowski, & Tolan, 2013, pp. 158–210 and the four chapters included in "Part Three: Still Gifted After All These Years—Lifespan Intensity and Gifted Adults" in Daniels & Piechowski, 2009, pp. 167–184.

202   An internet search resulted in a plethora of "hits" under "Wellness at Work programs." General information is available from the Center for Disease Control at http://www.cdc.gov/features/WorkingWellness/.

203   This strategy is based on PMI, a thinking-skill tool developed by Edward De Bono, a physician, author, inventor, and consultant. He first published PMI in his 1982 book, *De Bono's Thinking Course,* and has included it in many of his other books. One source of information on using PMI for decision-making can be found at http://www.mindtools.com/pages/article/newTED_05.htm.

204   Fiedler, 2009, pp. 176–177.

205   Maslow, 1970.

206   Fiedler, 2012.

207   Streznewski, 1999, p. 237.

208   Cohen, 2005, p. 143.

209   Schacter-Shalomi & Miller, 1995, p. 103.

210 The information on the following website is a good example of what one such Lifelong Learning Institute is all about: http://medicine.nova.edu/lli/index.html. See also Shideler, 2014, p. 38.

211 Cohen, 2005, p. xviii.

212 Fiedler, 2013.

213 Webb, 2013, p. 158.

214 Tolan, 1994, p. 136.

215 Fiedler, 2009, p. 178.

216 Jacobsen, 1999, p. 355.

217 Jacobsen, 1999, p. 219.

218 Fonda, 2011, p. 255.

219 Bateson, 2010, p. 232.

220 See http://en.wikipedia.org/wiki/Compassion_fatigue.

221 Webb, 2013, p. 159.

222 From "A Light Woman," by Robert Browning.

223 Bateson, 2010, p. 232.

224 http://encore.org/encore-career-handbook/

225 Freedman, 2014.

226 Streznewski, 1999, p. 237.

227 Fiedler, 2013, p. 203.

228 A recent book on this subject is *Unretirement* by Chris Farrell.

229 An internet search reveals the huge number of available software programs for mind mapping. A free source that you might find worth exploring is http://freemind.sourceforge.net/wiki/index.php/Main_Page. Also, Life-hacker.com lists their five best mind-mapping tools, including Freemind: http://lifehacker.com/five-best-mind-mapping-tools-476534555/all.

230 Raines, 1997, p. 159.

231 One source for such experiences is the Bernard Osher Foundation that supports lifelong learning in conjunction with various universities across the nation with "non-credit educational programs specifically developed for seasoned adults who are aged 50 and older." See http://www.osherfoundation.org/index.php?olli.

232 "Road Scholar, the not-for-profit leader in educational travel since 1975, offers 5,500 educational tours in all 50 states and 150 countries." See http://www.roadscholar.org.

233 A friend described some people in her life were "garden party only," indicating that she might (metaphorically) invite them to a garden party but not into her house. In other words, she was willing to have a casual relationship without wanting to get particularly close to them or have them become too involved in her life.

234 Information about amateur radio and licensing by the Federal Communications Commission can be found at http://www.arrl.org/ham-radio-licenses.

235 The website for Habitat for Humanity can be found at http://www.habitat.org.

Senior Corps is one of the largest volunteer networks for people 55 and over and is designed to "use the skills and talents you've learned over the years, or develop new ones while serving in a variety of volunteer activities within your community." For details, see the website for the Corporation for National and Community Service: http://www.nationalservice.gov/programs/senior-corps/rsvp.

For details on the "Create the Good" program, see http://createthegood.org/articles/jan15acquisition?CMP=EMC-SNG-OVS-ACQ-012115.

236 The APTA home page is http://www.apta.org/AboutUs/.
237 Streznewski, 1999, p. 236.
238 Fiedler, 2013.
239 Downs, 2007.
240 Cohen, 2005, p. 83.
241 Roeper, 2011, p. 23.
242 Bateson, 2010, p. 233.
243 Keillor, 2014.
244 Erikson & Erikson, 1997, p. 118.
245 Bateson, 2010.
246 Buettner, 2012.
247 Butler, 2010.
248 Cohen, 2005.
249 Ellis, 2004.
250 Fonda, 2011.
251 Hollis, 2005.
252 Lawrence-Lightfoot, 2009.
253 Pauley, 2014.
254 Schacter-Shalomi & Miller, 1995.
255 Pipher, 1999.
256 Chittister, 2008.
257 Poo, 2015.
258 Sheehy, 2006.
259 Webb, 2013, p. 164.
260 This growing trend has been described by a number of sources including: http://www.nytimes.com/2014/04/05/your-money/college-retirement-communities-expected-to-grow.html?_r=0, http://www.huffingtonpost.com/2012/05/29/college-towns-draw-retirees_n_1431694.html, and http://www.aarp.org/home-garden/housing/info-01-2009/university_based_retirement_communities.html.
261 In a study in Maryland to investigate the frequency of people who have completed advanced directives, Morhaim and Pollack (2013) found that 60 percent of individuals age 18 and over wanted their end-of-life decisions respected, but that only about a third of them had completed the forms for advanced directives.

262 High levels of internal motivation are typical of bright individuals throughout their lifespan, from childhood on.

263 Webb, et al., 2004, pp. 246–248, includes good information about this. The
Internet also has information about how to do an ethical will, including:
http://celebrationsoflife.net/ethicalwills/ and http://www.agingcare.com/
Articles/ethical-will-legacy-letter-150151.htm.

264 Retrieved from http://www.agingcare.com/Articles/ethical-will-legacy-let-
ter-150151.htm. See also Baines, 2006.

265 Jacobsen, 1999, p. 374.

266 Several sources of relevant information on this topic are available
online—e.g.: http://www.thesimpledollar.com/personal-finance-101-the-
basics-of-estate-planning/ and https://personal.vanguard.com/us/insights/
retirement/living/estate-planning. However, Cruisers need to be aware
that sources such as these are offered by companies that want to sell them
something, and they should act accordingly.

267 Roeper, 2011, p. 55.

268 Downs, 2005.

269 Armstrong, 2007.

270 Buettner, 2012, p. xxi.

271 Roeper, 2011, p. 16.

272 Pipher, 1999, pp. 42–43, citing author Joe Starita's book *The Dull Knifes of
Pine Ridge* and his discussion of "the differences between the way most
Americans view the elderly and the way the Lakota view their elders."

273 http://www.roadscholar.org/about/history.asp

274 Pipher, 1999, p. 20.

275 Pipher, 1999, pp. 20–21.

276 Pipher, 1999, p. 28.

277 This is one of Dan Buettner's "9 Lessons for Living Longer" from his book
The Blue Zones, based on research on people who have lived to age 100 and
beyond. This idea and his suggestions of how to implement it are on pp.
281–283.

278 Most cruise lines are skilled at accommodating people in this age group
and provide an abundance of opportunities for them.

279 This is another of Dan Buettner's "9 Lessons for Living Longer" from his
2012 book, *The Blue Zones*. This idea and his suggestions of how to implement it are on pp. 267–269.

280 At the age of 92, Marion Downs published a self-help book called *Shut Up
and Live: You Know How* on how to live a vibrant, active old age into one's
80s, 90s, and beyond.

281 Canes, walkers, wheelchairs, or scooters can be used when truly necessary,
but avoid becoming overly dependent on them too soon; also, if you are
less physically active, you need to watch your diet closely to prevent weight
gain, which may cause problems for physical activity.

282 Butler, 2010, pp. 27–28.

283   Smith (2013) includes interesting exercises related to this. Another option for putting this into action is to work through the CPS process. See http://www.creativeeducationfoundation.org/creative-problem-solving/the-cps-process/.

284   Information about AAA's driver safety courses can be found at http://seniordriving.aaa.com/maintain-mobility-independence/driver-improvement-courses-seniors.
      Information about the driver safety course from AARP is available at http://www.aarp.org/home-garden/transportation/driver_safety/.

285   Uber's website is https://www.uber.com.

286   See https://www.craigslist.org/about/sites.

287   Parents who homeschool their gifted children may be a good place to look for someone who would like to do this sort of exchange.

288   Mashable.com lists "50+ Places to Buy Groceries Online": http://mashable.com/2008/06/05/online-grocery-shopping/.

289   An arrangement like this can be in exchange for room and board—a win-win for both of you.

290   Webb, et al., 2004, pp. 246–248 includes good information about this. The Internet also has all kinds of information about how to do an ethical will, including the following sources: http://celebrationsoflife.net/ethicalwills/ and http://www.agingcare.com/Articles/ethical-will-legacy-letter-150151.htm.

291   The Shift Network describes itself as "a global movement of people who are creating a shift of consciousness that in turn leads to a more enlightened society, one built on principles of peace, sustainability, health, and prosperity." http://theshiftnetwork.com/main.

292   See Appendix 8 for instructions for the S.P.I.C.E.S. activity related to risk-taking.

293   This question came from legendary baseball pitcher Satchel Paige and can be found with others from him at http://www.satchelpaige.com/quote2.html.

294   See http://www.contemplativemind.org/practices for suggestions.

295   Fiedler, 2013, p. 206.

296   Tolan, 1994, p. 136.

297   Maisel, 2013, p. xviii.

298   Webb, 2013, p. 127.

299   Webb, 2013, pp. 145–160.

300   For comprehensive information about bright students and these behaviors, see Maupin, K., 2014.

301   For example, "You're so good at arguing; you should be a lawyer when you grow up." Or, "You're so good at science; you should be a doctor when you grow up."

302   Jacobsen, 1999, p. 125.

303   Two sources for relevant information about this are Miller, 2008, and Bowlby, 1969.

304 The emphasis in schools in recent years has been to bring the slow and average students up to a certain level of achievement, and schools more or less assume that the gifted can and will "get it on their own." Therefore, special programming for gifted students has been eliminated in many schools. The National Association for Gifted Children stated, *Most gifted students receive the majority of their K-12 education in a regular classroom, taught by teachers who have not been trained to teach high-ability students. For many gifted students, much of the time they spend in school is wasted; they have already mastered the material and are simply marking time until they are allowed to skip a grade or are permitted to take college-level courses.*

305 Temple University psychologist Frank Farley, Ph.D., a former APA president, has developed a personality model that describes the Big T (thrill-seeking) personality. (Munsey, 2006). Stimulation seeking has been correlated with intelligence by Raines, et al., 2002.

306 Freeman, 2010.

307 Kerr & McKay, 2014, p. 114.

308 One good source of detailed historical information about this can be found in Pulitzer Prize winning author Susan Faludi's 1991 book, *Backlash: The Undeclared War against Women.* Another valuable book about issues related to gender is Levinson's 1996 book, *The Seasons of a Woman's Life.*

309 Kerr & Cohn, 2001.

310 Kerr & Cohn, 2001.

311 Kerr & Cohn, 2001, p. 159.

312 Good resources for in-depth information about how giftedness affects men and women can be found in Kerr, 1991; Kerr, 1997; Kerr & Cohn, 2001; and Kerr & McKay, 2014.

313 Lovecky, 1986, p. 574.

314 For information about imposter syndrome, see Clance, 1986.

315 Tolan, 1994.

316 Jacobsen, 1999, p. 135.

317 Jacobsen, 1999, p. 138.

318 See Webb, et al., 2007.

319 Included in twice exceptionality are gifted individuals who have one or more of the following: learning disabilities, attention deficit disorders (with and without hyperactivity), vision and hearing impairments, autism spectrum disorders (including Asperger's Syndrome), sensory/motor integration issues, physical challenges, and behavior/emotional disorders. For comprehensive information about gifted individuals with other exceptional educational needs and the multitude of ways in which they are missed, misunderstood, and often ignored, see Webb, et al., 2005.

320 According to the NAGC, "For many years, educators in the field of gifted education have advocated that a disability does not preclude the presence of giftedness and, increasingly, researchers are generating evidence-based practices for working with twice-exceptional students." National Association for Gifted Children, 2009, p. 4.

321   One excellent source of information about this is the book by Webb, et al., 2005: *Misdiagnosis and Dual Diagnoses of Gifted Children and Adults.*

322   The Internet is loaded with examples of famous people who had disabilities and achieved outstanding, remarkable success.

323   Webb, 2013, p. 63.

324   The popular media seems to revel in focusing on the high IQs of noted criminals and regularly seems to imply connections between intelligence, psychopathology, and criminal behavior. Another interesting perspective on bright people who are psychopathic was offered by Kevin Dutton in a podcasted interview from *Scientific American*: http://www.scientificameri-can.com/podcast/episode/psychopathys-bright-side-kevin-dutt-12-12-28/.

325   Streznewski, 1999, p. 173.

326   Streznewski, 1999, p. 163.

327   Cross, Gust-Brey, & Ball, 2002, p. 248.

328   The U.S. Census finds that suicide increases with age, and the highest rate of suicide is in persons age 75 and older. These data thus raise the possibility that Actualizers and Cruisers may be more likely to attempt or commit suicide.

329   Goertzel, Goertzel, Goertzel, & Hansen, 2004, p. 344.

330   See http://www.collegedropoutshalloffame.com/xyz.htm.

331   See Chapter 2 in this book for more information about this, as well as Silverman, 2013, a chapter that clearly describes the two opposing views of giftedness that underlie this confusion.

332   A good place to start is with the list of resources provided in Appendix 2 of this book.

333   See especially Fiedler, 2013, and Gatto-Walden, 2013, and the four chapters included in "Part Three: Still Gifted After All These Years—Lifespan Intensity and Gifted Adults" in Daniels & Piechowski, 2009, pp. 165–235.

334   You may find that some of your responses might need more than one label and that the labels might change the longer you think about this.

335   Some people who provide this type of counseling even do so via phone or Skype.

336   See especially http://www.hoagiesgifted.org/gifted_adults.htm for the relevant articles on Hoagies, http://www.sengifted.org/search-results?cx-=003473141502989371879%3Ae7t044sohde&cof=FORID%3A11&q=-gifted%20adults&sa for information on the SENG website, and http://www.gifteddevelopment.com/search/node/gifted%20adults for articles on gifted adults provided by the Gifted Development Center.

337   Some suggestions included here are variations of strategies recommended for specific stages (Seekers, Explorers, etc.); others are new to this chapter.

338   Many useful tools for value clarification are available for free download—e.g., http://faculty.weber.edu/molpin/healthclasses/1110/bookchap-ters/valueschapter.htm or http://www.smartrecovery.org/resources/library/Tools_and_Homework/Other_Homework/values_clarification.htm.

339   This is a variation of a strategy suggested for Seekers that is applicable here as well. It comes from Kerr & Claiborn, 1991, p. 164.

340   In addition to the suggestions in Chapter 4, another helpful source of information about decision-making is http://www.skillsyouneed.com/ips/decision-making.html.

341   The "Expectations Chart" in Appendix 4 is useful for comparing your own expectations of yourself with those of others. If any of the other people you have listed on your chart are available, you might check with them to see how accurate your perceptions are of their expectations of you.

342   This concept of an unlived life comes from Schacter-Shalomi & Miller (1995), who describe its meaning and implementation on pp. 103–105.

343   Webb, 2013, p. 137.

344   A good source of information about this is *Living with Intensity*, especially the four chapters included in "Part Three: Still Gifted After All These Years—Lifespan Intensity and Gifted Adults" in Daniels & Piechowski, 2009, pp. 165–235.

345   This suggestion and others offered by Webb in his 2013 book, *Searching for Meaning: Idealism, Bright Minds, Disillusionment, and Hope*, can be very helpful. See especially pp. 164–172.

346   Webb, 2014, pp. 146–148. Also see Tolan, 2011, for her recommendations of how you can change your life by changing the stories you tell yourself about it.

347   Counselors and various programs are available to help unravel the emotions underlying drug and alcohol abuse, food addictions, gambling, and smoking.

348   These questions were adapted from p. 417 in Levinson, 1996, and are equally relevant for men and woman.

349   Kerr, 1997, pp. 219–220.

350   See additional information included among the resources in Appendix 2. Also, check out the 2e Newsletter, as well as the resources listed on their website: http://www.2enewsletter.com.

351   Hoagies' Gifted Education Page has good information about finding psychologists familiar with testing gifted and exceptionally gifted children and adults to do an assessment for you to find out if you might be twice exceptional: http://www.hoagiesgifted.org/psychologists.htm. Look especially at the links at the bottom of the page for ideas to help you select the right person for you.

352   In an early chapter of her book *Change Your Story, Change Your Life*, Tolan suggests the following steps for starting to put what she calls "Story Principle" to work: 1) Listen to other people and the stories they tell themselves; 2) Listen to yourself, hearing what you are saying; 3) Experiment with changing a story; 4) Take notice of how the story feels; 5) Get yourself an Easy Button (or make one for yourself); and 6) Find an ally or two or three. Tolan, 2011, pp. 25–39.

353   See Appendix 10 for instructions on how to deal with "Yes, buts..."

354 http://www.amnesty.org/en/library/info/ACT70/003/2009/en
355 This is a quite different meaning from the colloquial use of this phrase related to a marriage ceremony.
356 I crewed for Bob in the Mediterranean and again on Lake Huron and Lake Michigan when he brought his boat back to Chicago to complete his journey around the world.
357 Personal communication via email from Bob Bilhorn, April 18, 2014.
358 http://www.ask.com/question/i-am-the-master-of-my-fate-the-captain-of-my-soul
359 Lawrence-Lightfoot, 2009, p. 238.
360 "The Crossroads of Should and Must" by elle luna, retrieved from https://medium.com/medium-long/90c75eb7c5b0.
361 Jacobsen, 1999, p. 376.
362 Erikson, 1951.
363 Fiedler, 2013, p. 192.
364 Shaffer, 1988.
365 Levinson, 1978.
366 Armstrong, 2007, p. 257. His subtitles for his five stages of adult life are as follows: Early Adulthood—Building an Independent Life; Midlife—Moving through Muddy Waters; Mature Adulthood—Scaling the Peaks; Late Adulthood—Approaching the Horizon; and Death and Dying—Crossing the Bridge.
367 Jacobsen, 1999, p. 8.
368 Streznewski, 1999, p. 6.
369 Kuipers, 2010, p. xiii.
370 Rush NeuroBehavioral Center, http://rnbc.org/education/a-focus-on-executive-function/.
371 Mach, Vatcha, & Harris, 2008.
372 Kane, 2009.
373 Fiedler, 2007.
374 http://en.wikipedia.org/wiki/Mind_map
375 Personal communication, Betty Meckstroth, March 19, 2012.
376 Reprinted with permission from Linda K. Silverman.

Index

needs, 28-35, 36, 37, 51, 52, 64, 65, 81, 85, 88, 113, 123, 131, 132, 138, 159, 161, 172, 177, 182, 188, 193-4, 251, 255, 272, 283
neotraditional, 106
no, saying, 127
nontraditional, 106, 108, 186
numbing, 58, 185, 197, 201-2
nursing homes, 154, 160

obituary, 38, 273
obligations, 104, 213
obstacles, 34, 54, 172, 187, 194, 246, 257
OCD, 19
opportunity, 68, 86
optimism, 43, 121, 166, 186, 202
options, 2, 35, 36, 38, 46, 47, 52, 53, 59, 60, 63, 64, 71, 84, 85, 87, 88, 116, 130, 131, 132, 138, 159, 160, 163, 168, 175, 178, 189, 197, 199-200, 273
organizing skills, 34, 126, 145, 179, 245-9
organizations, 34-5, 57, 58, 67, 85, 88, 114, 119, 121, 123, 129, 132, 136, 138, 139, 141, 143, 148, 151, 154, 157, 159, 162, 166, 175, 206, 207, 237
out of sync, 1, 14, 15, 16-8, 41, 49, 119, 128, 190, 270
overexcitabilities, 12-3, 32
overqualified, 48
overwhelmed, 42, 64, 83, 94, 199
pace, 23, 45, 51, 60, 74, 109, 153
Palmer, P. J., 108
partners, 36, 70, 77-8, 80, 105, 107, 122, 125, 143, 160, 203

passion, 16, 18, 29, 32, 34, 37, 48, 52, 57, 58, 68, 71, 75, 76, 77, 85, 88, 91, 98, 102-3, 112, 113, 118, 121, 123, 129, 133, 136, 138, 142, 143, 144, 148, 149, 151, 173, 175, 179, 180, 196-7, 206, 215
peace, 103, 104, 106, 122, 124, 140, 144, 146-7, 152, 181, 206, 207, 208, 282
peers, 29, 39, 73, 75, 81, 188, 212
perceptions, 5, 17, 20, 217, 233, 238, 285
perfectionism, 14, 54, 189, 255
performance, 5, 14, 15, 16, 17, 34, 128, 137, 194, 197, 237
personality, 21, 62, 77, 90-1, 162, 218, 283
perspective, 1, 3, 5, 14, 23, 30, 59, 84, 92, 108, 113, 118, 121, 123, 136, 141, 142, 146, 147, 151, 159, 161, 165-6, 191, 255, 284
pessimism, 67, 202, 246
philosophy, 30, 48, 98, 121, 138, 139, 180
physical/physiological changes, 4, 23, 122, 154-6, 163-4, 167, 170-2, 193, 281, 283
Piechowski, M. M., ix
Pipher, M., 158, 165, 166
planning, 44, 160, 162, 170, 177, 249
politics, 57, 67, 98, 104, 136, 142, 149, 181, 196
positivity, 6, 44, 52, 102, 106, 115, 120, 123, 140, 144, 155, 157, 162, 211, 240-1, 277

About the Author

Dr. Ellen D. Fiedler, a professor emerita from the Master in Arts in Gifted Education (M.A.G.E.) program at Northeastern Illinois University in Chicago, is currently a private educational consultant. She regularly provides professional development strategies for school districts and other educational agencies, presentations for parents, and a wide range of consultation services related to gifted students and their education. She received her master's degree in elementary education, with an emphasis on gifted children, and her Ph.D. in counseling and guidance from the University of Wisconsin–Madison where she worked at the Guidance Institute for Talented Students as a research assistant to the director. She has been a gifted program coordinator and a state consultant for gifted and has provided consultation services, webinars, and presentations locally, regionally, nationally, and internationally, including at state, national, and international conferences. She was chair of the Counseling and Guidance Division of the National Association for Gifted Children (NAGC), co-chair of the Global Awareness Division, and newsletter editor for the Global Awareness Network of NAGC. She is a published author, including numerous articles in professional journals, a chapter on psychosocial issues for the gifted, and chapters on gifted adults in *Living with Intensity* and in *Off the Charts: Asynchrony and the Gifted Child* and books regarding giftedness.

Ellen lives in Florida during the winter and in southwest Lower Michigan in the summer. She is a member of the Florida Association for the Gifted; a member and past president of the Michigan Association for Gifted Children; and a member of the Illinois Association for Gifted Children, the NAGC, and the World Council for Gifted and Talented Children (WCGTC). She co-authored the state guide to diversity and equity for gifted programs in Illinois and serves as a state of Illinois trainer for the gifted education seminars. She is an avid sailor with an old wooden sailboat that she typically sails single-handedly on Lake Michigan. She initially became involved in gifted education as a parent of two profoundly gifted children.